INTERGOVERNMENTAL PERSPECTIVES ON THE CANADA-U. S. RELATIONSHIP

INTERGOVERNMENTAL

PERSPECTIVES ON THE

CANADA-U. S. RELATIONSHIP

ROGER FRANK SWANSON

New York • New York University Press • 1978

Copyright © 1978 by New York University

Library of Congress Cataloging in Publication Data

Swanson, Roger F.
  Intergovernmental perspectives on Canada-U.S.
relationship.
  Includes bibliographical references.
  1. United States—Foreign relations—Canada.
  2. Canada—Foreign relations—United States.
  3. United States—Foreign relations administration.
  4. Canada—Foreign relations administration.
  I. Title.
JX1428.C2S9   327.71′073   77-25747
ISBN 0-8147-7789-9

Manufactured in the United States of America

To William Y. Elliott

CONTENTS

INTRODUCTION

One of the more significant features of the postwar international community has been the increasing economic, strategic, and cultural interpenetration that has grown between Canada and the United States. By almost any standard of comparison, the degree of this "interdependence" between two sovereign nations is without parallel in modern history. The interpenetration of the Canada–U.S. relationship is in effect a theater of interactions involving a host of actors. The interactions are both tangible and intangible, ranging from the transborder flow of goods to the flow of ideas. The actors are both governmental and nongovernmental. But who is "managing" these interactions? The governments of Canada and the United States are, or at least we think they are. But how are the two governments organized to deal with these bilateral interactions?

Utilizing a series of intergovernmental perspectives, the purpose of this book is twofold. First, it identifies the relevant U.S. and Canadian governmental actors who are actually managing the relationship, and the institutional milieus in which these actors function. The organizational structures of these governmental actors are described; functional responsibilities are defined; and interrelationships are examined. What is the nature of the policy processes in Ottawa and Washington that deal with the bilateral relationship? How do the Canadian and U.S. embassies and consular posts operate? What is the role of the joint Canada–U.S. organizations? These basic institutional questions have been relatively neglected in the literature on the Canada–U.S. relationship, and yet they are essential to an understanding of the dynamics of the relationship.

Just as we cannot neglect the study of governmental institutions, neither can we stop there, for it is also important analytically to go beyond the descriptive focus of institutional studies. This brings us to the second purpose of this book. While the approach in this book does not purport to offer a rigorous "theory" of governmental decision-making in the Canada–U.S. context, this book does present actor-based theoretical frameworks that delineate factors which the author feels should be considered in analyzing the relationship at the intergovernmental level, either as a generalized decision-making process or as a process in the resolution of specific issues.

In the broadest sense, this book was written with the conviction that one of the most important questions facing the Canada–U.S. relationship concerns this intergovernmental "managerial" dimension.[1] How can Canadian and U.S. officials translate national policy goals into operable programs (whether in the area of energy or environment or economics) in the context of an interpenetrated bilateral system that is without precedent in the international community? This question can be answered only if we take a fresh institutional look at those governmental actors who are at the same time the agents dictating the framework of the Canada-U.S. relationship and the major agents in attempting to deal with the dynamics that inhere in this relationship.

Indeed, an understanding of the Canada-U.S. intergovernmental relationship is even more compelling given the November 1976 Quebec election of René Lévesque's government with its commitment to national sovereignty. While it is more exciting to speculate about the future of Quebec and its impact on the Canada–U.S. relationship, it is more useful first to understand the mechanics of the overall Canada–U.S. intergovernmental relationship. The Canadian attempt to absorb centrifugal forces in the pursuit of national unity could subject the Canada–U.S. relationship to great stress. It is the usage of these intergovernmental channels which will determine to a great extent how effectively Canadian and U.S. officials absorb this stress and stabilize an ever changing North American environment. In short, one of the prerequisites to meaningful speculation about the future is a firm grasp of the current Canada–U.S. intergovernmental infrastructure.

The chapters in this book are presented in a self-contained manner, thereby allowing the reader either to examine the intergovernmental dimensions selectively or to read them collectively to get an overview of all dimensions. Chapter I examines policy-making in Ottawa and Washington as it affects the Canada–U.S. relationship. The fundamental differences and similarities of the policy processes in the two capitals are explored. The policy-making systems in Ottawa and Washington are then individually examined, so that the implications for the Canada–U.S. relationship can be drawn. After this institutional interpretation, the concluding section develops the concept of "constellations," which provides a conceptual framework for a discussion of the two policy processes. Constellations, in the simplest sense, are defined as clusters of Canadian officials in Ottawa, and U.S. officials in Washington, who regularly interact with each other concerning matters affecting the other country.

Chapter II examines U.S. diplomatic and consular representation in Canada. This includes the delineation of the major components and subcomponents of the U.S. Embassy and seven consular posts in Canada, their organizational structures, and their functional responsibilities and procedures. Following an assessment of the origins and evolution of U.S. representation in Canada, including profiles of ambassadors serving in Canada from 1943, the U.S. Embassy is examined in detail. This includes its internal organization, functions, and operations and its interrelationships with Washington. The third section examines the U.S. consular posts in a similar manner. Communication flows between and within the posts are described, and individual consular functions and their execution are discussed. A concluding section discusses problems of coordination and assesses diplomatic and consular effectiveness. Chapter III examines Canadian diplomatic and consular representation in the United Sates, using a format identical to that of Chapter II.

Chapter IV examines the intergovernmental role of the bilateral Canada–U.S. organizations. A standardized definition of bilateral organizations is presented; distinctions are drawn between the different types of joint organizations that are active; and a three-quarter-century-era analysis is presented regarding their evolution. The subsequent five sections examine the individual seventeen joint organizations. concentrating on the origins of each organization, its organizational structure, and its functions and operations. This includes an examination of the six joint military committees and the North American Air Defense Command, the three joint economic committees, the six joint commissions, and the Interparliamentary Group. A concluding section summarizes the findings, assesses the overall function of the bilateral organizations, and discusses the extent to which these organizations have furthered political integration between Canada and the United States.

It is all very well to examine the institutional dimensions of the Canada–U.S. intergovernmental relationship, but how do these institutions come together in dealing with specific issues? Chapter V develops an issue-flow paradigm which permits empirically grounded consideration of the interrelationships among the actors, their organizational milieus, and the concomitant standard operating procedures (SOPs) through which issues are processed. This paradigm goes beyond the intergovernmental dimension to include an analytical treatment of transgovernmental and transnational forces. Although applicable to other transborder interactions in all issue areas, the paradigm is tested by examining the Canada–U.S. defense issue area. This is not, of course, to suggest that the defense area has an illustrative universality, but rather that the analytical properties of the paradigm have a wider applicability. This chapter utilizes case studies and examples which have been intentionally selected to cover a maximum historical time span. The threefold nature of transborder dealings are identified and analyzed: pure intergovernmental transactions involving only governmental actors; mixed transactions involving actors other than governmental, but who do not alter the outcomes; and transformative transactions involving the activities of new actors who significantly alter the outcomes of the transaction. This chapter also disaggregates issue flows into a three-stage process and examines the impact of transnational and transgovernmental activity on these flows. Finally, those factors encouraging and discouraging this activity are considered, as is the impact of differing perceptions and cost benefits of issue involvement.

Chapter VI adds a rather new dimension, in that it holds the intergovernmental perspective but drops it a notch by examining the nature and scope of subgovernmental relations between U.S. states and Canadian provinces. The policy implications of state/provincial activity are assessed. A standardized definition of state/provincial interaction is presented; three types of interaction are identified; and eleven functional categories mapping overall governmental activity are delineated. Pairs of states and provinces, as well as individual provinces, are then examined to determine levels of activity. Charts are presented which indicate levels of state/provincial activity both by types of interaction and by functional categories. This is followed by a concluding assessment of the analytical ramifications of state/provincial relations, including an analysis of how U.S. states are internally organized to deal with the Canadian provinces and what transborder techniques state officials utilize in dealing with their provincial counterparts.

Much of the material in this book originally appeared as articles in journals. Accordingly, the author is indebted to the following journals for giving permission to use these published materials: the Canadian Institute of International Affairs' *International Journal,* the Canadian Institute of Public Administration's *Canadian Public Administration,* the World Peace Foundation's *International Organization,* and the Canadian Department of External Affairs' *International Perspectives.* The author is also indebted to the U.S. State Department's Bureau of Intelligence and Research and the University of Manitoba's Natural Resource Institute for permission to use materials that originally appeared under their auspices.

The author is especially indebted to hundreds of Canadian and U.S. governmental officials, both at the federal and state/provincial level. Without their cooperation through interviews and correspondence, this book would not have been possible. The conclusions in this book remain, of course, the sole responsibility of the author. The author is also indebted to those former graduate students who participated in parts of this project as research assistants: Larry Kohler, John Kirton, Robert Simmons, Laurette Watts, and Joel Sokolsky. Finally, and very importantly, the author is indebted to Linda Ross for her typing and secretarial assistance.

NOTE

1. This emphasis on the intergovernmental dimension might seem curious since the claim can be convincingly made that the Canada–U.S. relationship is not determined in the first case by governmental actors at all, but rather by such transnational institutions as corporations, unions, and so on. It is of course these transnational institutions which are responsible for much of the interactive dynamics of the bilateral relationship involving such tangible transborder flows as goods and capital. However, it is only the governmental institutions which have the "right" to authoritiatively formulate rules and implement procedures applicable to all other actors. In the Canada–U.S. context, this means that these transborder flows of goods and capital occur under, or in the absence of, federal governmental control. (E.g., even the absence of tariff barriers in trade can be construed as resulting from governmental policies.) It should be emphasized that this intergovernmental approach does not neglect the importance of transnational forces in the relationship, but is analytically extended to include them within the context of government-to-government relations. Indeed, the possibility exists that there could be an erosion of overall governmental authority resulting from these transnational institutions. However, as Chapter V demonstrates, even with the acknowledgment of this possibility, the focus should still hold an intergovernmental framework.

I

WASHINGTON, OTTAWA, AND THE CANADA-U.S. RELATIONSHIP

In the 1940s Canadian Foreign Minister Louis St. Laurent could declare that "it is not customary in this country for us to think in terms of having a policy in regard to the United States. Like farmers whose lands have a common concession line, we think of ourselves as settling, from day to day, questions that arise between us, without dignifying the process by the word policy." [1] In the 1950s a Report of the Foreign Affairs Committee of the U.S. House of Representatives could state: "Canadian and United States interdependence demands a new category of relationship. Canada does not stand in a position towards us of a 'foreign' country." [2]

In the 1960s President Johnson could observe that "Canada is such a close neighbor that we always have plenty of problems there. They are kind of like problems in the hometown." [3] By 1965 the U.S. and Canadian governments could agree in the Merchant-Heeney Report that "the nature and extent of the relationship between our two countries is such as to require, in the interests of both, something more

1

than the normal arrangement for the conduct of their affairs with one another." [4]

The Canada-U.S. relationship had evolved into a unique relationship. It was unique in terms of the strategic, economic, and cultural intimacy that had developed during the postwar period. It was unique in terms of the bilateral relationship's own history, for this intimacy exceeded anything that the two nations had previously experienced. The relationship was unique in terms of the consultative procedures used by the two governments to handle issues generated by this intimacy. And the relationship was unique in terms of the rhetoric that grew up to describe both this intimacy and these consultative techniques.

The blossoming of the Canada-U.S. relationship resulted, not from any imperialist designs of the U.S. government, but rather from the open dynamics of the relationship. Canadians as well as Americans encouraged and luxuriated in it, but Canadians, unlike Americans, were worrying about it. While Canadians acknowledged the benefits they derived from their interdependence with the United States, they were also concerned about the extent to which this interdependence, particularly in the economic and cultural sectors, was eroding Canada's distinctiveness as a nation.

From the Canadian standpoint, the advent of the Trudeau government in 1968 had major implications for the Canada-U.S. relationship. The new prime minister called for a foreign policy review, which resulted in the June 1970 governmental publication *Foreign Policy for Canadians*. According to the review, one of the "inescapable realities" facing Canada was that of "living distinct from but in harmony with the world's most powerful and dynamic nation, the United States"; the other reality was national unity.[5] The foreign policy review was followed up in the autumn of 1972 with a special policy paper on Canada's relations with the United States. Three options were listed, the first two of which were dismissed:

status quo and closer integration with the United States. The Canadian government opted for the "third option," which consisted of "a comprehensive long-term strategy to develop and strengthen the Canadian economy and other aspects of our national life and in the process to reduce the present Canadian vulnerability to the United States." [6]

These governmental statements, and a blizzard of other governmental white papers in the areas of economics, defense, and culture, were essentially conceptual documents outlining objectives. As such, they could have been dismissed were it not for the fact that they were accompanied with significant Canadian legislative and regulative attempts to reduce the U.S. impact on Canada. Indeed, it was clear that Ottawa was pursuing national and internal policies that were distinct from those of the United States. Examples include Canada's 50 percent NATO force reduction; its recognition of mainland China prior to the Nixon initiatives; its law-of-the-sea initiatives; and domestically, the passage of the Foreign Investment Review Act and broadcasting regulations.

From the U.S. standpoint, the advent of the Nixon administration in 1969 had major implications for Canada. Given President Nixon's global view of foreign affairs under the tutorship of Henry Kissinger, the Nixon approach toward Canada constituted somewhat of a departure from previous U.S. administrations. President Nixon and his staff tended to deal with Canada-U.S. relations as an integral part of U.S. foreign policy, indeed, as a part of a global U.S. strategy. This led to a more rigid and formal approach, a greater sense of detachment, and a tendency to deal with bilateral issues at a somewhat higher level in the Nixon administration. President Nixon, in his April 1972 speech to the Canadian Parliament, assessed the bilateral relationship as follows: "It is time for Canadians and Americans to move beyond the sentimental rhetoric of the past. It is time for us to recognize that we have very separate identities; that we have significant differences; and that nobody's interests are furthered when these realities are obscured." [7]

Alterations in the U.S. approach toward Canada of course went beyond presidential and prime ministerial approaches, for in effect, the Canada-U.S. relationship was adjusting to a rapidly changing international system. The rigidities of the cold war period were softening in the name of détente, and the stability of the postwar economic system was deteriorating. It was President Nixon's August 1971 New Economic Policy that became the most dramatic symbol of the altered Canada-U.S. relationship. The unique relationship seemed to be evaporating at Canada's expense, given the U.S. refusal to grant Canada an exemption from the import surcharge as it had done in previous balance-of-payments measures, and given the rumbling about of the *enfant terrible*, Secretary of the Treasury John Connally. All this resulted in the death of several rather sacred conceptual cows. If the United States was energetically linking bilateral and multilateral issues using national rather than "continental" Canada-U.S. criteria, was not there a need in Ottawa for a conceptually integrated and distinct Canadian policy toward the United States? The Nixon administration in effect became the salesman for those Canadians advocating a less dependent bilateral posture, because the policies of the Nixon administration seemed clearly to demonstrate Canadian vulnerability to U.S. actions.[8]

By the summer of 1974, Canada-U.S. relations were badly in need of normalization. Not only had the surcharge demonstrated to Canadian officials the vulnerability that inheres in special concessions from the United States; there was also a host of abrasive bilateral irritants, ranging from energy matters to beef quotas, all of which were occurring in an atmosphere of increasing Canadian public concern about the U.S. hegemonic impact on Canada. At the intergovernmental level, consultations dropped sharply in frequency and productivity, with Canadian officials maintaining a watchful eye on Washington and venturing forth only when there was a cabinet consensus on a specific issue. President Nixon's Washington in the meanwhile was becoming increasingly absorbed in the Watergate morass. The traditional Canada-U.S. dialogue had deteriorated into a strained silence, seldom had the need for normalization in the bilateral relationship been greater, and never had a U.S. president been less able or less inclined to direct his attention to Canada.

With President Nixon's resignation, Gerald Ford became the first nonelected president in U.S. history, only to be rejected by the American electorate two years later in his own bid for the presidency. However, in an overall sense, President Ford's approach toward Canada was positive and effective. The Ford interlude normalized a highly unstable period in the Canada-U.S. relationship and neutralized volatile issues. For example, during the first Ford-Trudeau summit meeting held in December 1974 in Washington, the two leaders defined two managerial ground rules. First, when either government contemplated a major action affecting the other government, officials would inform their counterparts. Second, they would do so by giving the other officials an opportunity to reply (e.g., not the irksome half-hour warnings before a major announcement). These two rather simple ground rules were made explicit between the two leaders, but significantly, the rules were not described in any public announcement by either of the two governments. Indeed, there was even private caution on the part of Messrs. Ford and Trudeau in emphasizing that this was not a question of making joint decisions whereby one government was surrendering sovereignty by seeking permission from the other government. Rather, it was a question of each government notifying the other government of a policy direction so the latter could assess how a contemplated policy would affect its interests. Corresponding with this "issue warning system" was an equally explicit deemphasis on formal joint organizations (particularly the Canada-U.S. Ministerial Committee on Trade and Economic Affairs), with a corresponding emphasis on ad hoc consultations between U.S. and Canadian officials at the working level.

The net effect of the Ford-Trudeau approach was that it defined bargaining parameters within which U.S. and Canadian officials had to work, and it definitionally precluded public displays of abrasiveness while fully absorbing very tough unpublicized bargaining at the working level.[9] In effect, the president and the prime minister placed a lid on U.S.-Canadian consultative decision-making. Indeed, this lid was sufficiently tight that when departing U.S. Ambassador to Canada William Porter was reported to have stated that Canada-U.S. relations were "deteriorating" (referring to the U.S. congressional and corporate sectors), he was instantly challenged by Prime Minister Trudeau and Foreign Minister MacEachen. Even more significantly, he was just as quickly challenged by both President Ford and Secretary of State Kissinger.

President Carter, upon taking office in 1977, in effect continued the legacy of normalization left by the Ford aministration. The second foreign leader to visit the Carter administration was Prime Minister Trudeau. From the outset, Carter seemed even more interested in Canada than President Ford, given his administration's emphasis on good relations with U.S. allies (as opposed to the Nixon and Ford emphasis on bridging East-West conflicts which some charged was at the expense of allied relations). Even more important was the November 1976 election in Quebec of René Lévesque's secessionist government. Clearly, the Carter administration was in favor of a unified and politically stable Canada, and would take care not to exacerbate matters for the government of Prime Minister Trudeau in dealing with the separatist issue. And clearly, from the Canadian stand-point, the preoccupation of national unity coupled with economic difficulties began to supersede the preoccupation with the hegemonic impact of the United States. The prime minister himself, throughout his visit to Washington, including his address to the U.S. Congress, tended to deemphasize Canada's "third option" of differentiation from the United States while emphasizing Canada-U.S. similarites and complementary interests.

The presidential and prime ministerial approaches toward the Canada-U.S. relationship are important but of course do not constitute the totality of the policy approaches in Washington and Ottawa. While it is at the head-of-government level that the tone of the respective approaches are set, the actual formulation and implementation of these approaches take place through complex policy processes.

The first part of this chapter assesses the differences and similarities between Washington and Ottawa, while the second and third sections examine policy-making in the two capitals. Such an examination of extremely complex policy processes is of necessity selective, and the coordinative roles of the Departments of State and External Affairs are emphasized. While all this is useful, it still does not answer a basic question: What is the best way to conceptualize the role of the two capitals in the intergovernmental relationship? A concluding section defines the concept of "constellations" as clusters of officials in the two capitals who deal with bilateral matters. For purposes of illustration, several constellations are then tentatively identified.

DIFFERENCES AND SIMILARITIES

In examining Washington and Ottawa, it is tempting to assume that the respective centers of policy formulation and implementation operate on the same, or at least similar, institutional principles. While Washington and Ottawa have responded to similar influences over the past several years, there are fundamental differences between the two capitals which, in turn, affect the conduct of their foreign policy vis-à-vis each other. Indeed, an understanding of these differences is essential to an understanding of the policy processes in the Canada-U.S. intergovernmental relationship. Four major factors account for these differences: constitutional and political frameworks, size of the two federal governments, number and priority level of bilateral issues processed, and permanence and organizational traditions of the two civil services.

Even the most cursory glance at the U.S. and Canadian constitutional frameworks reveals fundamental differences which are, to a surprising extent, unrecognized by Canadians, and especially by Americans.[10] To begin with basics, if the United States is a republic with an elected president as the chief executive authority, Canada is a parliamentary democracy with a monarch as head of state and a prime minister as head of government.[11] The monarch (Queen Elizabeth II) is symbolically represented by the governor general, with the real executive authority resting in a cabinet consisting of ministers headed by the prime minister and responsible to the legislature. Thus, in Canada, the prime minister and his cabinet are all elected and have seats in the legislature, where they also direct its operations. In the United States, the nonelected cabinet is responsible to the president alone, and neither the president, nor his cabinet sit in the legislature. In the simplest sense, the U.S. system is therefore characterized by a separation of powers in which there is a division of authority between the executive, the legislative, and the judiciary; while the Canadian system is characterized by a single chain of authority involving the cabinet (the executive branch) and the House of Commons (the legislative branch).[12]

The differences between the two governments mean that Washington is more compartmentalized than Ottawa, not only in terms of executive-legislative functions, but also within the executive. In the United States, the executive branch, and more specifically, the president, obviously has a formulative and implementative centrality in the foreign policy process.[13] This centrality is derived from such sources as constitutional authority, congressional grants of power, "inherent powers" through decisions of the Supreme Court, and the president's role as national political leader. It is therefore within the president's prerogative to make long-range policy, to administer the day-to-day response to external events, to have access to extensive and confidential information, and to represent the United States in its foreign relations. The president's powers over foreign affairs are restricted in that the Senate has the twofold constitutional authority to approve treaties and confirm appointments, while the legislative power regarding the appropriation of funds needs no elucidation. Nor should such congressional roles in the areas of legislation, investigation, and resolutions be ignored. Thus, although the legislative branch lacks a foreign policy centrality, it is an essential component of the Washington foreign policy process. Indeed, its assertiveness and relevance have markedly increased in the wake of U.S. presidential supremacy throughout the 1960s, triggered by the Vietnam war. Moreover, a distinction must be made between the finite nature of legislative power (e.g., power to ratify treaties) and the theoretically infinite nature of legislative influence (e.g., the Congress as a forum of public opinion). In short, there is in varying degrees a built-in tension between the executive and legislative branches which Ottawa does not share.

Another illustration of the contrast in policy compartmentalization between Washington and Ottawa is that while in the United States there is one man at the apex, in Canada there are approximately thirty, of whom one, the prime minister, is "first among equals." The Canadian parliamentary/cabinet system, with its collegial executive style, therefore ensures that individual governmental departments exert less independence in the policy process than their U.S. counterparts who operate within a one-man executive separation-of-powers framework. Given its collective executive, the policy process in Ottawa tends to be less compartmentalized than in Washington, in that each member of the Canadian executive must theoretically be aware of, and have an opportunity to participate in, governmental policies for which he shares a collective responsibility.

A second factor explaining the differences in decision-making between Washington and Ottawa concerns the size of the two federal governments. Size refers both to budgets and to the sheer number of personnel. This disparity in size directly affects the availability of "decisional resources" which can be brought to bear by Canadian and U.S. officials in dealing with a particular issue.[14] Because of budgetary limitations in Ottawa, Canadian officials simply cannot indulge in the luxury of duplicating expertise and functions in specialized fields among several departments. For example, in Washington there can be half a dozen different uncoordinated studies of the multinational corporations, recommending measures that would have to be implemented by half a dozen departments and agencies. For Ottawa, this disparity in the size of the two governments militates against the highly competitive bureaucratic warfare characteristic of Washington, which is based upon independent departmental data and personnel resources. In addition, there is not the private expertise that Ottawa can draw on, as can Washington with its host of available "think tanks" ranging from the Brookings Institution to the Rand Corporation.

A third factor accounting for the differences between Washington and Ottawa is the number and priority level of issues which are defined and processed by the two governments as bilateral questions [15] Quite simply, U.S. global perceptions of its responsibilities tend to minimize the number of high-priority Canada-U.S. issues which require handling at high government levels in Washington. These issues are handled at comparatively lower levels than in Ottawa and are processed within the confines of individual departments or relatively low-level ad hoc interdepartmental gatherings. In short, U.S. officials spending most of their time on Canada are primarily middle level, and since matters concerning Canada are relatively of lesser importance, the communication flows concerning Canadian issues are generally horizontal, or among these middle-level officials. This can cause problems in terms of vertical communication, for the more important an issue, the higher the level of the official who handles it. The result is that when there is a high-level Canadian issue, these high officials oftentimes lack an adequate familiarity with things Canadian, and policy distortions can result unless they fully utilize the expertise that does exist on this middle level.

Partly because of the size of the two governments, and partly because of the difference in which U.S. and Canadian officials regard matters as priority, there is a ritual complaint in Canada that "Washington does not know or care about Canada." Such a complaint goes to the heart of misunderstanding about the Washington policy process. Quite simply, the vast majority of Washington officials are not interested in Canada per se. The primary point of entry for the majority of executive and legislative actors is through a specific issue. Thus, an official interested in general monetary policy is therefore interested in this facet of the Canada-U.S. relationship but not in the relationship as a whole. Indeed, with the exception of the State Department's Office of Canadian Affairs, all the other organizational units in Washington dealing with Canada have a highly specialized, as opposed to a general, interest in Canada. Many officials in Washington therefore both "know and care" about Canada, but their knowledge and concern is issue specific.

The situation is of course entirely different in Ottawa, for certainly no one would charge that Canadian officials don't "know or care" about the United States. Because of the disparity between the United States and Canada, and because of the generalized U.S. impact on Canada in all areas, ranging from economic to strategic matters, there is an overall awareness and knowledgeability about the United States, and those issues emanating from the United States are therefore consistently handled at higher levels in Ottawa.

A final difference between Washington and Ottawa concerns the comparative permanence and organizational traditions of the respective civil services. Given the relative permanence of most of the senior levels of the Canadian civil service, there is greater continuity and professional expertise brought to bear on a given issue than is the case with the more transient political appointees in Washington. Thus, interactions among these Canadian officials over time give not only a sense of ongoing familiarity with given issues but also established procedures among individuals who personally know each other. In addition, and notwithstanding Ottawa's recent attempts at policy coordination, Washington remains more preoccupied with formalized structures and systematic organizational techniques when compared with Ottawa. Also a function of the respective size of the two federal governments, Ottawa can be satisfied with less structured consultative procedures among relevant departments and agencies than can Washington.

Notwithstanding these differences between the United States and Canada, there are two similarities which should be noted. One need not dwell on the interpenetration between the United States and Canada, whether in environmental, economic, strategic, or transportation matters. This is probably the single most common theme in the literature on Canada-U.S. relations. However, the policy importance of this intertwining has been rather neglected. The net effect of this interpenetration is that traditionally domestic issues become, in the Canada-U.S. context, "foreign," and there is no governmental machinery in Washington and Ottawa to deal with them adequately. To take the United States as an example, decisions in Washington are obviously made in terms of U.S. interests. U.S. law invests authority for domestic issues (e.g., environment) in departments and agencies, and yet these issues can have an impact on Canadian interests in a way they do not for other countries. A full-fledged "foreign" component is therefore unnecessary in U.S. departments dealing with these issues, but at the same time, a domestic component is not well equipped to deal with Canada. In short, there has not been an adequate Canadian policy coordinative dimension built into U.S. governmental organizations that can absorb these transborder issues. Although lip service is paid to this attempt to deal with these issues, the fact remains that the U.S. government is not organizationally equipped to take them into account. This is not to denigrate the usefulness of those attempts to solve this problem, including the use of such joint organizations as the International Joint Commission, but one need only look at a recent checklist of recent Canada-U.S. irritants, ranging from the deletion of television commercials to the Garrison Dam project, to see the impact of this phenomenon. It should be emphasized that Ottawa fully shares these difficulties in dealing with the United States.

A second similarity between Washington and Ottawa concerns attempts at policy coordination. Prior to the governments of President Nixon and Prime Minister Trudeau, the handling of bilateral issues by officials in Washington and Ottawa tended to be fragmented. This fragmentation manifested itself on the organizational and conceptual levels. On the organization level, both countries had witnessed growth in their federal government departments, while the issues confronting them have become increasingly complex. Not only had the traditional foreign-affairs-related departments grown (i.e., Department of State and Department of External Affairs), but new departments and agencies emerged in response to new needs and growing specialization in such areas as energy and environment. Many departments and agencies, aware of the bilateral and international implications of what until recently were considered domestic issues, incorporated international sections as an integral part of their operations. Complicating all this were the vocal interests and increasing relevance of state and especially provincial governments in external matters. In short, problems of policy coordination that had always existed were exacerbated if only because there was more to coordinate.

In addition to this organizational proliferation, there was a conceptual fragmentation. For those U.S. and Canadian officials handling bilateral matters, there was oftentimes lacking an expanded awareness of the implications of the issue they were dealing with. Instead of exploring the interrelationships among issues and assessing the long-range effects of these interrelationships, issues tended to be compartmentalized. Within this limited perspective, which was confined to those officials immediately involved in a particular issue, the question generally asked was: Is this course of action inherently beneficial? In short, there was a lack of effective coordination and policy overview in both capitals. The difficulty was that enduring bilateral commitments could be triggered, but without a careful assessment of what the long-range implications of these commitments would be, including how far they would or should go. In addition, this lack of coordination in Washington and Ottawa tended to encourage transborder contacts between governmental officials. Hence, transborder identities of interest, grounded in "old-school ties" (e.g., having attended the same universities) and "nuts-and-bolts ties" (e.g., sharing specialized professional expertise), were formed and flourished. While these ties facilitated the resolution of bilateral issues, they also seriously complicated problems of coordination in the two capitals.

The degree of organizational and conceptual fragmentation that existed in Washington and Ottawa prior to the governments of Nixon and Trudeau can easily be exaggerated, as can the effects of this fragmentation. Moreover, the extent to which Washington and Ottawa have become better coordinated in their policy processes since then can just as easily be exaggerated. But the fact remains that since the late 1960s there has been a conscious effort in both capitals to develop processes that are more systematic and coordinated. It is useful to examine in a more concrete sense the policymaking setting in Washington and Ottawa.

THE WASHINGTON SETTING

On the executive side, the president, as administrative head of the executive branch, is situated above some fifteen organizational units in the Executive Office of the President (ranging from the White House Office to the National Security Council); twelve executive departments (ranging from State to Energy); and fifty-seven agencies (from the Arms Control and Disarmament Agency to the International Communication Agency).[16] The cabinet, a creature of custom and tradition, functions at the discretion of the president, advising him on those matters regarding which he wishes advice. Unlike the Canadian cabinet, it does not constitute a collective decision-making body. The cabinet consists of the heads (secretaries, and the attorney general in the case of the Justice Department) of the twelve departments. In addition, the vice-president participates in all cabinet meetings, as do others upon invitation.

In examining the role of the executive in the foreign policy process, it is essential to bear in mind that while responsibility is concentrated in the president, authority to act is diffused throughout the executive structure. The president, while making major, final policy decisions, delegates much of his operational authority to his subordinates. These subordinates, as recipients of derived presidential power, operate subject to the president's final (and in many if not most cases, implicit) approval. Accordingly, the president normally establishes a general line of action in which objectives are formulated; these objectives are then transmitted to subordinate officials for elaboration and implementation. The president's function is therefore largely one of administrative supervision. However, this varies with the holders of the office, with Presidents Nixon and Carter, for example, utilizing their indisputable power to intervene in the foreign policy process at rather specific points.

Several organizational units in the Executive Office of the President deal with matters affecting Canada. The National Security Council (NSC), established in 1947, is responsible for advising the president on the integration of domestic, foreign, and military policies relating to the national security.[17] Located within the Executive Office of the President, the NSC consists in law of the president, the vice-president, the secretaries of state and defense, and other ranking officials on precedence or invitation.[18]

It is not surprising that the NSC, as an organizational assistant to the president, reflects the style, both organizational and intellectual, of each president. For example,

President Eisenhower's utilization of the NSC reflected a military staff preference and constituted what was perhaps the most highly structured presidential staff in history. Under President Kennedy the system underwent a relative breakdown, with the Council embodied in the person of McGeorge Bundy. Major crises were handled, not through the NSC, but through ad hoc groups (e.g., during the 1962 Cuban missile crisis). Under President Johnson, the NSC adjusted to the different style of Presidential Assistant Walter Rostow, again existing in name only. President Nixon, as Mr. Eisenhower's vice-president and therefore as a student of the highly structured Eisenhower approach, unequivocally registered his preference for a tight staff organization, and the NSC system again adjusted, this time to the style of the then Presidential Assistant Henry Kissinger.

Each presidential approach has its advantages and disadvantages. For example, with President Eisenhower there was literally a deluge of papers, but it was relatively easy to determine what presidential policy was. Under the Nixon approach many decisions formerly made in the bureaucracy (e.g., the State Department) were made in the NSC. However, the amount of decision-making in the NSC can easily be exaggerated, for the nature of foreign policy demands ensures that only a relatively small percentage of policy problems reaches the NSC. Those that do are of course major, ranging from the Chinese initiatives to the India-Pakistan war. The Nixon approach, under the direction of Dr. Kissinger, and continued under the administration of Gerald Ford, showed itself capable of a profound conceptual sweep and a sometimes equally profound conceptual overextension. One of the primary problems created by the Nixon/Ford approach was that the expertise of the State Department was not fully utilized on high policy matters. The result was a functional shift on the part of State (and other departments) toward a role associated more with a parliamentary than a presidential system. That is, the Department of State had to take over the role of congressional relations in the foreign policy field, spending an increasing amount of time directing Capitol Hill activities (from preparing and presenting budgetary to policy defenses).

The approach of the Carter administration, with Zbigniew Brzezinski as head of the White House National Security Council Staff, is to rely less on one man and more on a team effort, with the president making it clear that it is he who will execute final authority in foreign policy matters. This means that the other departments involved in foreign policy such as Defense, Treasury, and especially State, play more significant roles in the formulation of U.S. policy. Indeed, under Carter, the staff of the National Security Council was cut and reorganized. There are presently two major NSC committees, one on policy review which deals with interdepartmental issues. Membership consists of those departments affected by the issue at hand. The chairmanship rotates depending on the issue. The second committee is on special coordination, is chaired by Brzezinski, and deals with crisis management and shorter-term issues. Thus, there has been an attempt to institutionalize a greater role for other departments and a lesser role for the NSC.

While most of the executive departments in Washington handle Canadian matters in varying degrees, the department which handles most matters affecting Canada is the Department of State.[19] That department's Office of Canadian Affairs (EUR/CAN) was established in 1966 as one of the consequences of the Merchant-Heeney Report.[20] Prior to its establishment, the Canadian Desk ("desk" is defined as the administrative unit consisting of one or more officers responsible for relations with a specific country or countries) was an integral part of the Office of British Commonwealth, and Northern European Affairs, whose geographic responsibility included the British Commonwealth, British dependencies, and Scandinavia. Between two and three officials in this office handled matters relating to Canada. There were no Canadian specialists in any specific sense, and there was little continuity in area assignments regarding Canada. With the 1966 reorganization, EUR/CAN remained in the Bureau of European Affairs, one of five regional bureaus in the State Department, each of which is headed by an assistant secretary.[21]

EUR/CAN operates not as a "post office," but as a "nerve center," both in an operational and in a policy sense. It is not EUR/CAN's function to resolve technical matters; these it refers to the appropriate agencies. It is EUR/CAN's function to place the results of this technical expertise in the perspective of the Canada-U.S. relationship and to coordinate these results when necessary. In an operational sense, EUR/CAN is therefore charged with applying its political, military, environmental, and economic staff judgment to specific technical and nontechnical matters. It is also responsible for the preparation of basic policy papers on Canada. EUR/CAN is significant because it is the only organizational unit in Washington that has an overall geographic interest in, and responsibility for, Canada. The other organizational units dealing with Canada have a functional interest regarding that country (e.g., a department interested in defense policy is thereby interested in Canada).

The EUR/CAN staff consists of the director, three officers, and three secretaries. The responsibliities of the officers are divided functionally: one handles economic affairs, another environmental affairs, and a third politico-military and consular affairs; while the director, in addition to overseeing the entire office, handles political affairs. In a formal sense, the director is responsible for overall guidance and interdepartmental coordination concerning Canada. As such, he is the focal point in Washington for serving the needs of the U.S. ambassador in Canada. He works closely with the "country team" at the mission in Canada (which includes all section chiefs and is chaired by the ambassador) to ensure that all elements of the mission in Canada jointly pursue U.S. foreign policy objectives.

The most recent significant organizational development occurred in Washington in 1972 when the State Department established the position of deputy assistant secretary of state for Canadian affairs, the only deputy assistant secretary in the State Department responsible for a single country. Thus, the post of deputy assistant secretary for Canadian affairs was inserted between the assistant secretary for European affairs and the director of the Office of Canadian Affairs. In dealing with other departments and agencies on Canadian matters, the director of the Office of Canadian Affairs in an increasing number of cases was insufficiently authoritative to deal with these governmental officials, who were often of a higher level. The creation of the deputy assistant secretary position therefore raised the coordinative authority of the State Department a level, and has subsequently proven to be of great utility.

Within the State Department, the minimal vertical tie-off point on Canadian matters is the director of EUR/CAN: that is, a country desk officer would normally get clearance from the director before resolving an issue. For most operational problems, the highest tie-off point would be the deputy assistant secretary for Canada. In policy matters, the deputy assistant secretary and the assistant secretary would normally be involved. Should the issue necessitate higher-level attention, it would, depending on its nature, be handled with other State Department organizational components. However, a vast majority of Canadian issues would be handled within the Bureau of European Affairs and, more specifically, within the Office of Canadian Affairs. It must be added that this entire formulation is based on usage rather than on any institutional procedure.

In addition to the regular coordinative functions of EUR/CAN and the deputy assistant secretary for Canadian affairs, two coordinative techniques are utilized in Washington on Canadian matters—interagency weekly meetings and ad hoc interdepartmental groups. Once a week, some twenty governmental officials from different agencies and departments hold a one-and-one-half hour meeting, chaired by the deputy assistant secretary for Canadian affairs. Members represent other departments (i.e., Departments of Defense, Commerce, Energy, Interior, and Agriculture); agencies (International Communication Agency and Central Intelligence Agency); and other subcomponents of the State Department in addition to the entire staff of EUR/CAN (e.g., officials representing State's legal advisor and its economic and energy people). The Department of the Treasury attends some meetings, but not regularly. To ensure maximum attendance, memos are extended to all relevant departments and agencies, followed up by reminder memos. The deputy assistant secretary opens the meeting; the director of EUR/CAN presents a checklist of issues; and there is a round table discussion that is remarkably frank and entirely confidential in nature. Each official discusses problem areas, and generally a specific topic is designated for the next meeting.

The second coordinative attempt in Canadian matters involves ad hoc interdepartmental groups. In effect, informal interdepartmental working groups are set up whereby U.S. domestic objectives are synthesized. The State Department (e.g., the deputy assistant secretary for Canadian affairs) would generally chair such a group, but this is sometimes vigorously contested by other departments. The issue is reviewed internally and often includes contributions from the legislative branch (e.g., through congressional hearings or representation). Once a position is formulated, the U.S. negotiating team would confer with officials of the Canadian government. An example of this procedure occurred with the 1972 Canada-U.S. agreement on improvement of water quality in the Great Lakes, which in fact was followed up in Washington under the fifth-year review. Issues involving the highest matters of policy would go to the White House level, either through the National Security Council or the Council on International Economic Policy. However, most ad hoc consultations on Canadian matters in Washington take place at the officer level, whereby officials from different departments and agencies confer by telephone, through circulation of draft papers, or over lunch.

On the policy-planning side, there was an ambitious attempt under the regime of Henry Kissinger to move away from crisis management toward country managerial planning by decentralizing the policy-planning function to "where the action is." Hence, each geographic bureau had its own policy-planning staff headed by a director, who was responsible to the assistant secretary in charge of that bureau. For Canada, the relevant official was the director of the European Policy Planning Staff, which had as its primary responsibility the preparation of Policy Analysis and Resource (PARA) papers for each of the thirty-two countries within the purview of the Bureau of European Affairs. The confidential PARA paper on Canada, running approximately fifty pages, was completed and defended in January 1972. This was the first overall paper on Canada since May 1969, when the then-existing State Department Policy Planning Council completed a 135-page confidential study entitled *Basic Issues in U.S./Canadian Relations*. The Canada paper, like all PARA papers, was an attempt to link, analytically, policies and their costs. Both trend analysis and causal analysis were utilized (computers were not used) in invoking hard data in an overall attempt to give a sense of priorities of direction. In essence, the primary purpose of the Canada paper was to project an assessment to 1975 of anticipated Canadian policies toward the United States and vice versa. A follow-up PARA paper was scheduled for this later date and every subsequent three or four years, with in-depth analyses of specific aspects being prepared as the need arose.

Advantages of this policy planning were twofold: first, the process was valuable in shaping the officers' conceptual approach toward a decision (e.g., a checklist of variables that should be considered); second, the papers were valuable in orienting officers going to a particular country. However, the experiment ultimately failed. The officials responsible for originally drafting a paper (country officers or, in some cases, officers in the field) were precisely those who were most burdened with operational problems. Just as important, the impact of austerity drives on staffing made the process of policy planning more difficult at all levels.

Under the administration of Jimmy Carter, PARA became PARM. That is, the PARA system was replaced with a system of policy papers called Policy Assessment and Re-source Management (PARM). The PARA exercise had evolved into a less formal system than was originally planned, and the PARM exercise is in effect an adaptation of the original system. In an attempt to develop short-term policy objectives, the PARM process consists of an annual review and assessment of U.S. policy toward all foreign governments. In the case of Canada, the embassy in Ottawa submits a policy analysis of what transpired in Canada over the previous year. In addition, this analysis includes a one-year projection of anticipated developments, coupled with an assessment of precisely what U.S. interests are involved and how.

This embassy analysis is distributed by EUR/CAN to some forty governmental officials in Washington handling

Canadian matters, who review the document. An intergovernmental meeting is then held, chaired by the deputy assistant secretary of state for Canadian affairs, and attended by these forty officials. The U.S. ambassador to Canada has joined these meetings, where he elaborates on the embassy analysis. All areas of Canada-U.S. relations are discussed; disagreements are tabled; and there is an attempt to strike a consensus. A formal policy document is prepared on the basis of this meeting, which is then transmitted to all relevant U.S. and foreign-based governmental officers as official U.S. policy.

The PARM paper is useful more as a process than as a product. The paper itself is not a document that is continually referred to throughout the year. However, the process of producing the paper constitutes a useful interagency review and assessment of U.S. policy objectives toward Canada and gives a broad policy focus to specific issues. The PARM process has not to date been effective in relating policy objectives to allocation of resources, although EUR/CAN is now engaged in a zero-based budgetary effort. There are indications that there will be a future emphasis on more systematic integration between budgetary matters and policy formulation and implementation.

On the legislative side, the most important thing to bear in mind is that the Senate and House of Representatives are rarely concerned with Canada specifically, and there are no ongoing organizational structures directly geared toward handling Canadian matters. However, legislative activities are of extraordinary importance for Canada given the contiguity and interdependence between the two countries. The ways in which legislative activities can affect Canada are obvious: ratification of treaties and appointments, appropriation of funds, and of course legislation. In addition, congressional hearings can deal with Canadian matters (i.e., energy hearings), as can congressional resolutions (i.e., Saskatchewan potash) and legislative letters to the executive (i.e., commercial deletion).

The most obvious legislative focal points on Canadian matters are the Senate Foreign Relations Committee and the House International Relations Committee, with each committee having approximately ten consultative subcommittees. In the Senate's Foreign Relations Committee, the Subcommittee on Western Hemisphere Affairs deals with Canada. It is revealing that a Subcommittee on Canada was disbanded in 1969 after a decade of existence for lack of work. This clearly illustrates that an overall geographical perspective of Canada, as opposed to an issue specific one, is not useful in legislative circles. In the House International Relations Committee, the Subcommittee for Europe deals with Canada. However, as in the case with the executive departments in Washington, matters affecting Canada are permeative and are discussed not only on the floor of the Senate and House but also in the respective specialized committees such as agriculture, defense, foreign commerce, marine and fisheries, and so on. Indeed, evidence suggests that of the approximately forty Senate and House committees, at least half at some time have handled issues directly affecting Canada.

In a rudimentary attempt to gauge in a long-range sense the regional location of legislators interested in Canada and the nature of the issues with which they were concerned, the *Congressional Record* index was examined for the following congressess: the 86th Congress under Eisenhower, the 88th under Kennedy and Johnson, and the 91st Congress (first session) under Nixon. The findings were not unexpected. Legislators from the northern states made by far the largest proportion of entries referring to Canada. Roughly 88 percent of entries under "Remarks" in the Senate were from states which bordered Canada or the Great Lakes (but including Oregon), while 74 percent of the "Remarks" in the

House were made by congressmen from these same states. In terms of issue preoccupation, 66 percent of the remarks in the Senate and 89 percent in the House related to economic matters.

A more useful question is: Which current senators and congressmen are interested in Canadian matters? The answer to this question is again rudimentary in nature and is based upon interviews with officials dealing with Congress. At the same time, four distinct categories of legislators can be identified, even though the numbers of legislators included in the categories are rough estimates. First, there are the "friends of Canada" consisting of those legislators who are both knowledgeable about Canada and favorably pre-disposed toward the country. This interest and predisposition is attributable to their constituencies and background, and generally the legislators in this category are from border states. There are roughly ten senators and twenty-five con-gressmen in this category.

The second category of legislators are the "international-ists," consisting of those who are interested in foreign matters (especially European) and who have traveled fairly exten-sively. These legislators are somewhat familiar with Canada, but within this broader international context, and are generally of a favorable predisposition. However, their knowl-edge and predisposition is superficial in nature and somewhat unpredictable. There are approximately twelve senators and seventy-five congressmen in this category.

The third category of legislators would be the "anti-Canadians." Their knowledge of Canada would be similar to that of the internationalists, but their predisposition toward Canada is negative for ideological or other reasons. There would be roughly three senators and eight congressmen in this category. Finally, there is the category of "know-nothings." These legislators have never really thought about

Canada per se in a policy sense, and they have no particular predisposition toward Canada. Thus, matters affecting Canada would be largely judged in an issue-specific sense on their merits. This category includes the majority of legislators in both the Senate and the House.

Several concluding observations might be made about the U.S. legislative branch and Canada. While individual legislators interested in Canada can be identified, as can relevant legislative committees and subcommittees, the key element is the nature of the issue being processed. That is, the type of issue determines to a great extent the relevance of legislative actors. Secondly, notwithstanding the importance of a legislator's favorable predisposition toward Canada, such a predisposition will evaporate with astounding speed in the light of constituency interests, and after all, it is this constituency dimension that constitutes the legislator's raison d'être. Finally, mention should be made of those suggestions in Canada that the Canadian Embassy in Washington is not doing enough to influence the U.S. legislative branch. Such calls are naive unless a distinction is made between monitoring, providing information, and active lobbying. Certainly legislative developments should be followed closely by the Canadian Embassy, and information about Canada should be provided to responsive legislators to avoid decisions being made which might inadvertently disadvantage Canadian interest. However, active lobbying is a difficult and oftentimes counterproductive undertaking, especially to the extent that it can involve a foreign nation in the ongoing U.S. legislative-executive tug of war. Even though indications are that the legislative branch will continue to exert an increased influence on the executive domain under the Carter administration, the fact remains that the prerogatives and techniques of policy formulation and implementation rest with the executive rather than the legislature.

THE OTTAWA SETTING

The executive in Canada exercises a collective responsibility over government policies, be they domestic or foreign, with the Prime Minister serving as leader of a political party, as leader of the Government in the House of Commons, and as Chairman of the Cabinet.[22] Members of the Office of the Prime Minister (PMO), a partisan, politically-oriented Secretariat, advise and brief him on significant developments in the country, liaise with various party organizations, and prepare evaluations and recommendations. The special assistant to the prime minister is especially active within the Office of the Prime Minister (PMO) on United States-related matters.

The cabinet itself is a ministerial committee of the Privy Council, with members generally chosen by the prime minister from elected representatives sitting in the House of Commons.[23] It is the cabinet that provides the coordinative pull for the integration of policies, and its style of collegial responsibility and its committee structure reinforce this process. The preparation of a cabinet memorandum is a fundamental force in integrating policies. Indeed, Ottawa can in a sense be compared to a policy vacuum cleaner, with the cabinet providing the suction. There is an upward and coordinative draft emanating from the cabinet/ministerial level which is continually acting on lower levels of the policy process. Given the managerial problems of dealing with thirty or so ministers, an elaborate cabinet committee system has evolved [24] and now comprises four coordinating committees: Priorities and Planning; Legislation and House Planning; Federal-Provincial Relations; and the Treasury Board. In addition, there are five substantive or standing committees: Economic Policy; External Policy and Defence; Social Policy; Science, Culture and Information; and Government Operations.[25] Although the membership and terms of reference of the committees are determined by the prime minister, these committees make decisions which are annexed to the agenda of the weekly meeting of the full cabinet, and if there is no objection they are regarded as approved by the cabinet.

It is interesting to note the reaction of an American official in dealing with one of the cabinet committees. In 1948 after a meeting with the Defence Committee of the Canadian cabinet, the U.S. Secretary of Defense, James Forrestal, noted in his diary: "One of the deep impressions that I had as a result of this meeting was the contrast to the functioning of our government . . . This group not merely was the Defence Committee of the Cabinet . . . but they represented the control of the Canadian Parliament, because they are chosen Ministers of the Liberal Party now prevailing in power, as well as the chiefs of their respective (departments). Therefore, expressions of policy at this meeting are the statements of a responsible government."[26]

Two central agencies, the Privy Council Office (PCO) and the Treasury Board Secretariat, serve these ministerial bodies. Under the clerk of the Privy Council and secretary to the cabinet (the most senior Canadian civil service position), the PCO addresses itself to policies and strategies rather than to specific issues. As a secretariat to the cabinet, its officials prepare agendas, produce cabinet documents to ministers, and record and circulate decisions. The Treasury Board Secretariat, as the operational arm of the Treasury Board, is the management agency of a management committee responsible for government expenditures and internal policies.[27] This secretariat interacts with the PCO on agenda items, working of cabinet discussions, and discussion of "general climate." It is at the cabinet/ministerial level that issues being handled by the respective committees are synthesized and translated into government policy.

Policy proposals for cabinet submission are prepared on

the initiative of ministers and their departmental officials; and the proposals, to have status as a cabinet document, are submitted as a memorandum under a minister's signature. Usually when a department wants to send a memorandum to cabinet, it involves one or more of a combination of three things: a change of policy, a confirmation of existing policy, or an overlapping issue involving the mandates of several departments. The memorandum is forwarded to the PCO where it is circulated to ministers and assigned to one of the cabinet committees. Given the permeative and variegated nature of Canada-U.S. relations, there is no single cabinet committee or PCO Secretariat on these relations. However, the highest-priority issues, for example, the Auto Pact and the 1971 surcharge, would go to the Planning and Priorities Committee, which handles issues which are so all-encompassing and fundamental to Canadian governmental policy that it would be counterproductive to confine them to operational committees. The PCO Secretariat acquires additional information and coordinates with other relevant committees or secretariats. When the memorandum goes to the cabinet committee, the secretariat records the discussion, writes the minutes, and draws up the final report or recommendation which then goes to cabinet.

At this level, then, the secretaries of the PCO and the cabinet committees are the repositories of decision-making on United States-related matters. For example, a U.S. issue involving security matters that necessitated ministerial action (for example, the 1973 North American Air Defense Command [NORAD] renewal) would generally go to the PCO Secretariat servicing the cabinet committee on External Policy and Defense, and then to the cabinet itself. Likewise, a financial/commercial issue would go to the PCO's Secretariat for the cabinet committee on Economic Policy, an extremely active committee on U.S. matters in the past few years.[28] Issues involving transporation matters would go to the Government Operations Committee, which is concerned with renewable and nonrenewable resources and the infrastructure of government programs of an economic nature. The Government Operations Committee would also have handled such issues as the U.S. leasing of the Goose Bay, Labrador defense installation.

Deputy ministers and assistant deputy ministers constitute the hinge between the cabinet and the departmental working level. They are, unlike U.S. officials at this level, members of the Canadian civil service rather than political appointees, and it is they who constitute the rather sharp Ottawa distinction between political and professional. Deputy ministers (DMs) and assistant deputy ministers (ADMs) are therefore integral components of the working apparatus of departments, as well as constituting the department's ongoing executive structure. However, in addition, DMs and ADMs, and especially the latter, attend cabinet committee discussions, sometimes without their ministers. Deputy ministers are the chief source of policy inputs, and both DMs and ADMs are relevant on formal and informal interdepartmental committees, with the DMs having the authority coupled with the operational activity of the ADMs. Here it should be noted that issues generally go to the ministers after some sort of interdepartmental coordination at the DM/ADM level, and most items that require ministerial attention (e.g., items that cannot be resolved at the DM/ADM level or lower) involve interdepartmental consultation in some form. The form this takes varies, ranging from telephone calls to informal interdepartmental gatherings to formal standing interdepartmental committees. The way in which an item is processed depends of course on the nature of the issue, including its priority and subject matter, and the procedural predilections of the officials involved.

The interdepartmental committees are in effect clearinghouses, where information is tabled in an attempt to reach coordination and consensus among the various departments. Interdepartmental committees serve as a group for resource and task allocation, assigning working responsibilities, and deciding who will prepare discussion papers. There are over two hundred such committees, in varying degrees active. The PCO, and especially the Treasury Board Secretariat, are active on interdepartmental committees and informal inter-departmental discussions. Unfortunately, a complete listing of these committees, their departmental memberships, and their deliberations is not publicly available. However, it is known that these committees are involved on a range of subjects including defense, trade relations, economic issues, multinationals, restrictive business practices, and commercial policy. Functional committees to deal with matters like civil aviation also exist. Finally, in an overall coordinative sense, there is the Interdepartmental Committee on External Relations, established in 1970 and chaired by the Department of External Affairs (DEA).

Unlike Washington, the Canadian legislative branch is fully integrated into the overall policy-making process and does not have an independent existence. However, mention should be made of the two major standing committees in the House of Commons and Senate which have conducted extensive investigations into aspects of the Canada-U.S. relationship. Thus, the House Standing Committee on External Affairs and National Defence, and its Senate counterpart, have been especially active. In addition, the Parliamentary Center for Foreign Affairs and Foreign Trade has served in an advisory role.

As is the case in Washington, most of the executive departments in Ottawa handle bilateral matters in varying degrees.[29] The Department of External Affairs, like the Department of State, is the central coordinating point for such bilateral matters. Within that department, the recently created Bureau of U.S.A. Affairs serves a nerve-center function similar to that of the Office of Canadian Affairs in the State Department.[30] Its predecessor, the U.S.A. Division, had greater difficulty in defining its mandate and tended to be residual in its activities given the high rate of participation of other specialized organizational units in United States-related matters. However, the bureau now has greater centrality as a coordinating and monitoring unit in which it maintains an overview of U.S. issues and of other organizational units active in these issues.

In discussing the Department of External Affairs, it should be kept in mind that what a governmental department has the authority to do, and what it is able to do, are not necessarily synonymous. This is of course as true in Washington as it is in Ottawa. The Department of External Affairs must continually attempt to ensure formal acceptance by other departments and agencies of its coordinative primacy in all Canadian policies having external implications. The Trudeau foreign policy review, which culminated in the June 1970 publication of the five-part document *Foreign Policy for Canadians,* reflected a concern about this managerial dimension of Canada's external affairs.[31] The significant thing about this review was the explicit and implicit reaffirmation of the Department of External Affairs' coordinative centrality regarding Canadian-U.S. and other external matters. The lead booklet of *Foreign Policy for Canadians* stated that the "Government needs a strong and flexible organization for carrying out its reshaped foreign policy", which includes "modern management techniques" and "maximum integration in its foreign operations that will effectively contribute to the achievement of national objectives." [32] To accomplish these objectives, the government established the Interdepartmental Committee on External Relations (ICER), chaired by the Department of External Affairs, which met for the first time in July 1970. It is mandated with the goal of "guiding the process of integration during its initial phases and for advising the Government on such matters as the formulation of broad policy on foreign operations, the harmonization of departmental planning with the Government's external interests, the conduct of foreign operations, the allocation of resources for those operations." A subcommittee of the ICER, the Personnel Management Committee, concerned with the development of coordinative interdepartmental personnel policies, was also established. This subcommittee and the ICER itself continue to meet at irregular intervals. Since its creation, the ICER has addressed itself to two managerial dimensions of Canada's foreign operations: personnel integration whereby the supportive staff for most of Canada's foreign operations were integrated into a single system managed by the Department of External Affairs; and country planning whereby the plans and programs of all departments and agencies having foreign operations are tied together in a single conceptual package. The ICER subsequently has turned its attention to interdepartmental coordination in Ottawa.

It remains to be seen to what extent the Department of External Affairs is able to fully operationalize its coordinating and supervisory role, but several observations can be made at this point. Because the Department of External Affairs has the statutory authority for supervising and coordinating all external matters, there is the danger that it might become operationally irrelevant. The extent to which the department can maintain a comprehensive level of activity depends upon several factors. Examples would include budgetary allocations, quality of staff and staff procedures and the minister's leadership attributes, and the prime minister's orientation. Key to an effective level of activity is budgetary allocations, for obviously the resources to perform a task must be commensurate with the task assigned. The quality of External Affairs' staff, from the deputy minister to the section chief levels and below is another key factor and is related to salary and the department's ability to compete with the private sector, the department's rotational system, and the personal dynamics and effectiveness of individual officers. Just as important, the effectiveness and stature of the minister is an essential ingredient. Also key in any discussion of External Affairs' policy centrality is the prime minister's views of external affairs and the way in which he perceives the department as being relevant or irrelevant. In addition, the prime minister's most trusted advisors and assistants, for example, in the Prime Minister's Office, are important to External Affairs' centrality.

Curiously, other departments dealing with United States-related matters are in a sense more secure in the foreign policy process than is External Affairs. Moreover, this sense of security is increasing rather than decreasing, given the linkages between domestic and foreign issues. These other departments are more secure because they have indigenous resource bases grounded in their organizational structures, in economic and scientific matters, for example, thereby conferring upon them a high degree of functional or specialized relevance. The expertise of these departments is therefore essential in the processing of issues, and the departments themselves become essential, with a guaranteed centrality in the process depending upon the nature of the issue under consideration. Although the Department of External Affairs does have expertise in specialized areas, for example, in its Legal Bureau, there is no way the department can or should attempt to duplicate or compete with the specialized expertise of other departments.

Because its supervisory mission is so broad, External Affairs is less able to wait for an issue to flow into it, as the Department of Finance can, for example. A premium is therefore placed on contacts External Affairs officials are able to establish with other departments handling U.S. and other external matters. A related factor is the time External Affairs

officials have available to pursue these contacts in an effort to
detect active and potential issues relevant to its concern.
Continuity of External Affairs officials becomes essential in
maintaining an ongoing supervisory function per issue, a
continuity that is perhaps too often broken by the department's rotational system, exacerbated by the fact that the
department's most competent people often go to other
departments.

The Department of External Affairs is and should be a hub
with spokes radiating out to all departments dealing with the
United States and other external matters. The department's
role is essential because there must be some sort of coordinating at the deputy minister, assistant deputy minister, and
director general levels. The coordination which occurs at the
cabinet/ministerial level, which the department is also involved in, is too divorced from the operational departmental
bases of lower-level officials to provide adequate overall
coordination. Thus, External Affairs' attention might be
more assiduously directed at these two lower levels, and
especially at the director general level and below.

It might be useful at this point to illustrate how the
Ottawa policy process operates in handling a U.S. issue, using
as a case study the Michelin tire affair. By way of background,
the Michelin case involved the Canadian governmental
attempt to promote economic growth in one of Canada's less
developed regions as part of the work of the Department of
Regional Economic Expansion.[33] The Michelin Tire Company, with its major locations in Europe, received federal,
provincial, and local incentives in 1969 and 1971 to establish
manufacturing plants in Nova Scotia. While the Canadian
intention was to encourage production and employment in a
depressed area of Canada, the incentives provided by the
Canadian government to Michelin could be construed as an
export subsidy which would disadvantage interests in the
United States. At least this was the interpretation of the U.S.

Rubber Manufacturers Association, which filed a formal complaint wih the U.S. Treasury Department in May 1972, charging that the Michelin subsidies could adversely affect the output and employment of U.S. tire manufacturers. The Treasury Department announced that it would investigate the matter. Hearings were held over the summer, and the Candian government made direct representation by hiring a Washington law firm specializing in such matters, considered to be one of the best in this legal field. The U.S. Treasury Department, however, invoked a countervailing duty in January 1973, a decision that was not unexpected by the Canadian government.

Upon learning of the decision during the afternoon, a Canadian official (from the Department of Industry, Trade and Commerce [ITC]) in the commercial section of the Canadian Embassy in Washington telephoned the deputy minister of the Department of Industry, Trade and Commerce, who informed the department's assistant deputy minister for international trade relations. Also immediately notified were two other Canadian officials: the Department of Finance's assistant deputy minister, Tariffs, Trade and Aid Branch, and the Department of External Affairs' assistant under secretary (one of five "floating" under secretaries) responsible for economic matters. On an ad hoc basis, the Finance ADM called a meeting, and because he had the most expertise on this particular issue, informally became coordinator. The ministers were in the House of Commons until 5:00 P.M. and because more news services had picked up the story from an independent U.S. source, the problem was to brief the ministers so there would be a uniform response. A memo was rushed to the House by 4:00 P.M., while a press release was being prepared. The next day time was spent in preparing a response to put to the House of Commons. The three officials previously involved continued to be the core group, but, now included the Department of Regional

Economic Expansion. In addition, lower departmental levels became involved in the preparation of the memos: the U.S.A. Division; the Western Hemisphere Division; the Department of Industry, Trade and Commerce; and the Commercial Policy Division, Bureau of Economic and Scientific Affairs, Department of External Affairs. The House statement was then cleared interdepartmentally by telephone.

After the weekend, an interdepartmental committee held formal meetings to prepare a memo for the cabinet recommending what course of action should be taken by the Canadian government. Four departments constructed the core group: External Affairs; Finance; Industry, Trade and Commerce; and Department of Regional Economic Expansion. The next step involved getting interdepartmental agreement to a specific text. Problems were cleared by telephone. If there was a major change it was cleared through the Department of Finance, while the Department of Regional Economic Expansion was involved primarily as a data base. The process of interdepartmental clearance continued, where it went from lower department levels to the ministers. The text then went to the cabinet's Planning and Priorities Committee. The text was discussed and approved, but the committee wanted some changes in the note accompanying the text. After more departmental consultations, the note was delivered to the Canadian Embassy in Washington, to be formally delivered to the U.S. government. The minister of Industry, Trade and Commerce then made a statement in the House and tabled the note, a rather unusual occurrence.

CONSTELLATIONS

Given the policy-making processes in Washington and Ottawa, the question at this point is: How does one visualize the role of the two capitals in the Canada-U.S. intergovernmental relationship? A useful approach can be found in the concept of constellations. [34] In the simplest sense, constellations are defined as clusters of U.S. or Canadian governmental actors, empirically observed and analytically considered as a grouping, who have organizational responsibilities for matters affecting the other country, and who interact with each other about these matters over time in a patterned fashion.[35] As further refinements on this definition, it should be noted that the actors, while they may be individuals or organizational components, operate at the federal level. Moreover, while these actors are empirically observed and analytically considered as a grouping, they may or may not be aware of their membership in a given constellation or of the presence of other constellations.[36] The concept of constellations differs from more traditional perspectives in that the latter tend to concentrate on formal authority and formal organizational structures. The constellation approach includes formal organizational authority but goes beyond this to explore the actual patterned interactions of governmental actors to determine what actors are in reality acting together to process different issues. Hence, the constellations may or may not fall along formal organizational lines in that the observable interlocking activities of the actors define the boundaries of each constellation.[37]

Who are the members of these constellations in the two capitals? The answer depends upon the members' organizational responsibilities in conjunction with the nature of the Canadian or United States-related issue at hand. It is this set of organizationally relevant governmental officials who make up the core collection of the constellation. However, there is also a satellite collection of related actors who, while lacking the authority of the core group, nonetheless have peripherally related organizational authority which confers an interest in the issues being processed by the core group.

Thus, a constellation is viewed as having a center and a

periphery. At the center is the core set of continuing governmental actors, surrounded by a satellite set of related actors who, while lacking the consistent involvement of the core actors, nonetheless have peripherally related organizational responsibilities which confer an interest in the issues being handled by the core set. The exact membership of each constellation depends upon three factors: first, the actors' formal organizational authority or mandate (e.g., departmental and subdepartmental jurisdictional definitions of responsibilities); second, the specialized nature of the United States-related issues (e.g., whether it is economic, scientific, military, environmental, etc.); and third, the actors' decisional resources which enable it to operationalize its formal authority.

The constitutionally federal structure of Canada and the United States defines the overall context in which the national constellations operate. Within this context, the constellations constitute a dynamic process, in which there is a constant vying for authority on the part of specialized governmental actors, who utilize different forms of authority, invoke different decisional resources, and develop varied techniques—all in an attempt to influence the outcome of a particular process to their advantage. It should be noted that these constellations operate under very real constraints which tend to mitigate against any one member predominating. These constraints take several forms. Competition between members of the constellations themselves serves to restrict the degree to which any one constellation can prevail. In addition, constraints are imposed by other actors who are not members of the constellations, including nongovernmental pressure groups, the public, and state/provincial officials. Finally, constraints are imposed by events that occur outside the United States or Canada, including, for example, policy actions of the other nation in the bilateral relationship and developments in the international system.

The concept of constellations is introduced in this chapter as a conceptual tool, that is, as a means of visualizing how the governmental officials in the two capitals interact in handling bilateral matters. Further analytical work and fieldwork are required to systematically identify the constellations in the respective capital cities. In illustrating the constellations in Washington and Ottawa, the nature of the respective policy processes must be kept in mind. It will be recalled that Washington has executive departments that are relatively independent and budgetarily plump, while departments in Ottawa are comparatively less independent with smaller budgets. That is, the Canadian collegial system of collective responsibility, together with budgetary constraints and the sheer number of Canada-U.S. issues, tends to preclude any single department in Ottawa from acting as an independent unit in determining bilateral matters. Thus, the constellations in Washington tend to fall more along departmental lines than those in Ottawa (e.g., Ottawa's constellations are characterized more by interdepartmental clusters of actors as opposed to Washington's departmentally grounded clusters).

This suggests that Ottawa's policy planners might be less preoccupied with formal departmental autonomy, as is the U.S. system, than with the capabilities the departments' subcomponents can bring to bear in the respective constellations in which they are, or should be, most active. The key factor is therefore decisional resources, not organizational jurisdiction. Indeed, it could be that the organizational variable that most affects the policy outcome of issues processed by Ottawa is not the roles played by distinct and competitive departments as defined by statutes or the statements of political leaders but rather by the subcomponents of these departments as they act in multidepartmental constellations.

Two major constellations can be tentatively identified in both Washington and Ottawa: a security constellation and a financial/commercial constellation. The security constellation in Washington consists of organizational components of the Departments of State and Defense, while the Departments of the Treasury and Commerce are also active in matters concerning the Canada-U.S. defense production and development sharing agreement. In Ottawa, the security constellation consists of organizational components of the Departments of External Affairs and National Defence, as well as the Ministry of Transport. In terms of defense production sharing, the following units would also be active: Departments of Industry, Trade and Commerce; Supply and Services; and the Treasury Board's Secretariat. Satellite members of the security constellation would include the Departments of Communications and National Revenue.

The core members of the financial/commercial constellation in Washington would consist of subcomponents of the Departments of Treasury and Commerce. Satellite members of this constellation, depending upon the issue, would include the Departments of Agriculture, State, and Justice (i.e., anti-trust). In Ottawa the core members of this constellation would include components of the Departments of Finance; Industry, Trade and Commerce; and External Affairs. Other relevant members would include organizational units of the Departments of Agriculture; Energy, Mines and Resources; National Revenue; and Consumer and Corporate Affairs. It should be noted that in both of these major constellations other organizational units are active; for example, in Ottawa the Bank of Canada is a major actor in the financial/commmercial community.

In addition to these two major constellations handling U.S. matters, there are also several more specialized constellations that lack the coherence and sense of membership characteristic of the two major constellations, but that nonetheless appear to be active. Examples in the two capitals would include environment, energy, transportation, and legal. Three factors should, however, be borne in mind with respect to all these constellations. First, the same department or its components can be a member of more than one constellation. Second, these constellations can themselves be subdivided into more specific subconstellations. For example, the legal constellation handles law-of-the-sea matters in Washington and Ottawa, but law-of-the-sea itself has recurring departmental subcomponents which regularly interact. Third, the fact that actors in a constellation are dealing with bilateral matters does not necessarily mean that they are dealing directly with their counterparts in the other capital. Rather, the involvement of the actors can simply involve their assessments of the implications on their country of actions initiated by the other country.

Significantly, in interviewing officials in Washington and Ottawa, there does not appear to be a "political" constellation handling bilateral issues in the two capitals, unless the coordinative roles of the Departments of State and External Affairs are considered political. That is, the two foreign affairs departments are central in matters affecting the other country, but this centrality is grounded in their coordination and supervisory roles. Herein lies the distinction between these two foreign affairs departments and the other departments and agencies active on bilateral matters. These two departments are the only ones in the two capitals concerned with the overall impact of bilateral policies on their country and vice versa. In this sense, both the Departments of State and External Affairs constitute a coordinative constellation each unto themselves. The important thing to bear in mind is that the relevance of these two departments, both as a constellation and as a member of other constellations, is threefold: negotiating or consulting with their counterparts, assessing the potential impact of that other country's policies on their country, and assessing the impact of their policies on the other country.

The Canada-U.S. intergovernmental relationship is therefore an extraordinarily complex phenomenon. This chapter, introductory in nature, has of course had to be selective in highlighting dimensions of the relationship. The presidential and prime ministerial approaches to the bilateral relationship were surveyed, and fundamental differences and similarities between Washington and Ottawa were identified. The examination of Washington revealed a rather heterogeneous policy process, in which relatively independent executive and legislative actors deal with Canadian matters. In contradistinction, the assessment of policy-making in Ottawa revealed a more homogeneous policy process.

While it is commonplace in discussing Canada-U.S. relations to observe that Washington decided something, or that Ottawa is upset about something, this chapter revealed a far more complicated process. Washington and Ottawa operate in the relationship not as unitary actors but as clusters or constellations of actors. Instead of highly efficient monolithic decision-making systems in the two capitals, there are a neofeudal collection of loosely interconnected organizational components, each having an institutional life—and sometimes death—all its own. Thus, there is a Canada-U.S. intergovernmental relationship only to the extent that these constellations act in Washington and Ottawa; that is, as the organizational components perform their routine duties.

NOTES

1. "The Foundation of Canadian Policy in World Affairs," Toronto, January 13, 1947, *Statements and Speeches* 47/2.

2. Report of the Special Study Mission to Canada (Comprising Hon. Brooks Hays, Arkansas, and Hon. Frank Coffin, Maine) of the Committee on Foreign Affairs of the U.S. House of Representatives, 85th Cong., 2 Sess., House Report No. 1766 (Washington, D.C.: U.S. Government Printing Office, 1958), p. 15.

3. Remark made at LBJ ranch during visit of Prime Minister Pearson,

1965, as quoted in Dale C. Thomson and Roger F. Swanson, *Canadian Foreign Policy: Options and Perspectives* (Toronto: McGraw-Hill Ryerson Ltd., 1971), p. 129.

4. *Principles for Partnership: Canada and the United States* (Reprinted from the Department of State Bulletin of August 2, 1965), Washington, D.C.: U.S. Government Printing Office, August 1965, p. 6. This was the Report that constituted a formal agreement on how to disagree informally. It was written by the former ambassador to Canada and the former ambassador to the United States, undertaken at the request of President Johnson and Prime Minister Pearson. The Report defined special bilateral methods of resolving issues which came to be known as "quiet diplomacy." While all diplomacy, of course, may be quiet, both the phrase and the process have acquired a special meaning in the context of the Canada-U.S. relationship. It implied a close Canada-U.S. alignment manifested in pragmatic and informal contacts, through which difficulties were resolved quietly on the working level before they reached public attention.

5. *Foreign Policy for Canadians* (Ottawa: Queen's Printer for Canada, 1970), pp. 20-21.

6. Sharp, Mitchell, "Canada-U.S. Relations: Options for the Future," *International Perspectives*, Special Issue (Autumn 1972), p. 13.

7. Address of President Richard Nixon to Both Houses of Parliament in the House of Commons, Ottawa, April 14, 1972. *House of Commons Debates, Official Report*, 4th Sess., 28th Parliament, Vol. II, 1972, p. 1328.

8. These changes in the relationship also affected the informal transborder contacts between U.S. and Canadian officials. Many of these channels became not only less intimate but also less effective. The locus of decision-making in Washington was fluctuating, given the shift of issue priorities from strategic to economic. Even though a particular transborder channel remained open, its usefulness became variable as the relevance of that U.S. official in Washington altered. Those Washington officials favorably predisposed toward a particular Canadian position were less able to deliver. There was, for example, at the time of the surcharge a Canadian official accustomed to highly informal consultations with his American counterpart, who telephoned his colleague in Washington to informally discuss U.S. concern about the "dumping" of a certain product. The U.S. official said he would "check and ring back." Within twenty-four hours the U.S. secretary of the treasury telephoned the Canadian official's minister and said he was indeed willing to discuss the matter, inviting a Canadian delegation to come down to Washington. The Canadian officials remained in Ottawa.

9. This approach of managerial goodwill harked back to the Merchant-Heeney "quiet diplomacy" of the 1960s. By 1974 Canadian sensitivities about their sovereignty vis-à-vis the United States precluded a high degree of publicity about consultative arrangements that were too intimate. Nonetheless, the approach of President Ford and Prime Minister Trudeau

brought the Canada-U.S. relationship back full circle to this earlier approach.

10. For example, the experience is all too common that when an American is told that Canada has "responsible government," the reply is: "Well, I should hope so!" For the uninitiated, "responsible government" in the Canadian context refers specifically to the fundamental responsibility of the cabinet (executive branch) to the House of Commons (legislative branch).

11. This brief summary of the constitutional differences is from: John Ricker and John Saywell, *How Are We Governed?* (Toronto: Clarke, Irwin and Company, Ltd., 1971), pp. 170, 172, 173-174. This book is an example of a useful primer for Americans unfamiliar with the Canadian governmental system. For Canadians unfamiliar with but interested in the U.S. system, an easily available introductory source is: Gary Wasserman et al., *The Basics of American Politics* (Boston and Toronto: Little, Brown and Company, 1976).

12. Another major distinction between the two systems can be found in the authority of U.S. states as compared with Canadian provinces. While both countries have federal systems in which power is shared by the central and state or provincial governments, the Canadian federal system is weaker at the federal level and more decentralized than that of the United States. This means that the ten Candian provinces have a greater latitude than the fifty U.S. states in domestic and external matters. This, however, is discussed in Chapter VI.

13. See any source on the U.S. foreign policy process. This general discussion is from Charles O. Lerche, Jr., *Foreign Policy of the American People,* (2nd ed., Englewood Cliffs, N.J.: Prentice-Hall, 1961), pp. 60, 77-78.

14. "Decisional resources" refer to number of personnel, budgetary allocations available to those personnel, and degree of expertise that they have on matters within their jurisdiction, including research and intelligence capabilities.

15. Related to the factors of governmental size and priority level of bilateral issues is crisis management in Washington and Ottawa. An especially interesting area of research would be a Washington/Ottawa comparative study of definitions of crisis, the techniques of crisis response, and how crises catalyze issue resolution.

16. Parts of this section are excerpted from: Roger Frank Swanson, "The United States Canadiana Constellation, I: Washington, D.C.," *International Journal,* Vol. XXVII, No. 2 (Spring 1972), pp. 185-218.

17. At the risk of oversimplification, the economic and environmental counterparts of the National Security Council are, respectively, the Council on International Economic Policy and the Council on Environmental Quality. The Council on International Economic Policy, created in January 1971, has on its staff an official specifically charged with matters

pertaining to Canada among other functions. This council has the formidable tasks of achieving consistency between domestic and foreign economic policy, providing highest-level focus for the full range of international economic policy issues and maintaining close coordination with basic foreign policy objectives. Established in 1969 and situated in the Executive Office of the President is the Council on Environmental Quality. Responsible to the president, it develops and recommends to the president policies which promote environmental quality and conducts a continuing analysis of trends concerning the national environment. It is especially active in matters affecting Canada with a foreign service officer posted to the council to facilitate coordination with the State Department, generally working through the Office of Canadian Affairs.

18. It must be emphasized that the NSC system is the atypical channel for issue flows, reserved only for the highest-level issues. Three examples of issues involving Canada that were considered at least on the subcabinet level of the National Security Council system under the Nixon administration were: (1) energy resources and the question of a pipeline for Alaskan crude oil; (2) Arctic policy; and (3) mutual balance force reductions (MBFR).

19. Especially active on Canadian matters are the Departments of Defense, Treasury, Commerce, Agriculture, Interior, Transportation, Justice, and Labor. Mention should also be made of the Office of Special Representative for Trade Negotiations. Established in 1963, it is responsible for supervising and coordinating most aspects of high-level U.S. foreign trade policy. The Central Intelligence Agency (CIA), created in 1947 under the direction of the National Security Council, is directly responsible to the president and is charged with coordinating the intelligence activities of the several governmental departments and agencies. In addition, several of the thirty-three independent agencies responsible to the president are of special relevance concerning Canadian matters. Examples include the International Communication Agency, the Environmental Protection Agency, and the Federal Energy Regulatory Commission.

20. For a discussion of the establishment of EUR/CAN see Rufus Z. Smith, "Reflections on Canadian-American Relations," in R. H. Wagenberg, ed., *Canadian-American Interdependence: How Much?* (Windsor, Ontario: University of Windsor Press 1970).

21. Within the organizational structure of the State Department, there are, in addition to the five regional bureaus, some twelve functional bureaus of which the majority would deal with Canada. Examples include the Bureaus of Economic Affairs and Business, Intelligence and Research, Politico-Military Affairs, Security and Consular Affairs, Educational and Cultural Affairs, and International Scientific and Technological Affairs. Very important, the Office of Legal Advisor, technically not a bureau, is the principal advisor on all legal matters for the State Department and

overseas posts. It was and continues to be active regarding the unilateral Canadian declaration of sovereignty in the Arctic, and its Treaty Division plays a central role in matters affecting Canada.

22. This formal description of the organization and responsibilities of the cabinet/ministerial level is based upon Gordon Robertson, *The Changing Role of the Privy Council Office*, a Paper presented at the 23rd Annual Meeting of the Institute of Public Administration of Canada, Regina, Sask., September 8, 1971) (Ottawa: Information Canada, 1971); *Canada Year Book*, 1975 (Ottawa: Information Canada, 1975); *Organization of the Government of Canada* (Ottawa: Information Canada, 1976), and interviews.

23. Each cabinet minister usually assumes responsibility for one of the government departments, although four categories of ministers of the crown can be identified: departmental ministers, ministers without portfolio, and two types of ministers of state. Executive acts of the Canadian government are carried out in the name of the governor-general-in-council, and the cabinet (the Committee of the Privy Council) makes submissions to the governor general, who is constitutionally bound in almost all circumstances to accept them. These orders in council are utilized when a formal, legal instrument is necessary, but generally decisions taken by the cabinet are merely circulated to departments and agencies by the Privy Council Office through a "Record of Decision."

24. Major reorganizations of the cabinet committee structure were undertaken by Prime Minister Trudeau from 1968 to 1970.

25. In addition, there are special or ad hoc cabinet committees which meet as required.

26. James Forrestal, *The Forrestal Diaries*, ed. Walter Mills with collaboration of E. S. Dunfield (New York: Princeton University Library, 1961) by permission of the publisher, Viking Press, as quoted in D. C. Thomson and R. F. Swanson, *Canadian Foreign Policy: Options and Perspectives*, (Toronto: McGraw-Hill Ryerson Ltd., 1971), p. 14.

27. The Treasury Board consists of a president, the minister of finance, and four other cabinet ministers nominated by the governor-general-in-council. See, for example, W. I. White and J. L. Strick, *Policy, Politics, and the Treasury Board in Canadian Government* (Don Mills, Ontario: Science Research Associates, 1970).

28. Although classified, it can be speculated that membership on this committee would include at its core the Departments of Finance; Industry, Trade and Commerce; External Affairs; Agriculture; Energy, Mines and Resources; National Revenue; and the Treasury Board, in addition to such departments as Regional Economic Expansion; Consumer and Corporate Affairs; Labor; and Manpower and Immigration.

29. Especially active on United States-related matters are the Departments of National Defence; Industry, Trade and Commerce; Finance; and Agriculture. Other active units are the Ministry of Transport; and the

Departments of Energy, Mines and Resources; Consumer and Corporate Affairs; Environment; Justice; Regional Economic Expansion; Communication; Manpower and Immigration; and Labor.

30. Of the seven functional bureaus, the following would be especially involved in United States-related matters: Defence and Arms Control; Economic and Scientific Affairs; Legal Affairs; Public Affairs; and Consular Affairs. Special mention should be made of the Federal-Provincial Coordination Division which deals with United States-related issues in the context of provincial interests.

31. See, for example, Michael Henderson, "Policy Planning in Canadian External Affairs," a fifty-page paper prepared for the Canadian Political Science Association, June 3-6, 1974, Toronto Meeting; and Peter C. Dobell, "The Management of a Foreign Policy for Canadians," *International Journal*, Vol. XXVI. No. 1 (Winter 1970-71), pp. 202-20.

32. See *Foreign Policy for Canadians* booklet (Ottawa: Queen's Printer for Canada, 1970), p. 39.

33. For a background account, see: John Volpe, *Industrial Incentive Policies and Programs in the Canadian-American Context*, Canadian-American Committee, sponsored by C. D. Howe Research Institute (Canada) and National Planning Association (USA), January 1976, pp. 47-49.

34. The concept of "constellations" in the Canada-U.S. context was originally introduced in the article, Roger Frank Swanson, "The United States Canadiana Constellation, I: Washington, D.C." *International Journal*, Vol. XXVII, No. 2 (Spring 1972), pp. 185-218. However, the concept of clusters of actors in a decision-making process is of course not new, and has been applied in a variety of areas. See, for example, Wallace S. Sayre and Herbert Haufman, *Governing New York City* (New York: Russell Sage, 1965). One of the author's doctoral students has since modified and extended a "cluster" approach in an excellent examination of policy-making in Ottawa. See John J. Kirton, *The Conduct and Coordination of Canadian Government Decision-making Towards the United States*. Ph.D. Dissertation, Johns Hopkins University, Baltimore, Maryland, February 1977.

35. This is not to be confused with the popularly held notion of an "old-boy network" whose empirical existence is especially suspect given the higher degree of decisional specialization and the increased number of bureaucratic units involved in policy formulation and implementation. Conceptually these communities are empirically observable interacting sets rather than groups whose coherence and alleged effects are based upon such static attributes as similarities in background.

36. However, the officials' awareness of the existence of the constellations is an interesting analytical concern unto itself, both in terms of causation (e.g., the extent to which a sense of membership perpetuates the existence of that constellation) and in terms of outcome (e.g., those factors

which determine the sense of membership for each of the behaviorally identified constellations).

37. In this sense the concept of constellations can be viewed as a decision-making system in that the emphasis is on actors who can be typed and empirically identified as performing recurrent sequences of the activities of actors that originate in one subsystem and are reacted to in another. Here it should be reiterated that the identification of the actors is empirically grounded, and it is the observable interlocking activities of the actors that define the boundaries of each constellation (or subsystem).

II

UNITED STATES DIPLOMATIC AND CONSULAR REPRESENTATION IN CANADA*

United States representation abroad is extensive. It consists of 135 embassies, 10 missions, 67 consulates general, 48 consulates, and 12 consular agencies.[1] Of this international presence, U.S. representation in Canada consists of the embassy in Ottawa and seven consular posts located throughout Canada. This U.S. representational system, far from being a lower-order replication of the policy process in Washington, in fact differs from it substantially.

But first, a similarity must be noted between the two—their organizational constituency. Thus, the U.S. diplomatic and consular presence in Canada includes not just representatives of the Department of State but also of the Departments of Defense, Treasury, Agriculture, Justice, as well as of such independent bodies as the International Communication

* This chapter originally appeared as a published article entitled "The United States Canadiana Constellation, II: Canada" in *International Journal*, (Vol. XXVIII, No. 2 (Spring 1973), pp. 325-67. It was subsequently revised and updated for inclusion in this book.

Agency. However, the similarity between Washington and the U.S. representational system in Canada ends with this organizational constituency. If the Washington policy process is relatively heterogeneous, the U.S. representational system is, by contrast, homogeneous—a result of the organizational centrality of the ambassador as chief of mission.

The function of the ambassador as chief executive of the field mission is, of course, to represent all relevant departments in Washington, not just his parent organization, the Department of State. An ambassador's ultimate organizational superior is the president, and in fact he serves as the personal representative of the president in Canada.

The degree of homogeneity of the Canadiana field mission is a result of organizational factors within the overall U.S. decision-making process, and the decisional characteristics of the ambassador himself (e.g., his personal forcefulness, his predilection for coordination, etc.). From an organizational standpoint, the ambassador's authority had very seldom been challenged by other U.S. representatives abroad prior to World War II, primarily because of the small number and limited responsibilities of these other representatives. However, the immediate postwar years witnessed a proliferation of strong, semiautonomous U.S. missions and representatives overseas. The result was an erosion of the ambassador's organizational centrality to the point where he lacked the rudimentary authority to supervise or control these missions and representatives. By 1948, his authority had reached an all-time low.[2] This situation was subsequently rectified by a series of steps, the first being the 1951 "Clay Paper," which established the "country-team" concept and was the first explicit statement regarding the primacy of the ambassador vis-à-vis officials of other departments and agencies.[3] Since that time, the organizational centrality of the ambassador has been confirmed and embellished by every president (e.g.,

through executive orders and presidential communications),
by interdepartmental agreements, and by State Department
instructions. Perhaps the classic statement of the ambassador's organizational primacy was the May 29, 1961, letter
from President John F. Kennedy to all U.S. chiefs of mission
throughout the world:

> You are in charge of the entire United States Diplo-
> matic Mission, and I shall expect you to supervise all of
> its operations. The Mission includes not only the
> personnel of the Department of State and the Foreign
> Service, but also the representatives of all other United
> States agencies which have programs or activities in
> [name of host country].[4]

Thus, at the present time the organizational factors within
the overall U.S. decision-making process favor the primacy of
the ambassador in the field, notwithstanding the persistent
interdepartmental struggle for decisional centrality in Washington concerning such foreign policy issue areas as economics and defense. In short, the ambassador has sufficient
organizational authority to maintain a high degree of homogeneity in the field mission, with the primary variable now
being his personal decisional characteristics.

The purpose of this chapter is to identify the major
components and subcomponents of the U.S. representational
system in Canada and to define their procedures, functional
responsibilities, and organizational structures. The first section analyzes the evolutionary development of this field
mission, including compilations of data regarding the quantitative growth of the mission, and profiles of the twelve
ambassadors serving in Canada from 1943 to 1977. The
second section analyzes the embassy in Ottawa and its
subcomponents, while the third section analyzes the consul-

ates general in Canada and their subcomponents. The concluding section discusses problems of coordination and assesses diplomatic and consular effectiveness.

ORIGINS AND EVOLUTION [5]

U.S. diplomatic representation in Canada was formally established in 1927 when a legation was opened in Ottawa. In 1943 the legation was elevated to the status of an embassy. However, the origins of the United States Canadiana field mission go back much further in time. In June 1827 Henry M. Morfit was appointed commercial agent at Halifax, and the first consulate in what is now Canada was established in March 1833 in Halifax when John Morrow was appointed consul.[6] At that time, the United States was globally represented by approximately 150 consular posts. Thus, it was not until the 1830s that the first office of a consular network already global in scope was opened on the east coast of Canada, to be augmented, in succeeding decades, by extensions into the heartland.

The first U.S. consulate general in Canada was authorized by Congress in October 1857, and it opened the same year in Montreal under the title, Consulate General of the United States of America for the British North American Provinces. The period from Confederation to the turn of the century witnessed the numerical and geographical proliferation of consulates until, at the peak of the period from 1903 to 1913, the U.S. government had thirty-eight posts in operation across Canada. Although new posts have been established since that time, the twentieth century has been a period of reorganization and consolidation into the seven consulates general which exist today. Figure 1 illustrates the evolutionary development of the United States Canadiana field mission.

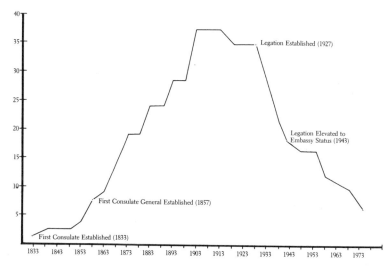

Figure 1. Number of consulates general and consulates in Canada 1833-1973.

Underlying this evolutionary sequence were a series of Canadian-U.S. societal factors and interorganizational forces in Washington. Of prime importance was the nature of the economic, political, and social interaction between the two countries. Proximity and complementary economies engendered a burgeoning commercial and societal intercourse which, together with its attendant functions, lay well within the purview of traditional consular responsibilities.

Thus, ever since the need to care for destitute U.S. seamen arose in Canada's eastern ports during the 1830s, it has been the extensive social contact between the two nations which has provided the basic justification for consular expansion. One of the major requirements for an increased network stemmed from the role of the consular posts in servicing the massive, if historically uneven, movements of people from

Canada to the United States. The enormous burden inherent in this service is illustrated by the resignation of the U.S. consul general at Vancouver in 1925 in response to the unmanageable volume of applicants following the U.S. Immigration Act of 1924.[7] That Americans residing in Canada could pose equally perplexing problems is exemplified by the case of a Montreal resident who, in 1857, sought consular assistance in hastening the delivery of the slaves he had ordered from the United States.[8]

No less important in stimulating consular expansion was the intense economic interaction between the two nations. Indeed, it was the east coast fisheries trade that had produced the initial demand for statutory consular services. With the development of the central provinces, and the Reciprocity Treaty of 1854, the tasks of export certification and commercial reporting increased rapidly. Even in periods when high tariffs constricted the volume of trade, the need for their initial application and administration in Canada made for no lessening of consular involvement.

The activity surrounding the Reciprocity Treaty of 1854 well demonstrates how indistinct the economic and political dimensions of the consular role can be. While political reporting dates back to the 1830s when the U.S. consul at Halifax submitted summaries of fisheries debates in the Nova Scotia House of Assembly, its major advance came in the late 1840s.[9] Personifying this role in an activist sense was Consul I. D. Andrews, appointed first to the post at St. John, New Brunswick, and later Montreal, who was particularly active in reporting on the prospects for reciprocity, lobbying on its behalf, and later claiming credit for its achievement. Reinforcing these expansive forces, especially in the earlier periods, was the political status of Canada as a colony. In the absence of a formal diplomatic presence within Canada, the United States was led to rely on the consular posts for activities of a more political nature.

If periods of close cooperation served to expand the political functions of the consular posts, so too could times of open hostility between the United States and Canada. As early as 1846, U.S. consuls were issuing intelligence reports on the strength and movements of the British fleet and local Canadian militia.[10] These concerns rapidly increased in the Civil War period with the influx of Confederate agents into Canada. Indeed, the suspicion between the U.S. and Canadian governments, and the sensitive nature of the activities of the former's representatives, were sufficient to induce a request from the U.S. consul in Montreal urging the State Department to be "uneasy for the safety of U.S. Consuls in the Province." [11]

It is important to note that the sheer number of U.S. consular posts in Canada cannot be taken as a reliable indicator of either the intensity of the U.S.-Canadian interaction nor the relative importance of these flows to the United States over time.[12] Inhibiting the growth these intersocietal factors engendered were constrictive factors of a technical and organizational nature. Advances in communications and transportation permitted a more compact operation in a centralizing Canada. Perhaps the most important cause of the rapid numerical decline of consular posts in the early years of this century was the new technologies that made much greater administrative centralization possible. This consolidation is reflected in the rise of higher-ranking consulates in this period, and the steadily increasing size of the districts which the consular posts covered. For example, six of the present seven U.S. posts in Canada were elevated to the status of consulate general between 1908 and 1964.

The size of the U.S. consular network in Canada is also a product of the largely independent organizational factors which have, on the whole, tended to exert a constrictive influence. Indeed, the U.S. Foreign Service apparatus seemed to possess an organizational logic of its own. Perhaps the primary Washington-based organizational relationship to affect the size of the U.S. consular network in Canada (and of course globally) was the Department of State's financial dependence on a Congress little impressed with the national importance of a substantial Foreign Service. The major result of congressional austerity in consular appropriations was an overworked, underpaid, and ill-supervised field staff. An interesting by-product of this situation, one which appears to have affected Canada, was a further expansion of the U.S. consular network. Before the drive for professionalization of the Foreign Service had secured adequate salaries for the local consuls, financial security could be obtained by the extensive, if illicit, practice of consuls appointing several cooperative consular agents with whom fee splitting was concluded.[13] By the latter decades of the nineteenth century, even the most unlikely Canadian town was liable to have a resident U.S. representative. However, these intermittent convulsions of consular abuses gave way to a series of statutory advances (for example, the Acts of 1906, 1915, 1924, etc.) which culminated in a reduced number of consular posts and, not incidentally, in the professionalism characteristic of the service today.

At this point, it might be helpful to examine briefly how the seven consular posts now active in Canada developed. In general, the U.S. consular presence responded to the westward extension of the commercial, societal, and political interaction between the United States and Canada. The first consulate opened in Halifax in 1833 to attend to the commercial and political aspects of an increasingly vigorous Maritimes-New England fisheries trade. The elevation of the post's consul, Mortimer M. Jackson, to the status of consul general in June 1880 coincided with the increased importance of the political-military dimension of the Canadian-U.S. relationship in the post-Civil War period.[14] The establishment of a consulate (now closed) in St. John's, Newfoundland, in 1852 is also largely attributable to the fisheries trade. Subsequent to Canada's attainment of formal autonomy in foreign affairs from Great Britain in 1926, the need to maintain U.S. representation in Newfoundland led to an upgrading of the post to consulate general, a status it maintained upon the province's admission to Canada in 1949. However, in a recent (August 1976) austerity effort, the Department of State closed the St. John's consulate, consolidating that district with the Halifax consulate general.

The mid-1850s witnessed the establishment of consulates in the growing financial and political centers of Montreal and Quebec in 1854 and 1855, respectively. In 1857 the Montreal post was elevated to consulate general, making it the first U.S. consulate general established in Canada. Quebec City's rise to consulate general status followed a century later in 1964. In addition to political factors, economic activity also explains the establishment of the U.S. consulate at Toronto in 1864 and its elevation to consulate general in 1933. The gradual westward extension of Canada is reflected in the early history of the Winnipeg consulate, which was established in 1869. Its first consuls, Gen. Oscar Malmros and James Taylor, were particularly active in supporting the annexation of the Red River colony to the United States. The post became a consulate general in the 1940s. The Vancouver consulate has a somewhat less activist history. It evolved from a consular agency in 1887, into a commercial agency in 1891, into a consulate in 1897, and finally, into a consulate general in 1908. The final post in the present U.S. network, Calgary, was opened as a consulate in 1906, one year after Alberta became a province. Its major period of expansion in staff came with the post-1948 development of oil and natural gas. The closure of the U.S. consulate at Edmonton led to the upgrading of the Calgary post to consulate general in 1963.

Prior to the establishment of the U.S. legation, the consulate general in Ottawa, which had been opened in 1889, was serving in a quasi-diplomatic capacity on a wide range of political matters requiring direct contact between the Canadian and U.S. governments.[15] While all U.S. consular posts were providing local or regional political reports, the Ottawa post had emerged as *primus inter pares*, with horizons and concerns that were unmistakably national. Since at least 1910, when a Canadian-German trade agreement was signed by the resident German consul general, the Canadian government had been using the consular posts in Ottawa to facilitate transactions (thereby contributing to the Canadian drive for autonomy), with the U.S. post constituting a part of this process. Even during World War I the U.S. post was submitting reports on important issues, such as the Navy Debate and the political prospects of the Reciprocity Agreement. By 1922 the U.S. consul general was dealing directly with Canadian cabinet ministers on commercial matters, and by 1926 the post was active on virtually all matters that were to concern the new U.S. minister of the legation the following year. With its major functions assumed by the legation, however, the consulate general at Ottawa entered a period of rapid decline culminating in its closure during World War II.

Thus, 1927 becomes a key year, with the U.S. government establishing a legation in Canada by appointing its first minister, William Phillips. The same year the Canadian government opened its first legation in Washington, D.C., with Vincent Massey as minister. A total of eight U.S. ministers were appointed to Canada in the years from 1927 to 1943 (see Table 1).[16]

TABLE 1   MINISTERS TO CANADA 1927–43

Minister	Tenure	President	Secretary of State
Phillips, William	June 1927–Dec. 1929	Coolidge (1923–9) & Hoover (1929–33)	Kellogg (1925–9) & Stimson (1929–33)
MacNider, Hanford	Aug. 1930–Nov. 1932	Hoover (1929–33)	Stimson (1929–33)
Robins, Warren D.	April 1933–April 1935	Roosevelt (1933–45)	Hull (1933–44)
Armour, Norman	May 1935–Jan. 1938	Roosevelt (1933–45)	Hull (1933–44)
Roper, Daniel	May 1939–Aug. 1939	Roosevelt (1933–45)	Hull (1933–44)
Cromwell, James	Jan. 1940–May 1940	Roosevelt (1933–45)	Hull (1933–44)
Moffat, J. Pierrepont	June 1940–Jan. 1943	Roosevelt (1933–45)	Hull (1933–44)
Atherton, Ray	Aug. 1943–Nov. 1943	Roosevelt (1933–45)	Hull (1933–44)

SOURCE: *Department of State Foreign Service Lists 1927–1943.*

The legation in Ottawa was formally raised to the status of embassy in 1943, the same year in which Canada elevated its legation in Washington into an embassy. Since then, twelve U.S. ambassadors have been appointed to Canada.[17] Table 2, based on the State Department's *Foreign Service List* and *Biographic Register* (1943-72) and other sources, gives some rudimentary data on these men. All the ambassadors attended four eastern universities as undergraduates, 80 percent going to the three Ivy League universities of Harvard, Princeton, and Yale, and 50 percent to Princeton. One of them also attended a business college. Over 30 percent studied at French universities, while only one studied at a university in the United Kingdom. The tenure of the ambassadors varies considerably; the shortest is ten months (Linder), the longest almost six years (Butterworth), the average for all ambassadors being two years and six months. The average age of the ambassadors at the time of appointment is fifty-eight and one-half years, ranging from forty-four (Enders) to sixty-eight (Linder). In addition, over 60 percent of the ambassadors were career officers, 50 percent of them having previous foreign experience of an equivalent nature

TABLE 2   UNITED STATES AMBASSADORS TO CANADA 1933–78

Name	Date of birth	Place of birth	Universities undergraduate (graduate)	Previous post	Career/ non-career	Length of service	President	Secretary of State
Atherton, Ray	1883	Mass.	Harvard (study in Paris)	EEMP Luxembourg	career	Nov. 1943–Aug. 1948, 4 years, 11 months	Roosevelt (1933–45) Truman (1945–53)	Hull (1933–44) Stettinius (1944–5) Byrnes (1945–7) Marshall (1947–9)
Steinhardt, Laurence	1892	N.Y.	Columbia	AEMP Czechoslovakia	career	Sept. 1948–March 1950, 1 year, 6 months	Truman (1945–53)	Marshall (1947–9) Acheson (1949–53)
Woodward, Stanley	1899	Penn.	Yale (Ecole libre des sciences politiques)	Chief of Protocol Division, State Department	career	June 1950–Jan. 1953, 2 years, 7 months	Truman (1945–53)	Acheson (1949–53)
Stuart, R. Douglas	1886	Ill.	Princeton (Northwestern)	President, Quaker Oats	non-career	July 1953–May 1956, 2 years, 10 months	Eisenhower (1953–61)	Dulles (1953–9)
Merchant, Livingston T.	1903	N.Y.	Princeton	Assistant Secretary of State for European Affairs	career	May 1956–Nov. 1958, 2 years, 5 months	Eisenhower (1953–61)	Dulles (1953–9)

Name	Born	State	Education	Previous position	Career status	Dates of service	President	Secretary of State
Wigglesworth, Richard B.	1891	Mass.	Harvard	Congressman	non-career	Dec. 1958-Oct. 1960, 1 year, 10 months	Eisenhower (1953-61)	Dulles (1953-9) Herter (1959-61)
Merchant, Livingston T.	1903	N.Y.	Princeton	UnderSecretary of State for Political Affairs	career	Feb. 1961-May 1962, 1 year, 3 months	Kennedy (1961-3)	Rusk (1961-9)
Butterworth, W. Walton	1903	La.	Princeton (Dijon, Oxford)	AEP European Economic Community et al.	career	Oct. 1962-Sept. 1968, 5 years, 11 months	Kennedy (1961-3) Johnson (1963-9)	Rusk (1961-9)
Linder, Harold F.	1900	N.Y.	Columbia	President, Export-Import Bank	non-career	Sept. 1968-July 1969, 10 months	Johnson (1963-9) Nixon (1969-74)	Rusk (1961-9) Rogers (1969-73)
Schmidt, Adolph W.	1904	Penn.	Princeton (Harvard, Dijon, Berlin, Sorbonne)	Vice-President, T. Mellon and Sons	non-career	Sept. 1969-Feb. 1974, 4 years, 5 months	Nixon (1969-74)	Rogers (1969-73)
Porter, William J.	1914	England	Boston C. Thibodeau Business College	UnderSecretary of State for Political Affairs	career	Feb. 1974-Feb.1976, 2 years	Nixon (1969-74) Ford (1974-77)	Kissinger (1973-77)
Enders, Thomas O.	1931	Conn.	Yale (Harvard)	Ass't Secretary of State for Economic and Business Affairs	career	Feb. 1976-	Ford (1974-77) Carter (1977-)	Kissinger (1973-77) Vance (1977-)

(e.g., rank of ambassador or envoy extraordinary), almost exclusively in European postings. Only three (Butterworth, Atherton, and Enders) have served consecutively under two different presidents for any significant length of time, and only one (Merchant) has been appointed for two nonconsecutive terms by two presidents of different political parties.[18]

THE EMBASSY[19]

The U.S. Embassy is located on Ottawa's Wellington Street, across from the Houses of Parliament. The embassy staff consists of the ambassador and the deputy chief of mission (DCM); approximately thirty-five officers; twenty-seven American personnel performing clerical, administrative, and cryptographic functions,[20] and forty-nine Canadians performing clerical and custodial services and some limited professional services. This is smaller than the Canadian Embassy in Washington. Indeed, in a wider sense, the U.S. Embassy in Ottawa is relatively small, having, for example, less staff than the embassies in Brasilia or New Delhi. This is a reflection, not of the comparative importance the United States attaches to its relations with Canada, but of the ease of communication between U.S. officials in Ottawa and Washington and the absence of a U.S. aid, Peace Corps, or military-assistance program in Canada.

Organizationally, the embassy consists of the ambassador and the deputy chief of mission (DCM) who constitute the Executive Section (EXEC), and nine major organzational units: Political Section (POL), Economic Section (ECON), Agriculture Section (AGR), Consular Section (CONS), Administrative Section (ADM), Defense Attaché's Office (DAO), Immigration and Naturalization Service (INS), Legal

Attaché's Office (LEGATT), and the International Communication Agency Post (ICA).

The functions of any ambassador are generally regarded as representation, information, negotiation, and protection.[21] However, to these traditional functions must be added a fifth—that of management. Essentially, the ambassador is the chief executive of a large and extraordinarily complex establishment, a task complicated by the fact that his authority is subject to all the vagaries inherent in his home capital. The U.S. ambassador to Canada is the personal representative of the president to the government of Canada. Whether he is partaking in a ceremony or negotiating with the Canadian authorities, he is doing so on behalf of the president. Moreover, he is responsible for the entire U.S. diplomatic presence in Canada, including not only the embassy and the seven consulates general but also, by special presidential direction, for all other official U.S. representatives in Canada, be they civilian or military.

While the U.S. ambassador is responsible to the president, his direct lines of communication run through the Department of State, and his instructions normally come through the secretary of state. Indeed, not only does the Department of State provide the ambassador's back-up, his diplomatic mission is staffed primarily by Foreign Service officers and other Foreign Service personnel.[22] Ambassadors are, of course, appointed by the president, a power defined in the U.S. Constitution. However, the Constitution also states that these appointments are subject to the advice and consent of the Senate. A notable example of the utilization of this power is the case of Nathan William McChesney, a Chicago lawyer and Republican stalwart, whom President Herbert Hoover nominated as minister to Canada in 1932. Despite this official endorsement and McChesney's vigorous efforts on his own behalf, the Senate, controlled by Democrats who had voted in conference not to accept any Hoover appointees, refused to act on the nomination. Mr. Hoover was subsequently defeated in the 1932 election by Franklin D. Roosevelt, who successfully appointed Warren D. Robins as minister to Canada the following year.[23] By constitutional authority, the Senate also has confirmation powers regarding the appointment of "other public Ministers and Consuls." This basic statutory authority of the Senate, coupled with a network of some fifty provisions of law establishing requirements for confirmation in the foreign relations field, confers upon the Senate confirmation powers regarding thousands of foreign appointments.[24]

The procedure for the appointment of an ambassador to Canada is as follows:[25] The U.S. ascertains before his appointment, according to international custom, that he will be considered *persona grata* by the Canadian government. After this request for acceptance (*agrément*) is received, the appointment is made public. The ambassador would then receive from the U.S. government his official letters (letters of credence), which in principle are opened by the Canadian governor general at the time of presentation. However, a *copie d'usage* is presented to the Canadian secretary of state for external affairs before presenting them to the governor general. The Protocol Division of the Department of External Affairs then arranges an audience with the governor general for delivery of the credentials. These letters of credence confer upon the ambassador the authority for his mission and determine the general bearing of his appointment.[26]

The deputy chief of mission (DCM), generally a career Foreign Service officer of proven capability, performs the threefold functions of serving as principal advisor to the ambassador, executive officer responsible for the efficient operation of the mission, and acting chief of the mission in the ambassador's absence (i.e., if the ambassador leaves the country, the DCM becomes *chargé d'affaires ad interim*).[27] Beyond these general functions, the DCM's specific roles depend on his relationship with the ambassador and the latter's organizational preferences. In recent years the DCM in Ottawa has had an efficient working relationship with the ambassador and consequently considerable responsibility for organization and coordination. While the nine organizational units have, as a matter of right, direct access to the ambassador, they are responsible to the DCM. In addition, the DCM sees every major incoming communication and clears in advance most outgoing communications.

The Political Section (POL) consists of three State Department officers and one trainee. Headed by a political counselor responsible for its overall direction, the two officers roughly divide their work between the internal and external dimensions of Canadian political developments. Most of this section's time is spent monitoring—acquiring and analyzing data—on the political aspects, compulsions, and imperatives of Canada. Because of its small size, functional responsibilities are flexibly assigned, and those political facets thought most important are emphasized. In addition, time is spent resolving specific issues in which the Political Section acts as an intermediary for the U.S. government vis-à-vis Canada. Finally, in resolving a specific issue, POL spends a great deal of time making operational policy recommendations—as opposed to long-range recommendations—while simulataneously pursuing specific instructions.

One of the officers has the responsibility of following developments in Parliament, knowing specific MPs, attending the question period, and so on. It is interesting to note, especially given the difference between the American and Canadian governmental systems, that the U.S. Embassy in Ottawa is more active than the Canadian Embassy in

Washington regarding the respective legislative bodies. (The Commons question period would also be attended by officers from sections other than POL should it appear that the discussions will involve their particular areas of interest.) Telegrams prepared for Washington by the reporting officers are subsequently on the DCM's desk before the close of the day.

The Economic Section (ECON) is headed by an economic counselor, and consists of six officials. In addition, there are the two collateral units, the Internal Revenue Service and the Agriculture Section. In the Economic Section half the time is spent on reporting, followed by operational policy recommendations and routine negotiations. Because of the size of ECON, there is a more formal distribution of functions than is the case in the other embassy sections, but like the embassy as a whole, ECON is characterized by an operational flexibility responsive to changing circumstances. In ECON, which is, in fact, the Economic-Commercial Section, there is first a commercial attaché who is a State Department official. He supervises and coordinates U.S. commercial work in the seven consulates general, administers Department of Commerce programs, protects U.S. business interests, and so on. Second, there is a transportation and communication officer, who is also a State Department official. His functions are reflected in his title. Third, there is a labor attaché who handles such matters as trade union, antitrust, and consumer issues. Fourth, a trade, energy and resources officer is responsible for trade and energy policy in general, including more specific aspects of oil exports to the U.S. and such other matters as fisheries. A financial and development aid officer deals with such specific facets as balance of payments and foreign investments. Finally, there is also a counselor for science and technology, who is a State Department official. The Internal Revenue Service (IRS) consists of two officials whose function is essentially that of liaison and income tax enforcement with respect to U.S. tax laws and regulations. The IRS officials report to their parent agency, the Department of the Treasury, but are responsible to the ambassador.

The Agricultural Section (AGR) consists of three officers, two of whom are from the Foreign Agriculture Service (FAS) of the Department of Agriculture,[28] and one of whom is a Canadian citizen. The two Americans are the agriculture attaché and the assistant agriculture attaché, while the Canadian is a reporting specialist. AGR is collateral to the Economic Section, with whom it works in close cooperation. The functions of AGR are special agricultural reporting (i.e., Canadian crop conditions and Canadian agricultural developments); specialized agricultural negotiations (i.e., resolving specific agricultural problems); and, in general, the facilitation of agricultural relations between the United States and Canada. AGR reports directly to the Department of Agriculture but is responsible to the ambassador. The Consular Section (CONS), consisting of two State Department officers, is responsible for such traditional consular services as visa and passport operations, welfare of U.S. citizens, and so on. Thus, it performs in the Ottawa area the same general functions as do the other U.S. consulates general located throughout Canada.   The Administrative Section (ADM) consists of six State Department officers and, quite simply, is responsible for the internal administration of the embassy. Its functions include such diverse aspects as personnel matters and the administration of the Marine Security Guard (MSG). It is also the centralized administrative headquarters for the seven U.S. consulates general for which it would, for example, draw up a lease for a building rental.

The Defense Attaché's Office (DAO) consists of four military specialists headed by a U.S. Air Force attaché with the rank of colonel. The DAO's primary function is to serve as liaison with the Canadian military. In addition, a great deal of time is spent in collecting, analyzing, and reporting Canadian military data. The DAO is responsible to the ambassador but reports to its parent agency in Washington, the Department of Defense. Not physically located in the embassy at 100 Wellington Street, the DAO, along with ICA, IRS, INS, the Consular Section, and the science counselor, have offices in four other locations.

The Immigration and Naturalization Service (INS) consists of one officer from the Department of Justice. He serves in an advisory capacity to the Consular Section in immigration and naturalization policies and deals with the U.S. immigration posts on the U.S.-Canadian border. He, too, is responsible to the ambassador but reports to his agency in Washington, the Immigration and Naturalization Service. The Legal Attaché's Office (LEGATT) consists of two officers posted from the Department of Justice in Washington. They, of course, have no enforcement authority in Canada, and their primary function is liaison with the Royal Canadian Mounted Police (RCMP). Responsible to the ambassador, they report to their parent agency in Washington.

The International Communication Agency Post (ICA) established in Ottawa in 1958, as the U.S. Information Service (USIS)[29] consists of three American officers—the public affairs officer (PAO), who is the ICA director in Canada, an information officer, and a cultural affairs officer. There are also seven Canadians on the staff, including three clerks, two information assistants, one public affairs assistant, and one administrative assistant. The PAO is responsible for advising the ambassador on Canadian public opinion with respect to U.S. policies that affect Canada and for fostering U.S. policies by attempting to make them understandable to the Canadian people. The information officer is responsible for press, radio, TV, and film distribution, utilizing resources from the ICA in Washington and, very importantly, in-house resources (e.g., work produced by the Ottawa staff). Both officers also work with universities and such cultural institutions as museums. In addition, there are three branch public affairs officers, each with a Canadian assistant, housed with the consulates general in Toronto, Montreal, and Vancouver. The Toronto office was established in 1960, that in Montreal in 1968, and that in Vancouver in 1976. The ICA Post in Ottawa is responsible to the ambassador but reports to its parent agency, the International Communication Agency. The overall functions of ICA/Canada can be grouped under the three headings of public information, public relations, and cultural activities. More specifically, it conducts the public relations program for the embassy, including distribution of documentation and periodicals; it administers the ICA film program and reading room, including an intralibrary loan service; and it provides a reference service by annually responding to over ten thousand individual information requests of Canadians.

The U.S. Embassy in Ottawa performs reporting services for the entire U.S. government, although the bulk of U.S. communications is addressed to the Department of State. It also corresponds directly with private parties such as corporate institutions or individuals. A relevant telegram may, for example, be sent to the U.S. Consulate General in Halifax, or to Washington for the attention of such Departments as Commerce, Treasury, Interior, or to the U.S. Embassy in Moscow (e.g., regarding a Canadian matter affecting the United States-USSR interaction). Most of the embassy's communications are sent to the Department of State generally in the form of telegrams or aerograms. The section chiefs either authorize or clear all outgoing communications, which are then read by the DCM. A section chief's signature generally ensures clearance by the DCM. The primary rationale for this layer of clearance (e.g., section chief, and DCM generally for the ambassador) is to provide an additional higher-level perspective and to prevent wasteful duplication.

There are essentially five methods of communication: letters, transmittal slips, aerograms, telegrams, personal calls, and meetings. Letters posted to the Washington (or Canadian) assistant secretary level are normally signed by either the DCM or the ambassador, while letters to subordinate levels are often signed by the section chief. The State Department's deputy assistant secretary for Canadian affairs receives copies of virtually all embassy correspondence with Washington officials.

Transmittal slips are used to send secondary materials (e.g., articles from newspapers) on specific subjects. While transmittal slips are sent to the appropriate functional addresses, three organizational units in Washington receive most of them: the State Department Office of Canadian Affairs, and the Canadian Desks in the Departments of Commerce and Treasury. Since aerograms generally take a week between the Ottawa dispatch and the Washington distribution, they are used for detailed reports when there is no time problem. The section chief authorizes those aerograms drafted in his section, the more important of which are then submitted for approval to the DCM.

Telegrams are used for more urgent matters, facilitated by direct-line transmission facilities to the State Department from the embassy. First-person telegrams necessitate clearance and classification by the section chief, approval by the DCM, and initials by the ambassador. Non-first-person telegrams necessitate section chief approval and classification and DCM initials for the ambassador. Personal calls to other officials and meetings of importance to other officials are recorded in memoranda of record, distributed to relevant officials or agencies.

An average of fourteen to sixteen telegraphic communications are sent out of the embassy each day. As has been stated, generally these are addressed to the U.S. secretary of state. The Communications Center in the State Department then decides on the distribution of the communication. The Office of Canadian Affairs, the deputy assistant secretary of state for Canadian affairs, and the assistant secretary for European affairs normally receive these communications; but beyond this the distribution is a function of the nature of the communication. The telephone is frequently used between embassy and Washington officials, because most of them know each other personally and because of the desire to circumvent the complicated and time-consuming procedural problems involved in written communications.

Incoming communications, again excluding telephone calls, to the embassy from either Washington or the consulates—not addressed to a specific individual or section—go to the embassy's Communication and Records Office, where it is marked for information or action and distributed to the proper officer. Should there be doubt as to whom it should be sent, it is forwarded to the DCM for a decision.

In addition to the DCM overseeing all incoming communications, the section chiefs see all communications relevant to their particular section. However, the section chief also depends on the action officer to bring to his attention special problems, including particularly those problems of sufficient importance to warrant attention at the weekly staff meetings. To enhance personal communications, the U.S. officer arranges for visitors to call on the ambassador. The officer would submit a memorandum through his section chief and the DCM to the ambassador stating the purpose of the visit. Likewise, visits by Washington officials to Ottawa are made known to all relevant embassy sections and individuals.

The U.S. Embassy in Ottawa is atypical relative to other U.S. embassies in that it tends to be more policy oriented in an operational sense (as opposed to merely reporting). For example, the embassy's opinion would normally be given great weight in Washington's decision whether or not to pursue a specific policy, and how this policy might be most effectively implemented. In addition, the embassy's submission of unsolicited policy recommendations in a specific issue area would again normally be given great weight in Washington. This centrality of operational policy relevance is a function of the embassy's expertise and of the reservoir of credibility it has established in the Washington policy process.

One of the fundamental objectives of the embassy is to prevent the U.S. government from being caught unaware, unthinking, or uninformed with regard to a development in Canada that might affect the United States. Attempts are presently being made to expand the reporting program and to commit more of the business to paper via telegram, since excessive use of the telephone has left embassy officials without adequate records for future reference. On a routine basis, topical articles from Canadian periodicals and newspapers, government reports and statistics, and such are sent by transmittal slip to Washington, accompanied by distillations and interpretations.

In the area of analytical reporting (e.g., in-depth analyses as opposed to transmission of secondary material with comments), the embassy's activities are extensive and profound. This is in conjunction with the embassy's threefold objective of providing information about development in a field in which there is a U.S. interest, defining that interest, and providing a sense of trend and policy implications. The embassy's reporting has a reputation in Washington for precision, incisiveness, and balance. Evidence suggests this reputation to be well deserved. Indeed, the reports are notable for the absence of linguistic malformations ("finalize"), hackneyed invocations ("life-style"), and euphemisms ("the Embassy thinks"). They are also distinguished by their clarity (e.g., "remark" versus "note," "advise" versus "inform") and by their accuracy.

With respect to issue resolution, whether the embassy will or will not be invoked in a negotiating capacity is dependent upon five variables: (1) a resident embassy authority on a special issue; (2) work load of embassy personnel; (3) amount of weight given to an issue or statement (e.g., Canadians can perhaps discount the statement of an Embassy official unless it is the ambassador or the DCM, but generally not that of the assistant secretary of state for European affairs or the deputy assistant secretary of state for Canadian affairs); (4) where the action is taking place; and (5) where the Canadian government requests the use of the embassy channel.

The permeative U.S.-Canadian interaction poses serious problems of coordination for officials in other departments, and especially for officials in State's Office of Canadian Affairs and in the U.S. Embassy in Ottawa. Due to the enormous multifarious contacts, it is difficult for embassy officials to prevent U.S. officials from working at cross-purposes in implementing U.S. interests. Because of staffing limitations, the embassy is equipped to deal only with problems having broader implications. Accordingly, the embassy has made no attempt to have all matters channeled through it. Its primary objective in this area, in conjunction with the State Department's Office of Canadian Affairs, is to keep informed of developments and coordinate these developments to the best of its ability.

It might be noted that the Canadian government, while sharing this problem of coordination, has the additional problem of personalized access to officials in the U.S. policy process. Because the American bureaucracy is so much larger than the Canadian bureaucracy, it is more difficult for the

Canadian official to know the higher-level American officials dealing with matters affecting Canada. This suggests that the Canadian government should utilize its embassy in Washington to a maximum extent—certainly more than is necessary for the U.S. to utilize its embassy in Ottawa—precisely because the Canadian Embassy is theoretically in the best best position to define and cultivate the most useful points of entry into the U.S. policy process.

The problem of coordination must also be confronted within the U.S. Embassy in Ottawa. Daily small staff meetings are held, chaired by the ambassador or the DCM. Once a week, there is a meeting of all section heads, which gives them a regular opportunity to inform the ambassador, the DCM, and other section heads of matters of specific interest to the mission. These meetings are supplemented by regular section staff meetings and, of course, by ad hoc meetings.

This coordination is also manifested on the individual officer level. Specific functions assigned to U.S. officers are cast in somewhat broad terms and are characterized by flexibility. Indeed, one of the primary characteristics of the embassy is its operational flexibility and its consequential responsiveness to changing circumstances. However, to enhance coordination and avoid overlap, functional and geographic responsibilities are assigned, and operating ground rules are defined. For example, the functional responsibility usually prevails should there be a jurisdictional dispute (e.g., an environmental issue would be handled by the officer responsible for the north).

THE CONSULAR POSTS [30]

The seven consulates general in Canada (Montreal, Toronto, Vancouver, Calgary, Winnipeg, Quebec City, and Halifax) [31] can be variously described as constituent posts of

the U.S. Embassy in Ottawa, as operating under the direct
and immediate supervision of the Embassy, or as extensions
of the Embassy. Several general observations might be made
about these posts. First, while they are an integral part of the
U.S. diplomatic presence in Canada, their functions are
distinct from those performed by U.S. officials in diplomatic
posts. Second, there is little variance among the posts in
general functions and organizational structures, but there is a
great variance in their respective sizes: the Montreal and
Toronto posts are the largest, followed by Vancouver,
Calgary, Quebec City, Halifax, and Winnipeg. Third, consulates general are encouraged to evaluate political developments, but this is done in close cooperation with the embassy
in Ottawa. Fourth, few major operational problems exist in
the posts that could not be corrected by increased staffng and
resources. For example, at a time of markedly increased work
loads, one post sustained a loss of two U.S. officials in three
years. Finally, in terms of appointment of U.S. officials to
these posts, special expertise on Canada is not considered a
requisite. This fact reflects a presumption of competence
about those who have been in the U.S. service for several
years.

The remainder of this section is devoted to an examination
of the procedures regarding consulates general, their functions and communication flows, followed by analyses of
specific posts. However, a slight but tedious digression is first
necessary to clarify the concept of consular activity. The
word "consul" is used in a general sense to refer to the person
and can denote a consul general, a consul, or a vice-consul.
The word "consulate" refers to the entire post or the
building. Consulates general, headed by consuls general, are
posts located in areas more important than consulates,
headed by consuls.[32]

A second point of clarification concerns the distinction
between heads of consular posts and diplomatic agents. The

ambassador, or chief of mission, represents the state that sends him to a foreign state, and his functions and powers are practically the same throughout the international system. He alone is the formal standing intermediary for the relations of two states. Consuls, on the other hand, are charged by the sending state to exercise specific functions regarding their nationals in their consular district. Each sending state individually determines the status, functions, and powers of its consular corps. Moreover, this authority of the consular corps as determined by the sending state is subject to the approval of the receiving state. With respect to immunities, diplomats enjoy practically the same immunities in all states, while those of consuls are determined bilaterally by consular conventions.[33]

The procedure for the United States establishing a consular post in Canada is as follows: The location of the post, its classification, and the size of the consular district are determined by the United States. This is then submitted to the government of Canada for approval. Any modification of this new post or, for that matter, of existing posts, can take place only with the consent of Canada. Consuls general, consuls, and vice-consuls (of career status) are technically, according to the U.S. Constitution, appointed by the president with the consent of the Senate. Noncareer officers such as vice-consuls (not of career status) and consular agents are appointed by the secretary of state·as the occasion may require. All must be U.S. citizens.[34]

Assume momentarily that the United States decides to send a new consul general to Canada. The U.S. government would first provide him with a letter confirming his appointment (e.g., a consular commission or patent). This document specifies his status and defines the area in which he will exercise his functions. The government of Canada would confer upon him the *exequatur* providing him the free exercise of his powers per local legislation and Canadian-U.S.

consular convention, as well as a guarantee of those privileges and immunities to which he is entitled. Canada could refuse to receive the U.S. consul general and in fact is not bound to communicate to the United States the reason for such a refusal. Should there be a rupture in Canadian-U.S. diplomatic relations, this would not lead, ipso facto, to the rupture of Canadian-U.S. consular relations. However, once Canada recognizes the official status of the U.S. consul general, it must grant him the necessary immunities to guarantee the full exercise of his functions. The United States must, on its part, notify Canada of the nomination of all members of the staff of a consular post—of their arrival, definite departure, and in general any change concerning their status. This requirement also applies to members of the consuls general families, service personnel, and any other American having a right to consular privileges.[35] This same formulation would apply in reverse to Canadian consular activity in the United States.

The U.S. consulates general in Canada perform essentially five functions: citizen assistance, immigrant and nonimmigrant visa processing, commercial activities, political-economic reporting, and general representation. The first function consists of assistance to U.S. citizens who are in Canada on business or pleasure. This function runs the entire gamut of service activities—U.S. citizens who violate Canadian laws, accident, discovering the whereabouts of citizens, lost articles, deaths of citizens in Canada, mental cases, services to veterans, destitute citizens, absentee voting, notarial services, issuance of passports, registration of birth of citizens, registration of citizens. The work of many consular posts throughout the world is expedited by U.S. citizens registering with that post, a voluntary, not a compulsory procedure. However, the political stability of Canada means that there is little incentive for Americans to register, and relatively few do. Proximity to the United States tends to minimize consular involvement in cases of destitution, although bus tickets to points south of the border are issued as required.

The ability of the U.S. consulates general to efficiently perform their citizen-assistance function is to a great extent attributable to the cooperation of the Canadian authorities. For example, the local police and the RCMP provide aid by reporting on arrests and deaths of U.S. citizens within the respective consular districts. Moreover, Canadian police and judicial traditions and practice are such that the U.S. posts' statutory "protection and welfare" activities for Americans are relatively small compared with other areas of the world. Nonetheless, the consulates are assured of an active citizen-assistance function due to the tremendous number of visits by American citizens to Canada each year (38,448,652 in 1971, according to Statistics Canada) and to the especially large number of Americans residing in Canada. For example, the American resident population in the consular district under Montreal is estimated to be at 60,000, and in any season on any given day there may be several hundred thousand American tourists.

The second function of the consulates general is that of immigrant and nonimmigrant visa processing. Permeative involvement in this function is attributable to several factors: the large American communities in the consular districts who require accreditation to go to third countries; the large non-Canadian immigrant population who require visas to go to the U.S.; the large number of Canadians desiring to emigrate to the United States; [36] an exceptionally large number of Stateside immigrant visa cases involving persons who are already in the United States and want to adjust their status, an arrangement established by the State Department with the approval of the U.S. Embassy in Ottawa. The number of visas given and the amount of time consumed processing them by the U.S. consulates general is extraordinary, especially given the fact that Canadian citizens themselves do not need visas to visit the United States. For example, the volume of visa traffic at the U.S. Consulate General in Toronto is the eighth highest of all U.S. visa-issuing posts throughout the world (according to 1975 figures). The consulate general in Montreal, on any given day, can expect to be visited by over 250 applicants and relatives.

The third function of the consulates general concerns commercial activities; that is, promotion of and assistance to U.S. business activity. Generally a library with economic materials is maintained, and there is an active monitoring of trade statistics with regularized surveys of market opportunities. It is interesting to note that the U.S. consuls general tend to see themselves as performing a dual commercial task—finding Canadian markets for U.S. exporters *and* facilitating Canadian producers in their American activities. This is perceived as being in the interest of economic rationality, or, as the expression states: "The flows have to be both ways." The consuls general maintain a wide range of contacts which are furthered by meetings with corporate and banking people, and such organizations as the chamber of commerce. Knowledge of specific opportunities is then transmitted to interested parties. The involvement of the consulates general in direct foreign investment as an issue area appears to be peripheral. The U.S. commercial program in Canada is countrywide, with a staff of seven specifically committed to it (i.e., economic/commercial officers) among all the consulates general. These seven are concentrated in Montreal, Toronto, Vancouver, and Calgary (and one in Ottawa), and all are from the Department of State.

The fourth function of the consulates general is political-economic reporting. It might be noted that the consular posts are often in a better position to report on attitudes and trends that might impact Canadian-U.S. relations than is the U.S. Embassy in Ottawa, especially in a nation the size and diversity of Canada. It also might be noted that the U.S. *Foreign Service Manual* is quite clear in stating that all U.S. consular posts throughout the world are expected to engage in political and economic reporting and in fact are not to subordinate such reporting to other activities except where necessary to fulfill such statutory consular functions as citizen protection and visa processing. U.S. consulates general in Canada not only generally report on political and economic trends but are sometimes directed by the embassy to report on specific topics. An example of regular reporting would be the post in Calgary. Because Calgary is the "oil capital" of Canada, the U.S. Consulate General does a heavy volume of economic and commercial reporting on energy matters. Likewise, the U.S. Consulate General in Halifax is responsible for reporting on fisheries, shipping, and industrial development. An example of political reporting would be the U.S. Consulate General in Vancouver recounting Canadian demonstrations against the U.S. nuclear underground test at Amchitka or, less dramatically, identifying issues in Canadian provincial and federal elections. It is interesting to note that the Canadian consular posts in the United States are not equipped for, and do not systematically partake in, this political-economic reporting function to the same extent that their American counterparts in Canada do; this, however, seems to be changing.

The fifth function of the U.S. consulates general in Canada is that of general representation, whereby the consul general is responsible for symbolically registering his presence in his consular district on behalf of the U.S. government. Representational activities would range from giving speeches, to playing a prominent role in social activities, to meeting with the press. A specific example of representation would be the courtesy calls made several years ago by the then newly appointed consul general in Halifax on the premier and lieutenant governor of Prince Edward Island and the mayor of Charlottetown; like calls were also made in New Brunswick and Nova Scotia, all of which came under his consular district. A more unusual and less pleasant form of representation occurred in December 1972 when the consul general in Toronto was awakened by a phone call from Washington and alerted to the desirability of going to Toronto International Airport to establish an official U.S. presence during the Southern Airways hijacking.

The U.S. consulates general in Canada are in constant communication with the U.S. Embassy in Ottawa. Indeed, the posts keep the embassy informed of everything except the most routine kinds of its activities. Lateral communication among the posts in Canada is maintained directly on general matters as the need arises. However, the embassy is invariably invoked if the matters have political implications. There is also direct communication on routine matters between the posts and other agencies of the U.S. government (e.g., the U.S. Immigration and Naturalization Service regarding border-crossing points, ports, and airports). Communications regarding personnel matters are generally dealt with through the embassy, as are budget and supply matters. Indeed, salaries for consular staff come directly from Washington, and expense vouchers are processed by the embassy in Ottawa. The consuls general go to Ottawa every year or two for a budget meeting, and no financial centers are maintained in the consular posts.

Normally, substantive communications are sent from the consulates general to Washington, with the embassy in Ottawa simultaneously being provided with a copy. All of the consulates general are connected to Ottawa and Washington via a direct telex line. Those communications that go to the embassy are generally solicited by the embassy. Economic and political communications go directly to Washington, with a copy to Ottawa unless they are a part of a comprehensive report being written in Ottawa. When communications are forwarded, supplemental observations or differences of interpretation are appended. Politico-economic reporting will often be coordinated from the embassy. That is, a specific project is undertaken in which the embassy wants the regional input but needs to correlate this input for a single report to the State Department. An example is the attempt, prior to the October 1972 Canadian federal election, to identify the most important issues in particular regions, through detailed instructions soliciting information from all the consulates general. There is also direct contact between the consulates general and various departments and agencies in Washington other than the State Department, but generally with copies being sent either to the embassy or to the State Department. End users of such communications include, for example, the Departments of Agriculture, Commerce, Labor, Treasury, Interior, Justice, and Defense, and such independent agencies as the Veterans Administration.

At this point it might be helpful to use two of the consulates general (Montreal and Toronto) as case studies in somewhat detailed analyses of large but not atypical consulates general in Canada. This is followed by a summary comparative review of the other posts.[37]

In 1857 the staff of the Montreal consulate general was three—two officers and a clerk. By 1920 it had grown to eight—the consul general, four vice-consuls, and three clerks. At present, it numbers forty-seven Department of State personnel—the consul general, six consuls, five vice-consuls, three other Americans, and thirty-five locally engaged. In addition, the Montreal post houses: the ICA—a branch public affairs officer (rank of consul) and a Canadian secretary; Customs—two officers and an American secretary; Drug Enforcement Administration—three officers and an American secretary; Immigration Service—two inspectors who are present periodically; one officer from the Department of Agriculture permanently on duty, with additional officers (housed elsewhere) on temporary duty as required to inspect grain shipments; a total of some 50 Americans constituting staffs of inspectors from the Customs and Immigration Service who perform preclearance inspection and clearance duties for commercial flights destined for the United States at Montreal's Dorval Airport.

The Montreal post is divided into five sections: executive, administrative, citizenship, economic, and visa. The Visa Section is by far the largest, with a staff of twenty-eight, reflecting the heavy demand for both visitor's and immigrant visas. The Administrative Section is next, with a staff of ten. The Executive Section is relatively small, consisting of the consul general, who is the principal officer; a senior economic/commercial officer, who is also the deputy principal officer; and two secretaries. There is no political section in this or any other U.S. consular post, but political reporting is regarded as an important function of all posts. For example, both the post in Montreal and the post in Quebec City report on the provincial and local political scene, including problems and orientations. Such work is handled in Montreal by the consul general and other officers designated by him for special assignments which do not interfere with their regular duties. The communication flows from Montreal are both to Ottawa and to the Department of State in Washington; that is, the post has teletype links with both and sends mail to both. The bulk of the post's direct communications with Washington is on visa matters. The Department of State generally handles onward distribution to other agencies in Washington.

The representational function of the Montreal consul general is especially demanding, arising from the fact that some sixty-five foreign governments now have consular or trade office establishments in Montreal. Thus, the consular corps is larger than the corps found in many foreign capitals and is unusually active. In addition, Montreal is the site of the International Civil Aviation Organization (ICAO), which affects the consulate general directly in the following sense: The United States has a delegation to ICAO which is housed separately, consisting of a minimum of four officials including the U.S. representative on the ICAO Council. The consulate general provides administrative support for them, consisting primarily of handling their communications, thereby adding greatly to the post's communication load. The large resident American community in the Montreal consular district and the large number of American tourists visiting the area ensures an active consular role. In addition, this post has been subjected to its share of political demonstrations, primarily over the Vietnam war and the U.S. Selective Service. However, in all cases the Canadian authorities provided alert and efficient protection as it was needed. Also, in the aftermath of the Front de Libération Québécois (FLQ) kidnappings and assassination in October 1970, the Canadian security authorities provided watchful attention to the U.S. consulate general as well as to some other foreign establishments in Montreal.

The U.S. Consulate General in Toronto has a large staff, of whom sixteen are American citizens appointed from Washington, the remainder being hired locally. All sixteen Americans are members of the U.S. Foreign Service.[38] There are a total of six consuls (in addition to the consul general) at Toronto. Most of the staff deals with the heavy volume of work relating to traditional consular services (e.g., visas, passports, notarials, adjudication, welfare, etc.). While the bulk of the resident staff is employed in this area, these operations are supervised by about half a dozen American officers, who come under the Visa, Passport and Citizenship, and Administrative sections. The next division in the Economic-Commercial Section, which absorbs the energies of three American staff members (two economic/commercial officers and one secretary). The Executive Section of the post consists of two Americans—the consul general and a secretary.

The functions of the staff, rather than being allocated on a discretionary basis, are quite rigorously defined. The primary movement of personnel among functions arises from the heavy demand in the summer period for visa applications and the need for personnel, including the consul general, to become involved in greater-than-usual nonroutinized problems. Little regularized political reporting is done by the consul general or his staff. Substantive reports about demonstrations—for example, those related to the war in Vietnam—were sent only if the consul general judged the demonstrations to be of sufficient intensity or sufficiently divergent from the usual; generally, they may be sent if he feels he has a unique perspective or special information. For example, a report was prepared on the Amchitka demonstrations, as this was a new issue. All matters of substance are reported through and to the appropriate officers of the embassy in Ottawa, while routine matters (e.g., visas) are sent directly to Washington.

The U.S. Consulate General in Vancouver has an authorized complement of nine American and nineteen Canadian employees. The Americans are the consul general and his secretary; two vice-consuls; the administrative officer; and two economic/commercial officers, one a consul and one a vice-consul. The consul general provides managerial leadership and is involved in, and responsible for, the operation of all sections. He also performs such political functions as reporting on elections and handles other questions which do not fit specifically within the purview of the post's organizational divisions. The Vancouver consulate general is divided into three major sections—Consular, Administrative, and Economic/Commercial.

The consulate general in Calgary has an authorized staff of four Americans; Quebec City and Halifax each have authorized staffs of three Americans—the consul general, a consul, and a vice-consul; and Winnipeg has two Americans. In addition, there are a varying number of Canadians employed at these posts—eight in Calgary, five in Quebec City, seven in Winnipeg, and eight in Halifax. Generally speaking, the consul general performs the fourfold functions of representation, trade and economic matters, reporting, and management. At the Winnipeg consulate general, the principal officer devotes approximately 50 percent of his time to representation and trade and economic matters and the remainder of his time to consular services and management. The vice-consul devotes almost all of his time to visa issuance, both immigrant and nonimmigrant, citizenship/passport services, and special consular services (which includes visiting American citizens incarcerated in Canadian jails). The Canadian personnel perform varied functions. For example, the eight Canadian employees in the Calgary office are classified as follows: administrative assistant; consular assistant/immigrant visas; consular clerk/immigrant visas; consular clerk/passport and citizenship, consular clerk/citizenship and special consular services; commercial librarian/consul general's secretary; receptionist clerk/nonimmigrant visas; and administrative clerk.

Because Quebec is the only province in which there are two U.S. consulates general, it might be helpful very briefly to examine the functions of the Quebec City post. During the last three decades, the size of its staff has remained constant, not deviating by more than one position from the present level. The functions of the post have also remained relatively constant through the years. Traditional consular work and political reporting on the activities and attitudes of that part of Quebec coming under its consular district continue to be most important. In the consular field, the issuance of immigrant visas has for several years accounted for approximately 50 percent of the work of the staff other than the consul general. The main burden of economic and commercial work within the entire Province of Quebec is presently carried by the consulate general in Montreal, which has an economic/commercial section.

SUMMATION AND ASSESSMENT

This examination of U.S. diplomatic and consular representation in Canada has revealed a highly coordinated operation. The relevance of this system is of course affected both by the fact of geographical contiguity and by technological advances in communication and travel which expedite intergovernmental communications. The U.S. consular posts and the embassy perform largely traditional functions, although the embassy is less oriented toward formal intergovernmental negotiations given such other channels of consultation and negotiation as ministerial visits, officials telephoning their counterparts, negotiating teams, and so on.

One of the fundamental objectives of U.S. representation in Canada is that of being informed and aware of developments in Canada that might affect the United States. It is tempting but inaccurate to equate this objective with the U.S. Central Intelligence Agency (CIA). That is, this objective refers to the fundamental function of any country's field mission, per international custom, and is precisely the same function that the Canadian Embassy and consulates perform in the United States. As for the CIA's intelligence-gathering function, obviously no exact information is available regarding this activity in Canada. However, it should be noted that it is U.S. policy not to undertake any CIA activities in Canada without the general knowledge and consent of the Canadian government. Likewise, the U.S. ambassador in Canada would be informed of the CIA's presence. This is, of course, mentioned to delineate standard procedures regarding possible processes, not to speculate on whether there is contemporary CIA activity in Canada.

Coordination within the U.S. representational system in Canada is not a problem area at this point because of its homogeneous nature (as opposed to the heterogeneity of Washington). This homogeneity is a function of the organizational centrality of the ambassador as chief of mission. Indeed, it is perhaps no exaggeration to note that the major problem facing the ambassador is less intrafield coordination than interfield Washington communication: the ambassador's proverbial problem concerns his difficulties in persuading the relevant departments and agencies in Washington to concur in actions he has recommended. It might be added that the ambassador's organizational centrality also ensures a certain State Department centrality in the field mission because the ambassador's line of communication and authority run through the Department of State. However, this State Department centrality in the field mission does not ensure a centrality in Washington, which is characterized by somewhat persistent interdepartmental decisional struggles of varying intensity.

The nature of U.S. representation in Canada is determined to a great extent by the orientation of the ambassador. For example, the incumbent's tenure is characterized by a very firm control of the overall U.S. mission in Canada, both within the embassy and between the embassy and the consular posts. In addition, the ambassador has invoked a public style of diplomacy in which he and his officers regularly comment on current issues confronting the Canada-U.S. relationship. Finally, the ambassador's dealings with Washington might best be described as vigorous.

In conclusion, mention must be made of the November 1976 secessionist victory in Quebec. This development has affected U.S. representation in Canada on two counts. First, it has placed a premium on political reporting so that the U.S. government is not caught unaware of new developments. Second, there has been an emphasis on the part of the U.S. Embassy and consular posts to painstakingly avoid even the appearance of becoming involved in such a highly internal Canadian matter and, in particular, not to give inadvertent signals of official approval or support to the separatist government. However, the extent to which the Quebec situation has affected the U.S. policy approach toward Canada can easily be exaggerated. In essence, the U.S. approach is simply to regard the separatist government as a fact of life and, within this context, to conduct business as usual, leaving the resolution of the issue up to the Canadians.

NOTES

1. U.S. Department of State, *Key Officers of Foreign Services Posts,* November 1976. Examples of missions are USUN (New York), USNATO (Brussels), and OAS (Washington). In addition to the representation already noted, there is one U.S. liaison office and one branch of an embassy.

2. See U.S. Senate, Committee on Government Operations, Subcommittee on National Security Staffing and Operations. *The Ambassador and the Problem of Coordination,* Document No. 36, September 1963 (88th Cong., 1st Sess.), p. 157.

3. The "country-team" concept has no legal status; its utilization by ambassadors is not mandatory; nor does it even have a formalized modus operandi. It is simply a managerial tool which has proven effective regarding field coordination and consensus. Although it is an evolutionary U.S. administrative concept, its first use referred to a 1951 interdepartmental agreement between the Departments of State and Defense and the ECA, based on the recommendations of the "Clay Paper," that the chief of the U.S. diplomatic mission and the heads of the military and economic aid programs in any given country were to "constitute a team under the leadership of the Ambassador." See W. Wendell Blancké, *The Foreign Service of the United States* (New York: Praeger, 1969), p. 137 and chap. 5.

4. U.S. Senate Document No. 36, op. cit., p. 156.

5. The dates and substantive information on U.S. consular activity presented in this section were obtained from such primary sources as the

Department of State's *Foreign Service Lists* (1833-1968); the National Archive's *Consular Despatches,* 1833-1926; and *Diplomatic Despatches,* "Ottawa From," 1927-1929; and from secondary sources such as R. A. Johnson, *The Administration of United States' Foreign Policy* (Austin: University of Texas Press, 1971). J. B. Brebner, *The North Atlantic Triangle* (New York: Columbia University Press, 1945); and D. F. Warner, *The Idea of Continental Union* (Kentucky: University of Kentucky Press, 1960). It should be noted that some of the dates and interpretations presented in this section conflict with prevalent conceptions.

6. For convenience, "Canada" will henceforth be used in place of "what is now Canada."

7. Historical Division, Department of State, "Highlights in the History of the American Consular Office at Vancouver, British Columbia, Canada." Research Project no. 144, May 1958, p. 32.

8. National Archives, *Consular Despatches,* Montreal, 1857.

9. National Archives, *Consular Despatches,* Halifax, 1837.

10. National Archives *Consular Despatches,* Halifax, 1846; Pictou, 1852.

11. National Archives, *Consular Despatches,* Montreal, 1862.

12. This may, however, serve as an indicator of the relative importance of Canada, vis-à-vis other nations, to the United States at different periods.

13. Johnson, op. cit., pp. 48-63.

14. These individual "histories" are based on correspondence received in 1972 with the then existing eight American consuls general in Canada, as well as the sources listed in note 1.

15. National Archives *Consular Despatches,* Ottawa, from 1910 to 1926.

16. As the definitional criteria are in the process of further modification, and the sample size is low, this information is to be regarded as tentative, and is offered only to indicate general patterns rather than to serve as a body of precise data.

17. As one individual, L. Merchant, served two distinct terms at different times, "ambassadors" should be taken to mean "ambassadorships." The percentages are thus calculated on the basis of the twelve ambassadorships to Canada that have been served rather than on the eleven individuals who filled the positions.

18. The H. F. Linder case is not judged to meet the temporal requirements. It should also be noted that not all ambassadors faced the test of surviving the advent of a new president.

19. This section is based on a series of communications in 1972 and early 1973 with Mr. Rufus Z. Smith (then deputy chief of mission in Ottawa) and in 1977 with Mr. Robert W. Duemling (minister of the U.S. Embassy in Ottawa) and with officials of the embassy staff.

20. These figures include for example, representatives of the Internal Revenue Service (three officers, one secretary), Drug Enforcement Administration (DEA) (one officer, one secretary), and a counselor for science and technological affairs.

21. See John R. Wood and Jean Serres, *Diplomatic Ceremonial and*

Protocol: Principles, Procedures and Practices (New York: Columbia University Press, 1970), pp. 9-13.

22. Burton M. Sapin, *The Making of U.S. Foreign Policy* (New York: Praeger, 1966), p. 254.

23. A full account is provided in Richard N. Kottman, "Hoover and Canada—Diplomatic Appointments," *Canadian Historical Review,* Vol. LI, No. 3 (September 1970), pp. 292-309.

24. While the Senate's full share of the appointment power has seldom been used in recent years with respect to lower-level appointments except in a pro forma sense, the laws technically require Senate confirmation of more than ninety individual officers in foreign affairs agencies, about forty U.S. representatives in international organizations, plus all ambassadors and ministers, Foreign Service officers (numbering more than 3,000 in 1971), and Foreign Service information officers (about 900, also in 1971). For additional information, see: U.S. Senate, Committee on Foreign Relations, *The Senate Role in Foreign Affairs Appointments* (Prepared by the FAR, CRS, Library of Congress), 92d Cong., 1st Sess., Committee Print, August 1971, p. 1.

25. It is interesting to note that the United States did not appoint any ambassadors abroad until 1893, when they were appointed to Great Britain, France, Germany, and Italy. In a diplomatic/consular appropriations act in this year, Congress approved for the first time the appointment of full ambassadors. Although the Constitution explicitly authorizes the appointment of "Ambassadors," no appointments higher than rank of minister had been made prior to this date, the reason presumably being that ambassadorial rank was considered a monarchical trapping inconsistent with principles of representation in a democracy. See Blancké, op. cit., p. 15.

26. This is customary international procedure. See Wood and Serres, op. cit., pp. 39-41.

27. See Sapin, op. cit., p. 282.

28. In 1930 the Department of Agriculture was authorized to post its own specialists to diplomatic missions abroad, its subsequent unification into the Foreign Service was not regarded as successful, and in 1954 the Foreign Agricultural Service was reinstated by Congress. Its general mandate is both to develop markets for American farm products and to gather economic information on foreign demand for, and competition with, American products. For more information, see Blancké, op. cit., pp. 166-68.

29. International Communication Agency Post are offices of the U.S. International Communication Agency located in foreign countries. Formerly, they were known as the United States Information Service (USIS), foreign office of the U.S. Information Agency (USIA). The ICA is organizationally seperate from the State Department but receives guidance from the secretary of state on U.S. foreign policy.

30. This section is based on October-November 1972 correspondence

with seven U.S. consuls general: J. L. Topping (Montreal), J. S. Henderson (Toronto), L. H. Stutesman (Vancouver), H. E. Hall (Calgary), E. K. Melby (Quebec City), W. B. Kelly (Winnipeg), and D. J. S. Manbey (Halifax); an interview on November 22, 1972, in Toronto between Consul General Henderson and the author's research assistant, Mr. Kirton; and 1977 correspondence with the U.S. Embassy staff.

31. Canada has a total of fifteen consular posts in the United States. Eight of these are consulates general located in Boston, Chicago, Los Angeles, Minneapolis, New Orleans, New York, San Francisco, and Seattle. Seven of the Canadian consular posts are consulates located in Buffalo; Cleveland; Dallas; Detroit; Philadelphia; Atlanta; and San Juan, Puerto Rico.

32. Vice-consulates, headed by vice-consuls, are posts located in the district of either a consulate general or a consulate whose head remains under the authority of the consul general or consul. Consular agencies, headed by a consular agent, are offices generally located in ports and deal essentially with commerce and shipping affairs. (In addition to referring to heads of posts, consuls and vice-consuls are also designations referring to staff members of a consulate general. For example, the U.S. Consulate General in Halifax has three American officials: consul general, consul, and vice-consul.)

33. Wood and Serres, op. cit., pp. 64-78. The rights and immunities of U.S. consular officials in Canada, and of Canadian officials in the United States, are prescribed by the 1963 Vienna Convention.

34. For further general information on U.S. consular activity (and per the next section of this article, on U.S. diplomatic activity), see, in addition to sources already noted, such works as: The Brookings Institution, *The Administration of Foreign Affairs and Overseas Operations* (Washington, 1951); Graham H. Stuart, *The Department of State: A History of Its Organization, Procedure and Personnel* (New York: Macmillan, 1949); William Barnes and J. H. Morgan, *The Foreign Service of the U.S.: Origins, Development, and Functions* (U.S. Department of State, Historical Office, 1961); Chester Lloyd Jones, *The Consular Service of the United States: Its History and Activities* (Philadelphia: University of Pennsylvania Press, 1906).

35. Wood and Serres, op. cit., pp. 66, 68-69.

36. The only visa required of Canadians is an immigrant visa. While there are generally no nonimmigrant visas required of Canadians, visas are required for those Canadians desiring to work or study in the United States.

37. These seven posts cover the following areas (i.e., consular districts): The Vancouver post covers all of British Columbia and the Yukon Territory; the Calgary post covers Alberta and parts of the Northwest Territories; the Winnipeg post includes Saskatchewan, Manitoba, and additional areas in the Northwest Territories as well as northern Ontario;

the Toronto post deals with southern Ontario; the province of Quebec is divided between the Montreal and Quebec City posts; the Halifax post covers Nova Scotia, New Brunswick, Prince Edward Island, and Newfoundland (including Labrador); and the embassy in Ottawa covers several surrounding districts in Ontario and Quebec as well as parts of the Northwest Territories. These consulates general no longer have any subordinate offices.

38. It should be noted that the Toronto post includes representation from the following agencies: ICA (one American officer and one Canadian secretary); DEA (one officer and one secretary, both Americans); U.S. Travel Service (three American officers, four Canadian employees); and Customs and INS preclearance staff (sixty-eight Americans). When all these agency representatives are included, Toronto becomes clearly the largest consulate general post in Canada. However, the Customs and INS preclearance staff, in particular, is a totally separate organization and does not really contribute to the daily business of the consulate general.

III

CANADIAN DIPLOMATIC AND CONSULAR REPRESENTATION IN THE UNITED STATES*

Canadian representation abroad can be described as a systematic "muddling through." It is not quite like the U.S. representational system, nor the British, nor the French. It has evolved as uniquely Canadian and directly mirrors the administrative strengths and weaknesses of Canada as a national unit. By any standards, Canadian representation abroad is extensive. Canada has eighty-nine embassies (forty-nine resident and forty nonresident); twenty-nine high commissions accredited to commonwealth nations (seventeen resident and twelve nonresident); eight permanent delegations to international organizations; fourteen consulates general; and eight consulates. The importance the Canadian government attaches to its relations with the United States

* This chapter originally was published as two separate articles in *Canadian Public Administration* entitled "Canadian Diplomatic Representation in the United States," Vol. XVIII, No. 3 (Fall 1975), pp. 366-98 and "Canadian Consular Representation in the United States," Vol. XX, No. 2 (Summer 1977), pp. 342-69.

in particular is suggested by the fact that over half of Canada's consulates general and seven of its eight consulates are allocated to that country. The Canadian Embassy in Washington has some three hundred employees and has been chaired by Canada's leading diplomatic professionals, making it one of Canada's largest and most important missions abroad.

More than a dozen departments and agencies in addition to the Department of External Affairs are active in the United States.[1] One is tempted to say that not one but a dozen Canadian governments are present, personified in such departments as External Affairs; Industry, Trade and Commerce; Manpower and Immigration; National Defence; and National Revenue. But that would do injustice to the historical roots of these departments' individual representation in Washington, to the Canadian concept of departments and their procedural roles, and to the fact that these departments have, although not without problems, effectively serviced Canadian national priorities.

Under the embassy and the fifteen consular posts, which act as institutional umbrellas, work the departmental field officers who constitute a direct extension into the United States of Ottawa's departmental decisional processes. These field officers perform diverse functions and generally report back directly to their respective departments in Ottawa. The embassy and consulates provide a focus of responsibility for the execution and management of the field officers' departmental programs. All Canadian governmental activity is formally subsumed under the embassy itself, although embassy control over the consular posts is nominal. In each consulate the pattern is repeated, the head of post managerially presiding over different departmental field officers reporting back to their parent departments in Ottawa.

The purpose of this chapter is to identify the major components and subcomponents of the Canadian diplomatic and consular representation in the United States and to define their procedures, functional responsibilities, and organizational structures. The first section examines the origins and evolution of Canadian diplomatic and consular representation in the United States and gives profiles of Canadian ministers and ambassadors, while the second section analyzes the components of the Canadian Embassy. The third section examines the consular milieu and its major components, and the concluding section discusses problems of coordination and assesses diplomatic and consular effectiveness.

ORIGINS AND EVOLUTION

Canadian immigration agents were active, although nonresident, in the United States as early as 1873 and 1874, attempting to encourage U.S. settlers to go to Canada and to persuade Canadians who had emigrated to the United States to return to Canada.[2] These early immigration agents are significant in that they constituted the first type of Canadian representation abroad. Although they enjoyed neither consular nor diplomatic status, they did, in the absence of other Canadian representation, perform functions similar to those performed by consular officials.[3]

The recognition of the need for a separate permanent activity—the promotion of trade—was reflected in the appointment of Canadian commercial agents abroad in the late 1880s and in the formation of the Department of Trade and Commerce in the early 1890s. The development of Canadian commercial representation from commercial agents to trade commissioners in 1907 is significant for the almost complete absence of activity in the United States. No trade commissioners were appointed in the United States except in Chicago (1905-6), with the rationale that Canada-U.S. trade was already very large and that geographical contiguity facilitated an ease of Canada-U.S. communication, thereby obviating the need for United States-based commercial representation.

Thus, notwithstanding extensive commercial Canadian representation abroad, the only resident Canadian agents in the United States prior to 1921 were the immigration agents. However, by the early 1920s, the Canadian government concluded that trade commissioners posted in the United States would result in an increase in Canadian exports, and although there were urgings for a comprehensive system of commercial representation, the actual steps taken were rather modest. In 1921 a Canadian trade commissioner was appointed to New York, thereby converting the information office which had been created during World War I to a trade commissioner's post, making this the first such post in the United States.[4] It was not until 1939 that trade officers were sent to Los Angeles and Chicago to supplement the activity of the New York office, heretofore responsible for all trade promotion activities in the United States. While trade commissioners performed functions similar to those of a consular or diplomatic agent, they did not enjoy the immunities of diplomatic and consular officials. The first consular post was established in April 1943, when Prime Minister King announced that a new consulate general would be established in New York.

Beyond these initial Canadian developments, Canadian consular expansion in the United States consisted of three developmental stages occurring between 1947 and 1972.[5] These developmental stages of Canadian consular development were less a response to a coordinated governmental policy of expansion than they were a reflection of often conflicting departmental and societal pressures. Rationales for establishing consular posts varied; for example, diplomatic versus trade, which in turn triggered interdepartmental struggles, especially between the Department of External Affairs (DEA) and the Department of Trade and Commerce (since 1969 the Department of Industry, Trade and Commerce, [ITC]). In addition, other Canadian departments or agencies also wanted consular status for their own representational activity; for example, the Department of Manpower and Immigration; the Department of National Defence; and the Canadian Travel Bureau, now the Office of Tourism. Moreover, varying degrees of pressure were exerted by economic interest groups in Canada, and in the United States through interest groups such as the chambers of commerce and local governments. However, the ensuing growth of Canadian consular activity in the United States was somewhat less haphazard and indiscriminate than might appear at first sight, for there were departmental attempts at coordinated programs, although interdepartmental attempts were rarer and not substantially effective until the early 1970s.

During the first stage of Canadian consular expansion (1947-48), the Department of External Affairs proceeded to open four consular posts: Chicago in November 1947; and in 1948, Detroit in April, San Francisco in July, and Boston in October. The selection of consular locations in this first stage was essentially based on considerations of representation and prestige. However, commercial rationales tended to predominate with the passage of time. It was during this first stage as well that a consular section was established in the Canadian Embassy in Washington, D.C.

The second stage of Canadian consular expansion, which occurred from 1952 to 1953, resulted in the opening of consular posts in New Orleans in January 1952; and in 1953, Los Angeles in September and Seattle in October. Significantly, the expansive rationales differed little from that of 1947. However, given the extent to which austerity measures in Ottawa had necessitated concrete and precise rationales for the expenditures involved in consular activity, the DEA tended to adopt commercial rationales vis-à-vis other depart-

ments as a justification for expansion. It is significant that the
1949 Turcotte and the 1952 Allard missions were the last
concerted attempts for some time on the part of External
Affairs to systematically define criteria by which consular
posts should be internally justified. This lack of internal
systematic criteria, coupled with the adoption of somewhat
ephemeral commercial rationales, resulted not only in an
elusiveness about internal departmental allocations of new
sites but also in an inability to respond to the more
systematic commercial rationales furthered by ITC for its
suggestions regarding the establishment of new posts. Thus,
pressure emanating from ITC began in 1951 for the establishment of consular posts. This pressure started with that for
the New Orleans post, continued through the 1950s, and
culminated in the third stage of consular expansion beginning in 1961.

The third stage of Canadian consular expansion occurred
from 1961 to 1972, during which seven additional consular
posts were established: Philadelphia in 1961; Cleveland in
1964; Dallas in 1967; San Juan, Puerto Rico, in 1968; Buffalo
and Minneapolis in 1970; and Atlanta in 1972. The Department of Trade and Commerce had initiated the establishment of only one consular post, in New Orleans, before this
stage began. However, from 1961 posts tended to be established on the basis of surveys by ITC, which included a
quantitative survey of the merits of several U.S. cities best
suited to the promotion of Canadian exports. Thus, by the
advent of this third stage in 1961, the DEA for all intents and
purposes became a reactor to the initiatives proposed by
ITC.

The opening of the last consular post, in Atlanta, is
especially significant in that, despite departmental preoccupations with their own objectives, a more integrated
interdepartmental approach was manifested to the extent
that the post would function within the context of a set of

interdepartmentally agreed-upon objectives. Indeed, events had proven that neither the DEA nor ITC could sustain separate rationales and the separate execution of these rationales. Quite simply, trade and consular functions, as they are executed in a consular post abroad, are intimately interrelated in that one set of functions generates demands on the other. The result is a gradual broadening of that post's activities. Thus, with the culmination of the third stage of Canadian consular expansion, there were strong indications that henceforth Canadian governmental activity in the United States would in fact be more representative of the overall interests of the Canadian government rather than of a specific government department.

If immigration and commercial representation were the ancestors of Canadian consular representation, the Canadian Embassy in Washington had more direct predecessors. The first was the creation of the International Joint Commission (IJC) authorized by the Boundary Waters Treaty of 1909, "to make provisions for the adjustment and settlement" of questions arising from the "common frontier." [6] However, the IJC was not a diplomatic or representative body; its purpose was to serve as a permanent joint organization outside normal diplomatic channels.

The next antecedent of the Canadian Embassy in Washington was even more direct in lineage than the IJC. In 1918 a Canadian war mission was established in Washington. Observing that the usual Canadian diplomatic channel, the British Embassy in Washington, already had an extensive wartime work load concerning matters not directly affecting Canada, the order in council noted that the desired Canadian-U.S. governmental interaction was less diplomatic than commercial, which required a different and more direct method of execution than could be provided by the British Embassy. The mission represented the Canadian cabinet and governmental departments rather than Canada itself or its head of state.

The Canadian war mission remained active until 1921. Before the Armistice, discussions had been held with the British government concerning some form of permanent Canadian representation in Washington, and pending satisfactory completion of these discussions it was decided to continue the war mission temporarily.[7] The mission therefore continued to function, concluding its wartime business and periodically conducting affairs with the U.S. government. Although members of the mission eventually returned to Canada, its secretary, Merchant Mahoney, remained after its closing. Acting as agent of the Department of External Affairs, he occupied an office in the British Embassy with the responsibility of keeping the Canadian government informed, particularly on commercial matters. Although he was not formally connected with the British Embassy staff and had no diplomatic status, Mahoney's position was the direct predecessor of the Canadian Legation. On May 10, 1920, a simultaneous announcement was made in both the Canadian Parliament and the British Parliament concerning agreement on Canadian representation in Washington. However, it was not until February 18, 1927, that the first Canadian envoy extraordinary and minister plenipotentiary presented his credentials to the U.S. president. By this time there was no doubt about Canada's independent status, as reflected in correspondence between the British Embassy and the U.S. secretary of state: "The Canadian Minister being responsible to the Canadian Government would not be subject to the control of His Majesty's Ambassador nor would His Majesty's Ambassador be responsible for the Canadian Minister's actions." [8]

Under the direction of the minister, Vincent Massey, the legation very soon replaced the British Embassy as a link between the U.S. and Canadian governments. Moreover, it also circumvented the governor general in Ottawa by assuming the duty of informing the Canadian government of communications from Washington. Although it performed regular diplomatic duties, conducting negotiations on issues and treaties and reporting on developments in the United States, commercial questions were the major reason for its creation.

Vincent Massey's first report at the end of 1927 is especially interesting. The task at hand included a "large and increasing volume of correspondence" with British consular officers, U.S. government departments, business firms, private individuals, and other diplomatic missions. Active problems included boundary waterways, movement of persons across the border, tariff and trade policies, allocation of radio broadcasting channels, smuggling by land and sea—all in addition to the general protection of the interests of Canadian citizens. Ceremonially, 1927 was apparently a busy year, with a November visit to the legation by Prime Minister Mackenzie King and a December visit by the governor general of Canada and Lady Willingdon. Also interesting is Mr. Massey's preoccupation with keeping watch on the Congress, a responsibility he presumably found rather demanding with a staff of only four officers.

From its opening in 1927 until its elevation to embassy status in 1943, five Canadian ministers served in the Washington legation. Table 1 gives basic information about them. Three could be called noncareer appointments, although because of the relative newness of the Canadian diplomatic service this description is less precise than its use in information on U.S. officials. This early group possessed a wide range of educational backgrounds: two came from the University of Toronto; one each came from McGill and Acadia Universities; and one was without formal university education. One did advanced academic work at Oxford; three were lawyers;

TABLE 1 CANADIAN MINISTERS TO THE UNITED STATES 1928-46

Name	Year of birth	Province of birth	Universities attended	Previous post	Career/ noncareer	Length of service	Prime Minister	Secretary of State for External Affairs
Massey, Vincent	1887	Ontario	Toronto Oxford	Minister without portfolio, delegate Imperial Conference	noncareer	Feb.1928–July 1930 2 years, 6 months	King (1926–30)	King (1926–30)
Herridge, William D.	1888	Ontario	Toronto Osgoode Hall	lawyer in private practice	noncareer	June 1931–Oct. 1935 4 years, 5 months	Bennett (1930–5)	Bennett (1930–5)
Marler, Sir Herbert	1876	Quebec	McGill	EEMP, Japan	career	Oct. 1936–Sept. 1939 3 years	King (1935–48)	King (1935–46)
Christie, Loring	1885	Nova Scotia	Acadia Harvard Law	Counsellor (External Affairs)	career	Sept. 1939–April 1941 1 year, 8 months	King (1935–48)	King (1935–46)
McCarthy, Leighton	1869	Ontario	legal clerking	businessman lawyer	noncareer	Feb. 1941–Jan. 1945 3 years, 11 months	King (1935–48)	King (1935–46)

SOURCES: *Who's Who in Canada*, 1923–44, and information supplied by the Historical Division of the Department of External Affairs

two trained at Osgoode Hall and Harvard, respectively; and one came to the bar through private training as a legal clerk. Three of the five ministers, the noncareer appointments, were born in Ontario; the other two ministers were born in Quebec (although not of French Canadian background) and Nova Scotia. The average age upon appointment was fifty-four, though there is a wide variance from Massey's appointment at forty-one to McCarthy's at seventy-two. The average ministerial tenure was three years.

Since the 1943 elevation of the legation to an embassy, ten Canadians have been appointed ambassadors to the United States. Table 2 gives background information for the Canadian ambassadors excluding Mr. McCarthy.[9] All but one of them have been career foreign service officers of the Department of External Affairs. The exception, A. D. P. Heeney, was a senior civil servant who before his first assignment to Washington had served as clerk to the Privy Council and secretary to the cabinet and as under secretary of state for external affairs, and before his second assignment as chairman of the Canadian Civil Service Commission. The post of ambassador to the United States has been quite senior in the Canadian foreign service, and most incumbents have come from other prestigious ambassadorial posts or ranking staff positions in the Department of External Affairs. For example, past ambassadors have included a former high commissioner to the United Kingdom and a former under secretary of state for external affairs. The sole exception was Lester Pearson, who was promoted from the post of minister at the embassy. All but three of the Canadian ambassadors had some education at Oxford University. The ambassadors' undergraduate Canadian institutions have been more diverse: two from the University of Toronto and one each from the universities of Manitoba, British Columbia, Mount Allison, McGill, Queen's, and Western Ontario. In addition to Oxford, advanced or professional studies were taken by two at McGill and one each at Harvard, the Brookings Institution in Washington, l'Ecole libre des sciences politiques, and Queen's. Four of the ambassadors were born in Ontario; two in Quebec (one French, the other English Canadian), and one each in British Columbia, Nova Scotia, and New Brunswick. The average age upon appointment was fifty-three, and the range of ages has not been great, from Pearson who was young at forty-seven, to Heeney who was fifty-seven at the time of his second appointment. The average tenure has been three years, eight months, slightly longer than the ministers and longer than their American counterparts.

THE EMBASSY

The Canadian Embassy occupies three major locations in Washington, with the main chancery located near Dupont Circle. The embassy staff consists of the ambassador and the deputy head of post, Canadian-based officers and support staff, military personnel, and locally engaged officers and support staff. This is the largest of any Canadian embassy, which reflects the relative importance of the United States to Canada. Organizationally, the embassy consists of the ambassador and the deputy head of post and ten major organizational units: Political Division; Economic Division; Public Affairs Division; Canadian Government Office of Tourism; Canadian Defence Liaison Staff; Supply and Services Division; Post Central Administration Division; Consular Division; RCMP; and the National Research Council.

Like the U.S. ambassador to Canada, the Canadian ambassador has five general responsibilities: representation, information, negotiation, protection, and management.[10] The Canadian ambassador not only represents Canada to the United States but also maintains ongoing contacts with other ambassadors in Washington. He undertakes speaking engagements in cities throughout the United States to present the

Name	Year of birth	Province of birth	Universities attended	Previous post	Career/ noncareer	Length of service	Prime Minister	Secretary of State for External Affairs
				TABLE 2 CANADIAN AMBASSADORS TO THE UNITED STATES 1946–78				
Pearson, Lester	1897	Ontario	Toronto Oxford	Minister at Washington	career	Dec. 1944–Sept. 1946 1 year, 9 months	King (1935–48)	King (1935–46)
Wrong, Hume	1894	Ontario	Toronto Oxford	Associate under secretary of state for external affairs	career	Oct. 1946–July 1953 6 years, 10 months	King (1935–48) St. Laurent (1948–57)	St. Laurent (1946–8) Pearson (1948–57)
Heeney, A.D.P.	1902	Quebec	Manitoba, Oxford, McGill,	Amb. to North Atlantic Council and OEC	noncareer	July 1953–May 1957 3 years, 11 months	St. Laurent (1948–57)	Pearson (1948–57)
Robertson, Norman	1904	British Columbia	UBC, Oxford, Brookings	High Commissioner, Great Britain	career	May 1957–Oct. 1958 1 year, 4 months	Diefenbaker (1957–63)	Diefenbaker (1957) Smith (1957–9)
Heeney, A.D.P.	1902	Quebec	Manitoba, Oxford, McGill	Chmn., Civil Service Commission of Canada	noncareer	Feb. 1959–April 1962 3 years, 3 months	Diefenbaker (1957–63)	Green (1959–63)

Name	Born	Province	Education	Position		Tenure	Prime Minister	Secretary of State
Ritchie, C.S.A.	1906	Nova Scotia	Oxford, Harvard, Ecole libre des sciences politiques, King's College	Amb. to United Nations	career	May 1962–July 1966 4 years, 11 months	Diefenbaker (1957–63) Pearson (1963–8)	Green (1959–63) Martin (1963–8)
Ritchie, A.E.	1916	New Brunswick	Mt Allison, Oxford	Deputy under secretary of state for external affairs	career	July 1966–Jan. 1970 3 years, 6 months	Pearson (1963–8) Trudeau (1968–)	Martin (1963–8) Sharp (1968–74)
Cadieux, Marcel	1915	Quebec	Grasset College, Montreal, McGill	Under secretary of state for external affairs	career	Jan. 1970–July 1975 5 years, 6 months	Trudeau (1968–)	Sharp (1968–74) MacEachen (1974–6)
Warren, Jack H.	1921	Ontario	Queen's	High Commissioner Great Britain	career	July 1975–July 1977 2 years	Trudeau (1968–)	MacEachen (1974–6) Jamieson (1976–)
Towe, Peter M.	1922	Ontario	Western Ontario, Queen's	Assistant under secretary of state for external affairs	career	July 1977–	Trudeau (1968–)	Jamieson (1976–)

SOURCES: *Who's Who in Canada*, 1945–76, and Canadian Embassy in Washington

Canadian position publicly. Although he does some reporting and an occasional overview, his primary activity is to ensure that the embassy staff is issuing reports in their functional areas. The Canadian ambassador performs less of a negotiating role than might be expected because of the geographical proximity of Ottawa and the preference of government departments for doing their own negotiating. Thus, the ambassador advises on the timing and context of policy and arranges the visits of, and generally accompanies, Canadian ministers and deputy ministers in Washington. Administratively, the ambassador is the manager of all the various functions for which the embassy is responsible. The ambassador heads a staff with officers from several different departments or agencies in Ottawa, but all of them are under the organizational jurisdiction of the ambassador as head of post.[11]

The ambassador holds a monthly coordinating meeting attended by the heads of the embassy divisions that covers all areas of activity, including the general state of Canada-U.S. relations, public affairs, internal embassy affairs, and specific political and economic conditions. The purpose of these meetings is to make the specialized divisions aware of the context in which they are operating, especially at higher levels of political and economic policy. The ambassador chairs the meeting, offers his comments at the beginning and on various topics as they are developed, and often calls for written reports. A second regular meeting held by the ambassador occurs at the beginning of every week and is restricted to the ambassador's ranking staff. The purpose of these weekly meetings is to plan the week's activities in areas of concern. Attending these meetings are the two ministers (economic and political), the minister-counselor (information), and the section heads in the Economic Division.

The ambassador does not attempt to keep track of the 42,000-odd messages routed to the embassy each year. These communications are sent to the relevant division. All but the most sensitive telegrams, incoming and outgoing, are routed to a maximum number of embassy officials for information. This represents full access to all of the relevant communications of the Department of External Affairs.

Communications come in two basic types: information and action. Many telegrams exchanged between Ottawa and other Canadian posts abroad are routed to the embassy in Washington merely for information and do not normally require action in Washington. Most of the messages received by the embassy are of this type. But communications requiring action by the embassy, usually received from Ottawa, occupy a greater part of the staff's attention. Thus, for the 42,000 messages received, some 4,000 are dispatched from the embassy. The embassy sender of a message routes it, after clearance by the appropriate embassy officials depending upon the priority level of the message, directly to the relevant office in External Affairs by a system of initial codes. The sender designates an action addressee, information addressees, and other departments and diplomatic posts to which the message should be sent. The embassy's activities therefore focus on Ottawa, and more specifically on the Department of External Affairs.

The deputy head of post is the minister in the Canadian Embassy with the greatest seniority (one minister is head of the Political Division, the other head of the Economic Division, the present deputy head of post being the former). This position is closer to the British head of chancery than to the U.S. deputy chief of mission (DCM). For example, the DCM in Ottawa is responsible not only for the efficient operation of the mission but also for all substantive matters as the ambassador's second in command and principal advisor. Indeed, all the organizational components of the U.S. Embassy are responsible to the DCM, who sees every major incoming communication and clears in advance, in the name of the ambassador, most outgoing communications. In contrast, the position of the Canadian deputy head of post is less formalized and centralized. His major functions are the direction of his own division and general administrative embassy matters. Beyond this, he serves as *chargé d'affaires ad interim* in the ambassador's absence. While he is responsible for the efficient operation of the embassy as a whole and is in charge of the country-programming process, he is neither a link between organizational components of the embassy nor concerned with incoming or outgoing embassy communications apart from those of his own Division.

The Political Division is in a sense residual to the other embassy divisions. It performs five activities: (1) reporting and analyzing the main lines of U.S. foreign policy in those broadly political areas that affect Canada; (2) reporting and analyzing U.S. information and assessments of developments in other parts of the world; (3) ensuring that Canadian government views on a range of matters are made known to the State Department and other departments and agencies, either because these organizations solicit the Canadian position or because the Canadian government wants its position known to them; (4) contacting, discussing, and negotiating specific questions with U.S. officials; and (5) advising other sections of the embassy on the implications of certain U.S. courses of action. To perform these five activities, the Political Division has seven officers, all from the Department of External Affairs, and is headed by a minister. Most of the officers working in Washington are dealing with subjects in which they have had some previous experience. These political officers are dealing with two levels, the Washington governmental milieu and U.S. activities abroad. The key to their effective functioning is to know when to comment or to intervene in business being conducted, and to anticipate the interests and needs of Ottawa or Canadian missions elsewhere. Over the past four years there has been a relative decline in international interests, as opposed to bilateral and domestic concerns, with correspondingly less time being spent on the former areas and more time on domestic and congressional politics.

The purpose of the Economic Division, which is headed by the minister for economic affairs, is to monitor and process issues of special interest in the extensive Canada-U.S. economic interaction, with a special attention to impending difficulties and problems. The Economic Division is divided into several sections: Trade and Industrial Development, Defence Production Programs, Energy, Provincial Interests, and General Economics, with section heads reporting to the minister.

The Trade and Industrial Development Section, under a minister-counselor (economic), consists of twelve officers, all of whom are from the Department of Industry, Trade and Commerce. On the bilateral side, it protects and promotes Canada's commercial interests vis-à-vis the United States, through representation, service, protection, and reporting functions. This section also monitors other U.S. bilateral trade relations, with the European Economic Community (EEC), the USSR, China, Japan, and the developing world. It follows the trade promotional techniques of the U.S. government (e.g., the Department of Commerce's export programs) to see whether they are complementary with Canadian needs. It also follows U.S. multilateral economic relations, including General Agreement on Tariffs and Trade (GATT) negotiations, the Organization for Economic Co-operation and Development (OECD), United Nations Conference on Trade and Development (UNCTAD), Food and Agriculture Organization (FAO), and relevant commodity conventions or study groups. Apart from the United States the section has a service and liaison function with such organizations as the Inter-American Development Bank and the World Bank intended to relate commercial operations agreed upon under bank auspices to Canadian industrial and engineering capabilities. Non-policy-related correspondence is simply channeled through ITC.

The Defence Production Programs Section, integrated into the Trade Commissioner Service (TCS) in mid-1974, falls under the minister-counselor (economic), who is the senior officer of the Department of Industry, Trade and Commerce at the embassy and is responsible for the promotion of defense production and development sharing. It works through the U.S. Department of Defense, the U.S. Armed Services, U.S. defense contractors, and a number of foreign embassies from countries whose defense procurement agencies are not represented in Ottawa. In a general sense, this includes the promotion of cooperation, including research and development, and the assisting of U.S. organizational agencies in finding competent sources of defense matériel in Canada.[12] This section consists of four officers, normally a counselor and three first secretaries (defense production). Responsibilities are divided along the lines of the U.S. service departments (army, navy, and air force).

The Energy Section of the Economic Division created in 1960 is headed by a minister-counselor (energy) from the Department of Industry, Trade and Commerce. It has two officers, one from the Department of External Affairs and the other from the Department of Energy, Mines and Resources. The activities of this section are fourfold. It provides a reporting function for relevant departments and agencies in Ottawa; second, it actively participates in the discussions of these departments while performing a steering function. Third, it liaises with such U.S. departments as Energy, State, Commerce, and Interior, in addition to governmental agencies and private organizations. Fourth, the Energy Section informs these departments and agencies of developments in Canada in the energy field. The Energy Section also deals with the Congress, both with individual members and with legislative committees.

The fourth section of the Economic Division is the General Economics Section; it is headed by a counselor and has several residual functions, including general analysis and reporting of economic trends and conditions in the United States on transportation; communications; development assistance; and environmental, scientific, and labor affairs. Within the overall Economic Division there is an embassy official designated as the Provincial Interests Section of the division.

The purpose of the Public Affairs Division, headed by a minister-counselor, is to register the Canadian national presence in the United States by making Canada better understood both generally as a distinctive political and cultural unit and specifically by explaining the Canadian government's positions on issues of concern.[13] This objective can be subdivided into four interrelated functions: media relations, academic relations, cultural relations, and general information programs. The division is responsible for both the execution of these functions and their overall policy coordination with Ottawa and with the other consular posts. In addition, the division coordinates the ambassador's travel and speaking programs and renders important assistance and advice to other divisions of the embassy on informational matters. The Public Affairs Division has five program officers from the Department of External Affairs, and its contact point in Ottawa is the Bureau of Public Affairs of the Department of External Affairs, particularly that bureau's Information and Cultural Affairs divisions. Interactions between the Public Affairs Division (PAD) and other Canadian consular posts are constant. Although the degree of informational activity in the consular posts varies, most have officers who handle information. As policy comes from Ottawa, the PAD plays a coordinative and guidance role, especially in the areas of media relations, academic relations, and national information relations.

The purpose of the Embassy section of the Canadian Government Office of Tourism (CGOT), including the International Meetings and Conventions Office (M&C), is, quite simply, to increase individual, group, and convention travel to Canada. With a staff of four (manager, assistant manager, travel counselor, and travel promotion assistant), the Washington office has jurisdiction over an area parallel to the consular district of the embassy, which includes Maryland, Virginia, and the District of Columbia. The manager of the Washington office of the Travel Marketing Branch has diplomatic status, but other officers in the United States are generally classed as foreign business agents, although in some cases they have consular status.

In addition to handling mail and telephone inquiries (some two million a year), detailed studies of the Washington region are undertaken to examine key market centers (cities and their populations) and the main travel interests of people in the region by age, salary, and education. The Embassy section of the CGOT also does promotional work concerning convention and association meetings in Canada; indeed, over 50 percent of the head officer's time is occupied by such activities. However, this work is distinguishable from that of the International Meetings and Conventions Office, also located in Washington and an independent division of the CGOT. The M&C Office works at getting U.S. meetings and conventions to be held in Canada. It functions both nationally and internationally, handling policy matters, capacity studies, and travel incentives. The general manager of the M&C performs the role of generator, while the CGOT manager does the servicing and implementation.

The Canadian Defence Liaison Staff (CDLS), the Department of National Defence component of the Canadian

Embassy, serves as Canadian Forces attaché to the U.S. Armed Services and as headquarters for Canadian military personnel in the United States. The general terms of reference of the Liaison Staff as attachés are contained in their accreditation to the Department of Defense and the three armed services. The commander of the CDLS is accredited to the department as a whole and to the Joint Chiefs of Staff, with open access at the highest levels of the U.S. military structure. Despite the unified nature of Canada's own armed forces, the CDLS is divided along functional lines to correspond to the triservice structure of the U.S. Armed Services.

The general terms of reference for the attachés, other officers, and their staffs, given this breakdown, are to get sufficient information for Canadian officials to carry out their functions as stated in government policy for the Department of National Defence (DND).[14] Within the embassy the commander of the CDLS is the advisor on military affairs to the ambassador, works closely with the heads of the embassy's Supply and Services Division and Defence Programs Division, and reports directly to the chief of the Defence Staff or the vice-chief, who are his military superiors in Ottawa.[15] Under the direct authority of the commander (CDLS) is the senior staff officer to the commander who has under him logistics, administrative, and finance officers as well as a staff officer with designated responsibilities for training, visits, and clearances. An officer with the rank of lieutenant colonel is responsible for liaison with all three U.S. Armed Services and reports directly to the commander of the CDLS. The Canadian Forces Communications Electronic Section has a lieutenant colonel in charge, a civilian officer, and a staff of noncommissioned officers. The Administration Division has two sections, personnel and finance, to service Canadian military personnel in the United States. The operational core of the CDLS is composed of the three Canadian Forces attachés' offices—maritime, land, and air—with a senior attaché in charge of each.

In March 1974 the Canadian Defence Research Staff was integrated into the Canadian Defence Liaison Staff as the Defence Research Section (DRS). Its purpose is to maintain a continuing exchange of scientific defense data between the United States and Canada. The chief and his staff maintain contact with research-and-development officers in the Pentagon and elsewhere in an attempt to acquire scientific defense information relevant to Canada. Reporting to the chief of research and development, Department of National Defence, Ottawa, the DRS consists of a chief, his deputy, and four liaison officers. Within the embassy, these officers are now under the authority of and report directly to the commander of the CDLS.

The purpose of the Supply and Services Division of the embassy is primarily procurement for the Department of Supply and Services (DSS) in Ottawa on behalf of the Canadian Forces, of items acquired through U.S. foreign military sales procedures. Procurement includes advising the Department of National Defence (DND) on projected U.S. Department of Defense production to enable the DND to plan their fiscal management of the most economic procurement; negotiating with the U.S. Department of Defense and related agencies on contract prices and deliveries; preparing contracts; and assuring promised deliveries, accurate accounts, and prompt payments. The director of the office is the senior Canadian Commercial Corporation (CCC) officer [16] and is responsible for representing the CCC in Washington in addition to his primary responsibility of procuring Canadian defense needs. There are six officers under the director in the DSS Division of the embassy dealing with procurement, emergency preparedness and industrial mobilization,[17] U.S. military contracts issued to the

Canadian Commercial Corporation in Canada, contractual statistics, scheduling and expediting of contracts, and industrial security.

The purpose of the Post Central Administration Division of the embassy is to provide an integrated administrative infrastructure for the entire Canadian mission in Washington. Since the Canadian mission in Washington is located in three separate buildings, the division is subdivided into eight subcomponents corresponding to functional areas of responsibility: general services, personnel, records management, finance, telecommunications, property matériel, telephone services, and transport services. The division is administratively under a head and his deputy, who report directly to the deputy head of post (at present the minister for economic affairs). The Interdepartmental Committee on External Relations (ICER) in Ottawa suggested that every embassy establish a committee on post management to handle administrative and support facets of their posts.[18] The embassy in Washington established such a committee, chaired on behalf of the ambassador by the deputy head of post and consisting of eleven senior members of the embassy.

The Post Central Administration Division of the embassy has gained importance through the Canadian government's objective of "maximum integration in its foreign operations," in the words of *Foreign Policy for Canadians* (June 1970). In January 1971 the cabinet announced that the support staffs for most foreign operations (whether clerical, locally engaged, or administrative) were to be integrated into a single system to be managed by the Department of External Affairs.[19] In Washington the Post Central Administration Division became responsible for implementing the integrated administrative support structure, which has since been completed. The division's responsibilities have also expanded through the "country program" whereby present and projected resources are annually outlined in detail and then related to specific functional goals. The results of this program are then fed into the Interdepartmental Committee on External Relations in Ottawa. The Canadian consular posts in the United States do their own country program, which are considered separately by ICER.

The Consular Section of the embassy is collateral to the Post Central Administration Division, with the head of the latter also being senior consul. In addition to him, the section has two officers from the Department of External Affairs and a clerical staff of three performing regular consular functions with the attendant matters relating to immunities and privileges for the Washington consular jurisdiction, which comprises the District of Columbia, Maryland, Virginia, and West Virginia.

The Police Liaison Division is the RCMP component of the embassy. It maintains contact continually with senior officials of various law enforcement agencies in Washington and periodically with other agencies to exchange criminal intelligence and information on problems of mutual concern. Representing the interests of Canadian law enforcement in the furtherance of domestic operations and/or criminal investigations, the division maintains contact with such U.S. agencies as the Department of Justice, the FBI, the Drug Enforcement Administration, Customs, and various state and municipal forces. The interests of the National Research Council of Canada are represented by individuals in different branches of the embassy. For example, the counselor (scientific) is responsible for liaison and cooperation with scientific agencies, especially the National Science Foundation, NASA, and the National Health Service.

THE CONSULAR POSTS

The context in which consular representation occurs may be described broadly as a consular milieu which encompasses elements of diversity and elements of continuity. The structural diversity of the fifteen posts, demonstrated most vividly by their lack of uniformity in size and functional orientation, can be traced to the individual and distinctive way in which each post was established and has evolved. While this may be desirable in servicing local needs, it creates problems of coordination on a more general level of servicing the goals and needs of Canada as a whole. Compensating for this to some extent are the characteristics which are common to all posts. These are the elements of continuity which link the various posts in a discernable network across the United States.

Within the Canadian government, the procedure leading to the appointment of the head of a consular post, whether he be a consul general or consul, takes into consideration the number and variety of departments which operate in consular posts. When there is a vacancy for a head of post, an interdepartmental committee at the deputy minister level— including the Departments of External Affairs; Industry, Trade and Commerce, and Manpower and Immigration— reviews the possible candidates and submits a name to the cabinet for appointment, taking into consideration a desired balance between the foreign services of each of the departments. Hence, the head of post can come from any one of the departments having representation in the United States; in some cases they can come from outside government service. (However, they generally come either from the Department of External Affairs or from Industry, Trade and Commerce.)

Upon appointment as head of post, a consul general or consul is considered an employee of the Department of External Affairs in that he is administrative head of a post serviced by External Affairs. The official may retain a rank from his own service, such as that of trade commissioner, while serving as head of post, and upon leaving that position can revert to the promotion line within his own service. Almost 40 percent of all consular officers in the United States have a trade commissioner designation. For consular officers at the post, the normal tour of duty is four years, and there appears to be no particular pattern concerning previous and subsequent postings, insofar as the United States is concerned. The criterion for selecting consular officers to serve in the United States is not specialized U.S. expertise. Instead, there is a presumption of functional expertise that is regarded as being applicable to the United States.

Another dimension of the consular milieu concerns communication flows between and within the posts, and the internal workings of the posts. While the structural diversity of the posts and their interactions make generalizations hazardous at best, some fairly consistent patterns do emerge which provide a unifying theme in consular representation in the United States.

The most frequent flows of communications are between the specific divisions of the consular posts and their parent departments in Ottawa. In order of decreasing intensity, these departments would include Industry, Trade and Commerce; External Affairs; and Manpower and Immigration. Thus, there is an organizational relationship only between the consular post as a whole and the Canadian government in Ottawa, stemming from the fact that the Canada-based officers of the consular post are appointed by the various departments to carry out programs decided upon in Ottawa. However, the consular post as a component organizational unit has significant impact on the nature of the departmental programs carried out in its consular district through its contribution to the conceptualization of the total "country program" which is submitted to the Interdepartmental Committee on External Relations in Ottawa.

A second generalization is that the contacts between the consular posts and the Canadian Embassy in Washington are essentially of a liaison nature whereby one keeps the other informed of what is going on. Moreover, this type of relationship also exists among the consular posts themselves. However, when activities overlap between consular districts, or between districts and the Canadian Embassy, consultations follow. Mitigating against closer contacts is the fact that the posts are unable to send out or receive correspondence at a higher security level than "Confidential," since they are not equipped with the system of communications required for higher classes. Thus, telexes, telephone, and written correspondence are normally used in communicating with the different Canadian consular posts in the United States, with the embassy in Washington, as well as with the different departments in Ottawa.

A further generalization concerns the relationship between the divisions of the consular post and the consul general or consul. The heads of the divisions consult with the head of post on all significant policy matters and are under his superintendence and guidance. It is the head of post who chairs the Post Management Committee meetings, and it is under the head of post's direction that the division heads participate in the preparation of the yearly "Post Program" for that particular consular district. (The "Post Program" is then submitted to the ICER in Ottawa by the head of post, with a copy for the embassy in Washington.) The administrative and support services for all divisions of the post, which have been taken over by the Department of External Affairs through the recent integration, are under the authority of the head of post. Any request or query from the embassy for analysis or information on any matter affecting its territory would be handled by the head of post.

A final generalization concerns the internal workings of the consular posts. Constant communications occur within the posts, and contacts are furthered by frequent staff meetings chaired by the head of post. While such divisions as the

Canadian Government Office of Tourism have often been located physically apart form the post itself, there is a tendency toward housing the diverse consular divisions under one roof, thereby enhancing intrapost communications.

There remains a discussion of the actual functions of the consular posts. In the broadest sense, the purpose of the consular posts is, to quote from one of the post's "Post Programs": "to realize for Canada the maximum possible economic (including manpower), financial, commercial, scientific, cultural, social and political benefits" of its presence in the United States, while protecting and assisting individual Canadian nationals and organizations in that consular district. This overall objective permeates ten major functions which are basic to Canadian consular operations in the United States, although the intensity of activity of each function varies by post, and not all posts perform each function. These ten functions are: trade and industrial development; tourism; manpower and immigration; public affairs; general relations; consular; administrative and support services; customs and excise; science, technology, and environment; and provincial interests.

Currently, the four consular functions with the highest priority at the majority of posts are trade and industrial development, manpower and immigration, administration and support services, and tourism. It is useful at this point to individually examine the ten functions.

The promotion of Canadian exports, the encouragement of relevant industrial development and investment in Canada, and the general servicing of the needs of the Canadian business community represent the threefold mandate for the trade and industrial development function. Officers of the Trade Commissioner Service (TCS) of the Department of Industry, Trade and Commerce (ITC) who generally constitute the staff of the Commercial Division of the consular post work full-time on the commercial program to meet these goals. Their work consists of maintaining ties with Canadian firms whose goods are sold in the consular district and with potential U.S. purchasers of Canadian goods; encouraging and assisting Canadian firms in promoting their goods; and assisting with the paperwork and other problems associated with carrying trade through to its conclusion. For the vast majority of Canadian consular posts in the United States, this function is the most important and demands the greatest allocation of resources.

Coterminous with the trade and industrial development function is the Defence Production Program. The Defence Production Sharing Agreement and the Defence Development Sharing arrangement between the United States and Canada give Canadian manufacturers access to the $38-billion-dollar defense market in the United States every year. The promotion of defense production has become an important consular function and can be disaggregated into the prime and subcontract fields of activity. This function is conducted under the auspices of the Department of Industry, Trade and Commerce in Ottawa. While the officers involved in the U.S. field offices have been integrated generally into the Trade Commissioner Service from their previous section, the International Defence Programs Branch (IDPB), since 1974, their special accreditation, which permits them access to U.S. military installations, distinguishes them from their colleagues involved in trade and industrial promotion.

In the subcontract area, the objective is to provide Canadian manufacturers maximum opportunity to compete with U.S. firms in supplying components and subsystems to U.S. defense contractors. In order to accomplish this objective, procurements in the area are monitored, U.S. defense contractors are advised of appropriate sources in Canada, and Canadian contractors are advised of subcontract opportunities and are assisted in their marketing attempts. In the second area, that of prime contract and development sharing, the activity is concentrated in those consular posts having major defense installations in their district. The defense production promotion function of the consular posts, unlike that of trade and industrial development, constitutes an integrated operation, although even here there are variances by posts, depending on the regional needs.[20]

The basic objective of the second function, tourism, is to encourage and sustain the orderly growth of tourism in Canada. Given the geographic continuity of the United States to Canada, it is not surprising to find that efforts to attain this objective are focused in the United States. The Marketing Branch of the Canadian Government Office of Tourism utilizes marketing techniques as a means of encouraging individual tourism from the United States to Canada, and meetings and incentives programs to encourage organized tours and conferences to select Canada.

The immigration function consists of counseling, selecting, and processing immigrants to Canada; issuing nonimmigrant visas (for certain tourists entering Canada from the United States) and employment visas; liaising with the host government over immigration procedures; and reporting on their work to Ottawa. The manpower function involves three general activities: reporting on legislative developments and trends in the area of human resource policies; liaising with U.S. universities to assist graduating Canadians concerning employment opportunities in Canada; and assisting Canadian employers in the recruitment of workers to fill vacancies for which qualified workers are not available in Canada. Officers from the Department of Manpower and Immigration are responsible for this function.

A relatively new function for consular posts, public affairs, consists of three major activities: infomation (including media relations), academic relations, and cultural affairs. The Department of External Affairs in Ottawa is responsible for this function, and its officers at the consular posts develop individual programs for their district.[21] The information activity involves providing materials and assistance to opinion leaders as well as critics from media, newspapers, and magazines. In the area of academic relations DEA officers assist universities and secondary schools in the consular district and act as a clearinghouse for information. The cultural sector promotes Canadian performers, artists, and writers through shows, exhibits, and cultural festivals.

The general relations function includes a broad range of somewhat nebulous but nonetheless important activities aimed at ensuring that the overall Canadian approach toward the United States is both consistent and services national Canadian needs. Management, representation, and reporting are the components of this function. Management requires administering and coordinating the other specific functions (e.g., trade, defense, energy) in order to present a consolidated Canadian policy approach toward the United States. Representation, through the medium of consultation and information, attempts to influence key opinion elites in the United States on Canadian actions and policies. Finally, the reporting function includes the monitoring and analysis of developments in the United States that can potentially have an impact on Canadian interests.

Basic to all systems of consular representation is the consular function. In this case, broadly defined as assisting Canadian citizens in the United States, the consular function, performed by personnel from the Department of External Affairs, includes a broad range of services from the issuance of passports and some types of nonimmigrant visas to the provision of legal, notarial, or advisory services.

The administration and support function includes staff services such as personnel and financial management, as well as country planning and the physical maintenance of the consular post. This function is carried out by Department of

External Affairs personnel, although much of the support staff includes nonconsular employees ranging from typists to maintenance personnel.

Participation in investigations under the Customs and Anti-Dumping Acts and related tariff legislation, and the provision of advice and information concerning technical information pertaining to customs regulations, constitute the two major activities for the customs and excise function. Officers from the Department of National Revenue are assigned to consular posts in Chicago, New York, and Los Angeles, as well as being located both along the Canada-U.S. border and at major points of departure for Canada such as airports, where they preclear trade goods.

The science and technology function involves reporting on relevant developments in U.S. technological advances and encouraging the transfer of advanced technology to Canada. For example, the Seattle consular post is active in this area, given the fact that The Boeing Company is located in its district; there is an extensive complex of research facilities in the Cleveland district, while the Philadelphia consular district has a broad industrial base ranging from aerospace and solar energy to electronics companies. The environmental function is regarded as complementary to the science and technology function. It consists of both presenting the Canadian position on specific environmental issues and monitoring U.S. environmental trends. This can include attending United States-based hearings, arranging visits, and reporting developments to the appropriate Canadian authorities in Ottawa.

The provincial relations function involves liaising with the provincial governments, particularly with the provincial Trade and Development ministries. Not surprisingly, the greatest activity occurs in those consular posts located near the U.S.-Canadian border, where there is ongoing transborder contact. Somewhat surprising is the general absence of a more systematic program to deal with the provinces. There are, of course, exceptions, with Seattle providing an example, for in this post there are considerable efforts expended in the area of state/provincial contacts. Most of the provincial interests function currently takes place in the area of trade and industrial development. For example, the consular posts in Seattle, San Francisco, Dallas, and Minneapolis are concerned with the economic interests of western Canada and draw on the expertise of manufacturers based there while also working with the provincial governments.

SUMMATION AND ASSESSMENT

The Canadian Embassy in Washington and the network of consulates are not without problems. The degree to which departmental programs in Ottawa are interrelated, and the fact that departmental jurisdictional responsibilities do not neatly divide along functional lines, complicate coordination in the field. Moreover, the ease of communication and travel between the two countries tempts high departmental officials either to telephone their counterparts in Washington or to travel south for discussion, thereby circumventing the embassy. Such "operational buddyism" and "diplomatic tourism" can be useful, but they can also be counterproductive if executed without regard for the coordinative departmental interrelationships within overall Canadian governmental policy. Certainly the number of Canadian officials descending on Washington is high; some Washington bureaucrats see Canadian officials "coming down like rain." And of course there are also regular visits by Canadian parliamentarians and provincial officials, which can, intentionally or inadvertently, undercut the government's position.

Canada is but one of 123 nations having embassies in Washington, all attempting to gain access to and influence U.S. policy-makers. Strangely, one of the major problems facing Canadian diplomatic officials in the United States appears to be a lack of understanding in Canada of the organizational milieus in which Canadian diplomats interact with Americans. To be effective the Canadian Embassy must adapt to, and manipulate, the procedural routines of the Washington diplomatic environment. This adaptability and manipulation can be misunderstood by the Canadian public unless a distinction is made between procedure and substance. Ironically, an informal technique, which may subject the Canadian diplomat to home charges of having been "Americanized," may be most effective in furthering Canada's position. In short, a procedural flexibility cannot be equated with a substantive policy adoption of the U.S. position. Whether the embassy is effective or not, components of the U.S. government sometimes irrevocably pursue policies that both surprise and distress even other U.S. departments and their secretaries. The Canadian Embassy also shares the proverbial problem of all embassies, including the U.S. Embassy in Ottawa: the difficulty of putting the embassy's position to its own capital.

The Canadian Embassy in Washington has five more specific problems. First, and quite simply, the embassy is understaffed and insufficiently funded for its assigned functions and the commensurate expectations of Ottawa. Second, the embassy lacks physical unity; its components are located in three different buildings, seriously complicating both substantive and administrative coordination. This situation, however, will change with the Canadian government's plans to construct a large modern building which will house all components of the Canadian delegation. The third problem is more complicated but at the same time has been partially resolved through the ICER's attempts at integration. How far personnel integration for Canadian officers abroad will go remains to be seen. If the Canadian Embassy is an example, an impressive degree of operational integration has been achieved so far, while the parent departments maintain responsibility for their officer's career patterns. The problem of policy balkanization, with different departments pursuing different objectives within the same embassy while lacking a conceptually integrated overall U.S. program, has again been at least partially resolved by the ICER. However, solutions can beget new problems, and now there is danger of rigidity, that is, country-programming projections can lessen or preclude staff adaptations to the rapidly changing Washington scene.

A fourth problem concerns the embassy and its contacts with Congress. The fact that there are 100 senators, 435 congressmen, and some 255 Senate and House committees and subcommittees, and the pervasiveness and complexity of Canada-U.S. interaction, make rather difficult any attempts to monitor or influence legislative opinion to Canada's advantage. A final problem area for the embassy is the question of representing provincial interests. The embassy is responsible for providing the provinces, through the federal government in Ottawa, with data on matters of provincial interest and in provincial areas of jurisdiction. The extent to which the embassy fails to perform this function will proportionately increase the desire of the provinces to establish their own reporting mechanisms. A certain balance appears to have been struck in which an embassy official is designated a provincial interests officer.. Beyond this, solutions to problems generated by legitimate provincial demands are being worked out.

The difficulties that inhere in consular representation in the United States may be stated as a question: What is the optimal level of coordination and integration required and desired to further Canadian national interests insofar as the United States is concerned, and how should it be institutionalized? At present, the degree of coordination exceeds that of integration. In spite of this, or perhaps more directly because of this, the posts have been flexible and effective in furthering Canadian interests by responding to the highly variegated regional conditions of their respective consular districts. In addition, the desirability and feasibility of greater integration are by no means self-evident. Some of the consular functions are more amenable to this schema than others, examples of which are public affairs and general relations where there is a higher degree of interdependence among the posts as well as between the posts and the embassy in Washington. Other functions, especially those under the purview and control of one department exclusively, such as trade promotion, tourism, and manpower and immigration, lend themselves to this approach less well. It might also be added that the embassy exerts only a formal and nominal control over the activities of the consular posts and that the interactions between the posts themselves is not structured. As such, any attempt beyond the limited approach to country programming in a coordinated fashion would require an extensive overhaul of existing reporting relations and systems of accountability.

It might be noted that the lack of organizational unity within a Canadian consular post, and the lack of coordination between them and the embassy, are significant areas where problems could arise, but there is the sense that the system functions well on an ad hoc basis and that there are no operating problems. Nonetheless, it would seem essential to have a more systematic coordinative interaction between the consular posts and the embassy, a coordination that would appear to be of mutual benefit to all organizational units involved. Those consular problems that do exist appear to be of a structural rather than of a personnel nature.

There are no panaceas for the difficulties of Canadian diplomatic and consular representation in the United States. The intimate socioeconomic transborder interactions between the two countries have relentlessly generated needs that require bilateral governmental servicing. The majority of these needs, though undramatic, constitutes the core of the Canada-U.S. relationship. The ultimate criterion of the effectiveness of the system is its degree of responsiveness to, and success in implementing, the policies and programs generated by the federal government.

NOTES

1. Internationally, a total of twenty-two Canadian departments, agencies, or other organizational units of government have some 1,880 Canadian and 2,228 locally engaged employees situated at 115 locations in 69 countries. See J. R. Maybee, "ICER and Its Two-year Search for an Approach to Integration," *International Perspectives* (September-October 1972), p. 40.

2. This section's historical account of the development of Canadian consular posts is based upon: (1) correspondence with the consuls general in Atlanta, Boston, Chicago, New Orleans, San Francisco; with the Canadian consuls in Cleveland, Dallas, Minneapolis, Philadelphia, San Juan; (2) W. R. Young and E. McAllister, *Development of Consular Operations in the United States 1940-1972*, a study prepared for the Department of External Affairs, May 1973; (3) M. Gordon Skilling, *Canadian Representation Abroad* (Toronto: The Ryerson Press, 1945); and (4) Don Page, *Selling the Canadian Image in the United States: The Consulates*, a paper prepared for delivery at the Canadian Studies Panels on "Canada and the United States, Decade of Decision: Energy, Ecology and the Economy," at the Western Social Science Association Annual Meeting, Arizona State University, Tempe, Arizona, April 29-May 1, 1976. 26 pages.

3. This paragraph is based upon Skilling, op. cit. pp. 6-7.

4. Ibid.

5. The remainder of this section is based upon correspondence with Canadian consular officials in the United States, and especially on the Young and McAllister study.

6. Young and McAllister, op. cit., p. 191.

7. Skilling, op. cit., p. 200.

8. Ibid., p. 214

9. This excludes Leighton McCarthy, who appears on the preceding minister's chart. As the incumbent minister, McCarthy was promoted to ambassador with the 1943 elevation of the legation to embassy.

10. For an account of customary international procedure see John R. Wood and Jean Serres, *Diplomatic Ceremonial and Protocol: Principles, Procedures and Practices* (New York: Columbia University Press, 1970), pp. 9-13.

11. Although not organizationally a component of the Canadian

Embassy and not included in the previous figures, other Canadian representation in Washington, D.C., includes the following: World Bank (two Canada-based officers); International Monetary Fund (two officers); Inter-American Development Bank (three officers); and the Canadian Permanent Observer Mission to the Organization of American States (two officers).

12. It is necessary to distinguish this section from the Supply and Services Division of the embassy (Department of Supply and Services), which procures Canadian defense needs in the United States. Both had their origins in a supply mission established for Canadian needs. The establishment of the Department of Defence Production in the early 1950s maintained the continuity of the mission's activity, and the declaration of Principles of Cooperation followed by the Defence Production and Sharing Agreements gave this agency the twofold responsibility for marketing and procurement. The creation of the Departments of Supply and Services, and of the Department of Industry, Trade and Commerce in 1968-69, divided the functions of marketing and procurement, the latter still being carried out by the DSS section of the Embassy. From 1969 to mid-1974, the involvement of Canadian industry in U.S. Department of Defense programs was the responsibility of an element of the Defence Program Branch and was separate and distinct from both the Economic Division of the embassy and from the Canadian Trade Commissioner Service. In July 1974, the foreign-based officers of the Defence Programs Branch were converted to the Canadian Foreign Service and integrated in the Trade Commissioner Service, maintaining, however, the right to direct communication with the Defence Programs Branch in Ottawa on program-related operational matters.

13. Although press, information, and cultural functions were part of the embassy's mandate since the early 1940s, the origins of the Office of Information date back to the mid-1950s when the first minister-counselor was assigned to the embassy. He set up a one-man shop and manned it until 1963, after which the post was left unoccupied until late in 1966 when the incumbent was appointed. The Office of Information underwent a major expansion in 1969 when it was established in separate headquarters on the third floor of the National Association of Broadcasters Building near the Chancery. The importance the Canadian government now attaches to the United States is reflected in the fact that well over one-third of its total information budget is expended there, and indications are that the information function of the embassy will undergo further expansion. There are Canadian cultural affairs offices and press offices in London and Paris, but they are not at present integrated into an information section. Nor are there Canadian information offices in Tokyo, Brussels, or other key centers. The office of Information of the Canadian Embassy in Washington is therefore unique, given the functional integration of information activities under two successive ambassadors in such areas as educational, informational, and cultural affairs.

14. In addition to liaison functions regarding information and contacts, the Canadian Defence Liaison Staff has the administrative responsibility of arranging for visits of, and courses attended by, Canadian officers in the United States, which are in the order of seven thousand each year. Beyond relations with the United States, the attachés meet regularly with their counterparts from the Commonwealth, NATO, and other international groups. Mostly these are just social sessions, but often are found useful for the contacts they foster. The Canadian Defence Liaison Staff also handles liaison with the attachés of those other nations who have dual accreditation to both the United States and Canada but who are normally resident in Washington, including Australia, New Zealand, Nigeria, and Greece. The Canadian forces attaché (maritime) is also the accredited Canadian representative to Supreme Allied Command Atlantic Fleet (SACLANT) with headquarters in Norfolk, Virginia.

15. The commander of the Canadian Defence Liaison Staff (Washington) is responsible for some five hundred Canadian military personnel in the United States, of which approximately ninety are located in the Washington area and the rest attached to 159 units of the U.S. Armed Services at eighty-seven locations in thirty-six states and in Iceland. The ninety in the Washington area include sixty-six members of the Defence Liaison Staff and twenty-four at various installations including the Pentagon, Quantico, and offices of the Standardization committees. Of the sixty-six officers and men on the Canadian Defence Liaison Staff there are three officers including the commander and three NCOs in the Command Section, plus a medical liaison officer who reports directly to the commander, six officers and one NCO in the Canadian forces attaché (land) section, eight officers in the Canadian forces attaché (maritime) section, six officers in the Canadian forces attaché (air) section, one officer in the Canadian Forces Electronic Communications Section, with fourteen other ranks in the Communications Section, and three officers and seventeen other ranks in the Administrative Finance sections. In addition, there are six civilian officers with the Defence Research Staff and one Department of National Defence Civilian employee in the Communications Electronics Section. All secretarial staff is furnished by the Department of External Affairs under the recent organizational reform. The commander is a two-star flag officer and the Canadian forces attachés are of one-star rank. They correspond to U.S. officers in Ottawa, who have the rank of colonel with similar responsibilities. Here it is interesting to note that the United States maintains lower-ranking officers in its embassy in Ottawa in order to not overwhelm the host state's military with rank, while Canada maintains senior officers in Washington because the rank is felt necessary to obtain increased access and support from U.S. counterparts.

16. Established in 1946, the Canadian Commercial Corporation is owned by the government of Canada. In 1963 it was subsumed under the Department of Defence Production and is now an interrelated component of the Department of Supply and Services, which provides the corpora-

tion's management and services and acts as the Canadian government's contracting and procurement agency on behalf of foreign nations who want to purchase defense or other supplies and services from Canada on a government-to-government basis. Evidence suggests that the defense business is relatively on the wane, with very roughly 60 percent of its business being in the area of defense, while 40 percent is commercial.

17. Canada and the United States have working arrangements concerning basic industrial-base activity whereby Canada would attempt to maintain a basic knowhow and industrial base in cooperation with the United States in the event of hostilities.

18. An interdepartmental task force had been set up in October 1969 under retired ambassador S. D. Pierce to study and make recommendations concerning the government's operations abroad, which was to concentrate on increased efficiency and the feasibility of greater integration. The task force's report was completed in March 1970, and after study by an ad hoc group the conclusions were publicly announced with the June 1970 publication of *Foreign Policy for Canadians*, which stated that the "Government needs a strong and flexible organization for carrying out its reshaped foreign policy." One result was the Interdepartmental Committee on External Relations (ICER), which met for the first time in July 1970 in an attempt to reshape foreign policy organizational processes. A subcommittee of ICER, the Personnel Management Committee, concerned with the development of coordinate interdepartmental personnel policies, was also established. Since its creation, ICER has addressed itself to two managerial dimensions of Canada's foreign operations, personnel integration and country planning, both of which have directly affected Canadian representation in the United States. See, for example, J.R. Maybee, op. cit., and Michael Henderson, "Policy Planning In Canadian External Affairs," a paper prepared for the Canadian Political Science Association, June 3-6, 1974, Toronto.

19. As a result, the support staff for most of Canada's foreign operation (e.g., administrative, clerical, local employees, stenographic) were integrated into a single system managed by the Department of External Affairs. This became effective in April 1971, involving the transfer of about one thousand employees, mostly locally engaged personnel, from other departments and agencies to External Affairs. Some $10 million in annual expenditures was involved.

20. The Defence Production unit of the Canadian Embassy in Washington is responsible for the overall monitoring of these arrangements. This unit maintains contact with relevant U.S. senior officials, in an attempt to identify U.S. military procurements which might be of advantage to Canadian industry.

21. The public affairs activities of the individual posts parallel those of the Public Affairs Division of the Canadian Embassy in Washington.

IV

THE FUNCTION OF BILATERAL CANADA-U.S. ORGANIZATIONS

The joint organizational experience on the part of Canada and the United States has resulted in an untidy web of no less than seventeen bilateral organizations. Although these organizations are in varying degrees active, the sheer number of them is significant. For example, there are approximately twice as many Canada-U.S. bilateral organizations as there are Mexico-U.S. organizations. Also significant are the sectors in which the Canada-U.S. organizations are active. There are bilateral organizations operative in the economic, strategic, environmental, and political areas of the Canada-U.S. relationship. The form these bilateral organizations take is also significant, and includes committees, commissions, an integrated military command, and an interparliamentary group of federal legislators.

This organizational network can be regarded as an institutionalization of the simple fact that regional coexistence between Canada and the United States necessitates transborder methods of resolving issues at the government-to-government level. The need for such methods is self-evident, given not only geographical contiguity but also the extraordinary economic, strategic, and social-cultural intertwining that exists between Canada and the United States.

It should be borne in mind that the use of bilateral organizations on the part of Canada and the United States is but one method of dealing with issues and is not the most important one. Here it is instructive to compare the Canada-U.S. experience with that of Europe. As a Canadian author has well pointed out, there is less of an emphasis on formal intergovernmental organizations in the case of Canada and the United States.[1] This reflects the important role of transnational forces (ranging from businesses to service clubs) in the Canada-U.S. relationship, as well as a predilection on the part of Canadian and U.S. officials for more informal methods of government-to-government interaction such as ad hoc working meetings and telephone calls. An additional factor reflecting the indigenous managerial nature of the Canada-U.S. experience is the Canadian concern about increased integration. While Canadians are interested in reaping the benefits of interdependence, they are congenitally wary about any form of economic, strategic, or political integration that might encourage Canada's absorption by the United States. In contradistinction, the European experience can be regarded as an attempt to deal with interdependence by selectively stimulating and furthering integration.

Notwithstanding Canadian reservations about the integrative dangers of organizational bilateralism, the twentieth century has witnessed a phenomenal growth of Canada-U.S. organizations as a means of regional management. Not only did these bilateral organizations, and particularly the International Joint Commission, seem to serve North American needs ideally; there also grew up a consciousness on the part of Canadian and U.S. officials that they were actively contributing to the solution of international problems by serving as an organizational model. For example, Canadian Prime Minister King could write in July 1923: "I am convinced that [the International Joint Commission] contains the new world answer to old world queries as to the most effective methods of adjusting international differences and avoiding the wars to which they give rise. In some respects it constitutes the most important contribution which has thus far been made to the practical solution of international differences." [2] By 1942 King's enthusiasm was unbounded, and he could suggest to President Roosevelt that the International Joint Commission might serve as the basis for postwar international organization.[3] Nor was this organizational enthusiasm confined to the International Joint Commission. The Canadian Minister of Defence, Brooke Claxton, could argue in 1948 that the Canada-U.S. Ogdensburg Agreement which had created the Permanent Joint Board on Defence "had far greater significance than the joint defence of North America." [4] He maintained that it symbolizes "friendship and co-operation between Canada and the United States" and "should point the way to that larger co-operation between nations on which alike depend the hope of peace and the promise of happiness to mankind." [5]

More self-serving than self-effacing and more pompous than prescient, this Canada-U.S. organizational enthusiasm had been largely dissipated by the early 1970s. Increasing internal Canadian sensitivities about the U.S. impact on Canada, coupled with increasingly divergent and abrasive issues (ranging from the 1971 Nixon surcharge to energy matters) made for a Canada-U.S. relationship that was less amenable to organizational panaceas. While not repudiating existing bilateral organizations (with the exception of the two ministerial level joint committees), there was a new commitment to "ad hocism" as a means of regional management on the part of Canadian and U.S. officials.

What, then, is the function of bilateral organizations in the Canada-U.S. context? The first section of this chapter provides a standardized definition of bilateral organizations, distinguishes between the different types of Canada-U.S. organizations that are active, and presents an era analysis of their seventy-five-year evolution. The subsequent five sections examine the individual seventeen bilateral organizations, emphasizing the origins of each organization, its structure, and its function. The second section discusses the six joint military committees and the North American Air Defense Command (NORAD); the third section discusses the three joint economic committees; the fourth discusses the six joint commissions and the Interparliamentary Group. A concluding section summarizes the findings, assesses the overall function of the bilateral organizations, and discusses the extent to which these organizations have furthered political integration between Canada and the United States.

ORIGINS AND EVOLUTION

There are few writings on the overall bilateral organizational structure between Canada and the United States, and the writings that do exist tend to encounter difficulties because there is no attempt to define "bilateral organizations." The failure to offer a standardized definition can affect the actual number of bilateral organizations that are thought to be operable. This definitional confusion is understandable given the hosts of ad hoc Canada-U.S. governmental meetings which at times seem to shade into formal organizations. Moreover, there is a variety of subcommittees and working groups of bilateral organizations that seem to have an independent existence; in fact, some of the existing bilateral organizations have as their origins such a subcommittee status. The variable levels of activity of the various bilateral organizations also present difficulties, for although some of the organizations have not met for a decade or two, they have never been officially disbanded.

The definition offered here is that a bilateral organization must have three ingredients: defined membership, defined statement of purpose, and anticipated ongoing meetings.[6] More specifically, a bilateral organization has an explicitly defined membership of Canadian and U.S. governmental officials, who are authorized by their respective governments to jointly discuss matters within their official jurisdictions through ongoing meetings that are explicitly anticipated to occur either on a regularized basis (e.g., once a year) or in response to defined issues (e.g., as the need arises). Thus, an organizational unit is not considered a bilateral organization if it is the subcomponent of another organization (i.e., the Regional Civil Emergency Advisory Committee is a subcomponent of the Civil Emergency Planning Committee) or if it is superseded by another organization (e.g., the 1905 International Waterways Commisssion was superseded by the International Joint Commission). In addition, a unit is not considered a bilateral organization, even though it is still "carried on the books," if it has not met since 1960 (e.g., the Industrial Mobilization Committee last met in 1953). Based upon discussions with officials, the probability of a bilateral organization being invoked after this time span is minimal, indicating that for all intents and purposes that organization is no longer in existence.

According to this definition, there are currently seventeen Canada-U.S. bilateral organizations. This Canadian-U.S. joint organizational structure is entirely a twentieth-century phenomenon. The chronological establishment of these joint organizations is revealing. Since the turn of the century, every decade has witnessed the creation of at least one additional ongoing joint organization. Indeed, four eras of Canadian-U.S. joint organization building can be identified: the era of commissions running from the turn of the century through the 1940s, the era of joint military committees during the 1940s, the era of organizational hyperactivity occurring during the decade of the 1950s and the era of organizational somnolence during the 1960s. The current era of the 1970s is characterized by a commitment to ad hoc consultative procedures as opposed to formal organizations.

The first era, running from the turn of the century to the decade of the 1940s, was the era of commissions. Four joint organizations were established during this era, all of them environmental, with the exception of the International Boundary Commission, which is political in terms of boundary surveys and maintenance. Indeed, four of the six existing Canadian-U.S. commissions were created during these forty years. More specifically, the International Boundary Commission was established in 1908; the International Joint Fisheries Commission in 1923 (whose name was changed in 1953 to the International Pacific Halibut Commission); and the Pacific Salmon Commission in 1930. In addition, the International Waterways Commission had been created in 1905 but was superseded by the establishment of the International Joint Commission, which became operational in 1912.

The second era of Canadian-U.S. joint organization building occurred during the decade of the 1940s. This was the era of the joint military committees. Beginning in 1940 with the establishment of the Permanent Joint Board on Defence, this decade culminated in the 1949 Military Cooperation Committee. But in addition to these two ongoing committees, a host of temporary wartime committees was established, including five bilateral Canadian-U.S. committees: the Matériels Coordinating Committee (1941-46), the Joint Economic Committees (1941-44), the Joint War Production Committee (1941-45), the Joint Agricultural Committee (1943-45), and the Joint War Aid Committee (1943-45) In addition, there was a host of multilateral wartime committees which included the United Kingdom and Canada. Examples include the Combined Production and Resources Board, the Combined Food Board, the Combined Committee on Air Training, and the Combined Policy Committee. In addition, the bilateral Canadian-U.S. Industrial Mobilization Committee was established in 1949, although it is now defunct. This second era is therefore important because it established the precedence of Canadian-U.S. committees, all military in nature, of which two survived—the Permanent Board and the Military Cooperation Committee.

The third and most important era of joint Canadian-U.S. organization building occurred during the decade of the 1950s. This can be regarded as the era of organizational hyperactivity. Eight of the existing seventeen joint Canadian-U.S. organizations were established during this period. The year 1958 was an extraordinarily active year, for in that year alone four joint organizations were created which are still active today. Of the eight joint organizations established during the 1950s, five are military in nature: the Regional Planning Group on NATO established in 1950; the Civil Defence Committee established in 1951 (renamed the Civil Emergency Planning Committee in 1963); the Senior Committee on Defence Production/Development Sharing created in 1958; the North American Air Defense Command (NORAD) formalized in 1958; and the Ministerial Committee on Joint Defence also created in 1958. Of the remaining three ongoing joint organizations established during the 1950s, one was economic (the Ministerial Committee on Trade and Economic Affairs created in 1953); one was environmental (the Great Lakes Fisheries Commission established in 1955); and one was political (the Canadian-U.S. Interparliamentary Group created in 1958).

The fourth era of joint Canadian-U.S. organization building can be described as the era of joint organizational somnolence. Only two ongoing joint organizations were established, one economic in nature (the Balance of Pay-

ments Committee established in 1963), the other environmental in nature (the 1964 creation of the Roosevelt
Campobello Park Commission). This fourth era is characterized not only by the establishment of fewer joint organizations but also by existing joint organizations falling into
disuse. For example, the Ministerial Committee on Defence
last met in 1964. The Senior Committee on Defence
Production/Development Sharing last met in 1968, and the
Ministerial Committee on Trade and Economic Affairs last
met in 1970. Perhaps symbolizing the new Canadian-U.S.
perspectives on joint organizations, a Technical Committee
on Agricultural Marketing and Trade problems was created
in 1967, only to be replaced in 1970 with a jointly defined
"agricultural trade consultation procedure" as opposed to a
joint committee structure.

The present era of U.S.-Canadian organizational activity
might be characterized as an era of periodic consultation.
Only one ongoing joint organization was established, the
1971 Committee on Trade Statistics, which of course is
economic in nature. An additional committee was created in
1972, the Committee on Water Quality in the St. John River
and its tributaries, but it accomplished its functions.[7]

A glimpse of what this fourth era will look like was
provided by the U.S. assistant secretary of state for European
affairs. During a press conference after the December 4, 1974,
Trudeau-Ford Washington summit meeting, a reporter asked
the assistant secretary if there was "any new machinery talked
about."[8] The assistant secretary replied, "No new machinery" and then proceeded to deliver himself of his own
views on joint consultation. "As we identify problems, it
seems to me we are going to get groups together to deal with
them. The idea of a general machinery that would be in place
to consult, I don't see that coming about. The example of
these experts getting together talking about the agriculture
problem I think is probably the way our consultative process

will go and should go in dealing with specific bilateral issues."
During the morning off-the-record press conference, a high-
ranking U.S. State Department official was even more
explicit regarding the viability of joint Canadian-U.S. consultative organizations.[9] The official stated that "[I] frankly
don't expect mechanism used in the past to be revived."
Referring "particularly to the Cabinet Committee on Trade
and Economic Affairs," the official stated that it "didn't
provide decisions and review that were helpful" because "the
interests of the members of the Committee were so diverse."
The official added that Canadian and U.S. officials "may be
discussing new methods of periodic consultation" which
would preclude the need for formalized meetings. An example of the new approach can be found in the June 1977
Ottawa meeting between the Canadian minister of justice
and the U.S. attorney general. In an attempt to resolve the
difficulties concerning the extraterritorial application of
American antitrust laws in Canada, this meeting resulted in
the establishment of a permanent long-term "consultative
mechanism" which will deal with future antitrust problems.[10]
In the short run, a set of general principles will be defined
which, when agreed to by both countries, will hopefully avoid
further difficulties in this area. The attempt is quite simply to
establish an "early warning system" whereby the interests of
both governments can be taken into account.

As this survey has shown, the first ongoing Canadian-U.S.
commission was established in 1908. However, the use of
commisssions as a technique of Canadian-U.S. issue resolution, especially concerning boundary settlements and fisheries
disputes, dates back almost two centuries to the Jay Treaty of
1794. In contrast, the use of Canadian-U.S. committees is a
relatively recent phenomenon, dating back to the 1940
establishment of the Permanent Joint Board on Defence.
Both commissions and committees have advantages and
disadvantages as methods of issue resolution.[11] Commissions

are generally created by formal treaties, and their mission is quite specifically stated. They are especially useful in depoliticizing issue areas; that is, in removing issues from normal diplomatic channels by redirecting them to technical experts. Thus, commissions are most effective, and most often utilized, in matters requiring a scientific, technical, or judicial approach. For example, three out of the six Canadian-U.S. commissions deal exclusively with fisheries matters; one deals with the maintenance of the international boundary between Canada and the United States; one deals with the administration of an international park; and one, which is the most important, deals with transborder pollution matters. Commissions, it should be added, are the most "equal" of joint organizations, a fact not irrelevant to Canada as the weaker economic and strategic component of the disparate relationship, because they confer both legal and operational parity.

Committees are generally established by less formal arrangements than commissions, ranging from an exchange of notes (Ministerial Committee on Trade and Economic Affairs), to a joint press release (Permanent Joint Board on Defence), to an unpublicized reorganization (the 1949 separation of the Military Cooperation Committee from the Permanent Board). The statement of purpose defining a committee's mission is cast in more general terms than that of a commission. Committees tend to be utilized most in strategic and economic matters, areas which do not lend themselves to scientific or judicial approaches. Indeed, areas of military and economic matters are those which are most heavily politicized in addition to being areas where governments tend to insist on a maximum amount of individual control and confidentiality. While committees do confer legal parity, operational parity is precluded because the disparity between Canada and the United States is not organizationally absorbed by the committee mandate or structure. For example, while the national capabilities of Canada and the United States are not directly registered, and are in fact irrelevant, in one of the joint fisheries commissions, the disparity is keenly felt in the Permanent Joint Board on Defence or the Ministerial Committee on Trade and Economic Affairs. In a general sense, committees tend to be more consultative in nature than commissions, which is exemplified by the Balance of Payments Committee.

With this overview as background, it is useful to turn to an examination of the individual Canada-U.S. organizations, beginning with the defense committees.

BILATERAL DEFENSE COMMITTEES AND NORAD

There are six bilateral defense committees between Canada and the United States: the Permanent Joint Board on Defence, the Military Cooperation Committee, the Regional Planning Group on NATO, the Ministerial Committee on Joint Defence, the Civil Emergency Planning Committee, and the Senior Committee on Defence Production/Development Sharing Program.[12] In addition, the North American Air Defense Command, which constitutes an integrated command structure between Canada and the United States, is discussed in this section. Of these six committees, two perform planning-recommendatory functions (Permanent Board and Military Cooperation Committee); one is concerned with liaison (Regional Planning Group on NATO); one with emergency planning and coordination (Civil Emergency Planning Committee); and one with the economics of defense collaboration (Senior Committee on Defence Production/Development Sharing).

The Permanent Joint Board on Defence was established by a press release issued on August 18, 1940, resulting from a meeting between President Roosevelt and Prime Minister

King at Ogdensburg, New York. The six-sentence unsigned Ogdensburg Declaration constituted a response to the worsening military situation in Europe. Within four days of the declaration the White House issued a press release announcing the constituency of the Permanent Board; and four days later, on August 26, 1940 the board held its first meeting in Ottawa. As an advisory rather than executive body, the board was responsible for two basic defense plans and thirty-three wartime recommendations.

The post-World War II existence of the board was officially confirmed on February 12, 1947, when the United States and Canada issued an announcement stating that "in the interest of efficiency and economy, each government has decided that its national defense establishment shall, to the extent authorized by law, continue to collaborate for peacetime joint security purposes." [13] Nevertheless, the functions of the board have been dictated by the changing nature of U.S. and Canadian defense requirements and the creation of other joint bodies (e.g., the Military Cooperation Committee and NORAD). Indeed, with the increased immediacy of the Soviet threat through the advent of first the long-range bomber and second missile development, the U.S. and Canadian military staffs assumed many of the board's functions. Direct post-World War II contributions of the board would include its participation in the planning of the Pine Tree, Mid-Canada, and Distant Early Warning lines. More indirect contributions include its involvement in the Ballistic Missile Early Warning System, the 1958 establishment of NORAD, the settling of the nuclear weapons controversy in 1963, and the NORAD renewals in 1968, 1973, and 1975.

The board's organizational structure remains largely the same as it was during World War II. There is a U.S. and a Canadian section, with each section having its own chairman (a civilian); four representatives from the armed services of general or admiral rank and four assistants of colonel or captain's rank; and two civilian members, for the United States from the State Department, and for Canada from the Department of External Affairs. Generally, representatives of the Canadian Departments of Transport and Supply and Services attend board meetings as observers. The chairmen are appointed by the president and prime minister, respectively, while the two State Department and DEA representatives serve as section secretaries. Membership in the Board is part-time. The board meets four times a year in locations of mutual interest, during which part of the time is spent touring that particular defense installation or area.

The Military Cooperation Committee was originally established in March 1946 under the auspices of the Permanent Joint Board on Defence in an attempt to provide a continuing structure for joint action by the Canadian and U.S. military. The first meeting of the committee was in May 1946, held in Washington, during which consideration was given to drafts concerning both Canadian-U.S. security requirements and a more general security plan. With the February 12, 1947, Canada-U.S. statement on the continuation of defense collaboration, the committee assumed primary responsibility for coordinating actions stemming from the implementation of principles contained in the February statement. In 1949, the Military Cooperation Committee was separated from the Permanent Board, and its membership thereafter consisted of military personnel only. It continues to operate as a binational, strictly military planning body, and has no direct relationship with NATO.

The committee is especially important because it is the primary Canadian-U.S. agency concerned with recommendations relative to military policy and planning for the defense of Canada and the United States. In addition, it handles those mutual defense issues that the Canadian Chief of Defence Staff and the U.S. Joint Chiefs of Staff might refer to it. Organizationally, the committee consists of two national sections, responsible to their respective Chiefs of Staff. Both the Canadian and the U.S. sections consist of a chairman, a secretary, and six members from the defense services (two from the army, navy, and air force for the United States, and two from each of the air, maritime, and ground components of the integrated Canadian Forces). The committee normally meets in combined session immediately prior to meetings of the Permanent Board. The agendas and proceedings of the committee are shrouded in secrecy, and until the early 1960s any information about it was classified. An example of the issues considered by the committee, from a meeting in early 1970, would include: basic security plan review, the NORAD Agreement, air defense, fighter dispersals, weather observational coverage, and joint military exercises.

It is with the Regional Planning Group that NATO, as a multilateral defense alliance involving both Canada and the United States, becomes organizationally relevant to the Canadian-U.S. bilateral defense alliance structure. The North Atlantic Treaty Organization was created with the April 1949 North Atlantic Treaty, and at its first meeting, held in September 1949, arrangements were made concerning the establishment of five Regional Planning Groups, of which the Canada-U.S. Group was one. In January 1950 a joint Canadian-U.S. Chiefs of Staff meeting was held "to consider the steps necessary to set up the Canada-U.S. Regional Planning Group in line with the other regional groups already organized in Europe," with the NATO Council having charged to the Canada-U.S. Group "the responsibility for planning the defence of North America, and for providing strategic support and reserves for the NATO forces in Europe." [14]

The Regional Planning Group therefore performs essentially a coordination liaison function. It is directly responsible to the executive agency of NATO, the North Atlantic Treaty

Organization Standing Group, and its function is the reporting to NATO of air and missile defense arrangements made
by the Canada-U.S. Military Cooperation Committee. The
Regional Planning Group has no direct relationship with the
Permanent Joint Board on Defence. The membership of the
group is the same as that of the Military Cooperation
Committee, a Canadian and American section consisting of
six representatives from the three defense forces of each
country. However, there is one exception. The Regional
Planning Group does not have a separate chairman in
addition to the other members as does the Military Cooperation Committee; instead it is chaired by one of the members
on a rotating basis among the services.

The organizational structure of the Regional Planning
Group is rather complex. It consists of a Chiefs of Staff
Committee, a regional Planning Committee, a Working
Team, a Secretariat, and such ad hoc subcommittees as
needed. The Chiefs of Staff Committee is composed of the
Canadian Chief of Defence Staff and the U S. Joint Chiefs of
Staff, although it last met in 1951 and delegated much of its
work to the Regional Planning Committee. The committee
itself consists of one representative each from the U.S. Army,
Navy, and Air Force and representatives of Canada's ground,
maritime, and air components, with an additional officer
from each of the countries' services serving as Working Team
members. The Working Team consists of one representative
of each member of the Regional Planning Committee, and
the U.S. Working Team members are the same as the
Assistant Military Cooperation Committee members and,
with few exceptions, serve also as assistants to the Permanent
Board. Finally, the Secretariat, located in Washington, D.C.,
consists of one U.S. officer and is provided with both
Canadian and U.S. civilian secretarial personnel. The U.S.
officer also serves as secretary for the Regional Planning
Group.

The announcement establishing the Canada-U.S. Ministerial Committee on Joint Defence was made on July 10, 1958, approximately two months after NORAD came into force. The two governments subsequently exchanged notes thereby officially creating the Cabinet Committee. The Cabinet Committee consists of Canada's secretary of state for external affairs, minister of national defense, and minister of finance and of the United States' secretaries of state, defense, and treasury, in addition to ad hoc participation of other ministers as needed. The exchange of notes establishing the committee state that, first, the "periodic review" to be undertaken by the committee would include political and economic matters of defense in addition to purely military matters.[15] Second, the committee's mission is further delineated under three points: first, general periodic consultation on "any matters affecting the joint defense"; second, "the exchange of information and views at the Ministerial level on problems that may arise"; and third, the reporting of the ministerial level discussions to the two governments, thereby enabling them to consider "measures deemed appropriate and necessary to improved defense cooperation." In addition, it is stated that the Cabinet Committee "shall meet once a year or more often as may be considered necessary by the two Governments," with the agreement remaining in force until either government serves a written notice requesting termination. Finally, it is significant that the exchange of notes expressly stated that "the agreement of the two Governments to integrated air defence arrangements increased the importance of regular consultation between them on all matters affecting the joint defence of Canada and the United States."

Using its own statement of purpose as an evaluative criterion, it can be concluded that the Canada-U.S. Ministerial Committee on Joint Defence has not been effective. Indeed, the committee has met but four times since its inception—in 1958, 1959, 1960, and 1964. Especially significant is the fact that the committee did not meet during the difficult bilateral controversy concerning the Canadian acquisition of nuclear weapons.

The Civil Emergency Planning Committee was established in 1963. Its origins lie in the creation of the 1951 Joint Civil Defence Committee. Confined to population matters in the event of an attack, Canada-U.S. civil defense cooperation was further extended with a 1963 agreement entitled "Defence: Civil Emergency Planning." Subsequently, there was an "Agreement on Cooperation between the U.S. and Canada on Civil Emergency Planning," signed by the two governments and entering into force on August 8, 1967. This agreement constitutes the currently active civil emergency accord.

With the 1967 agreement, which can be terminated by either government upon three months' written notice, the Civil Emergency Planning Committee continued, but in altered form. It consists of Canada's director general of Emergency Planning Canada, and a representative appointed by the Department of External Affairs; and the U.S. directors of the Defense Civil Preparedness Agency and Federal Preparedness Agency and a representative appointed by the Department of State. In addition, the Committee has a Secretariat provided by Emergency Planning Canada, and the two American agencies, Defense Civil Preparedness and Federal Preparedness. It is specifically stated that the committee will meet at least once a year, and four functions of the committee are defined. First, it is to "be responsible for supervising U.S.-Canada cooperative civil emergency planning and arrangements generally, including making recommendations and providing guidance." [16] Second, it is to arrange for necessary joint consultation and establish necessary subcommittees and working groups. Third, it is to facilitate "civil emergency planning and development of mutual assistance arrangements by adjacent states, provinces, and municipalities along the international boundary"; and fourth, it is "to facilitate the exchange of information . . . on civil emergency measures."

The organizational structure of the Civil Emergency Planning Committee is complex and in varying degrees active. The Committee itself, referred to as the Senior Committee, attempts to meet once a year (it did not, for example, meet in 1968), utilizing a prepared agenda and attended by officials of governmental agencies specified in the 1967 agreement. All decisions are made by unanimous consent.[17] Two other committees, the Regional Civil Emergency Advisory Committee and the Committee for Coodination of Emergency Economic Planning, are responsible to the Senior Committee.

The predecessors of the 1958 Senior Committee on Defence Production/Development Sharing can be found in the World War II Canadian-U.S. committee structure which implemented wartime economic cooperation and in the 1948 establishment of the Industrial Mobilization Planning Committee. Just as the August 1940 Ogdensburg Declaration constituted the initial step in overall Canadian-U.S. defense cooperation, the April 20, 1941, Hyde Park Agreement between Prime Minister King and President Roosevelt was an economic extension of Ogdensburg. The implementation of this wartime cooperation involved the establishment of numerous Canadian-U.S. joint committees and combined boards.

In the most basic sense, the Production Sharing Program "provides Canadian manufacturers with the opportunity to supply a wide range of defence supplies and services purchased by the U.S. armed forces in competition with U.S. industry"; while the Development Sharing Program, acknowledging the fact that research and development is essential to any success of the production aspects of the program, involves "Canadian industrial participation in Research and

Development leading to the production of modern defence matériel," including Canadian company involvement in research-and-development projects funded by the United States.[18]

While the Senior Committee on Defence Production, whose responsibility it is to oversee the Production and Development Sharing Program, met six or seven times in the late 1950s and early 1960s on a crisis basis, it has not been convened since 1968. The Steering Committee, also known as the Steering Group, whose mandate is to identify and fully describe any problems with the arrangement for action by the Senior Committee and whose role essentially is to facilitate the arrangement, has been relatively more active. Apart from a totally inactive period between 1968 and 1972, it has met more frequently than the Senior Committee, and it has agreed to meet annually since its revival in 1972.

The revival of the Steering Committee was initiated by the Canadian side and can be traced to the Canadian-U.S. trade problems of the early 1970s. In 1971, the U.S. Departments of Treasury and Commerce identified the production sharing imbalance and the auto pact as the major irritants between Canada and the United States, with the latter in severe balance-of-payments deficit overall. While a series of meetings was held outside of the Steering or Senior Committee,[19] the Canadian government, and most notably the Canadian Department of Industry, Trade and Commerce, saw it in its best interests to revive the Steering Committee to manage the problem better.

The Steering Committee, therefore, was reinvoked as a means of dealing with the American balance-of-payments deficit in defense matériel. Cochaired by the deputy assistant secretary (Procurement); the Office of the Secretary of Defense (U.S.); and the assistant deputy minister (Export Development) of the Canadian Department of Industry, Trade and Commerce, it reports to its respective senior managements. On the American side, representatives from the Defense Department, the State Department, and the U.S. Navy, Army, and Air Force are members of the committee. Representatives from the Department of Industry, Trade and Commerce; the Department of National Defence; the Department of Supply and Services; the Department of External Affairs; and the Canadian Embassy are members of the committee on the Canadian side. These representatives are at the senior working level and the host country usually has a larger delegation.

Meeting annually, the meeting place of the Committee alternates between Ottawa and Washington, with the host country responsible for establishing the agenda and clearing it with the other country; position papers on agenda items are circulated one month prior to the meeting whenever possible. A typical agenda would include the introduction of new members and status reports on the two programs, including "statistical monitoring" and special "issues." One interesting development typical of organizational proliferation has occurred. At the request of the United States a, separate Steering Committee concerning development sharing met on January 3, 1976, in Ottawa. Whether this committee will continue to have a separate life remains to be seen. In addition, some discussion has taken place about the eventual return of the Senior Committee itself, but the evidence, at this point, is inconclusive. Finally, on the development-sharing side, two joint Canada-U.S. working groups in the air force field meet twice a year to develop jointly shared "development" projects.

The North American Air Defense Command (NORAD) was established on an interim basis in August 1957, formally effected in May 1958 for a ten-year period, and renewed in March 1968 for an additional five years. It was renewed again in the spring of 1973 for three years, and again in 1975 for an additional five years.[20] The primary objectives of NORAD are: (1) assisting each country to safeguard the sovereignty of its airspace; (2) contributing to the deterrence of attack on North America by providing capabilities for warning of attack and for defense against air attack; and (3) should deterrence fail, ensuring an appropriate response against attack by providing for the effective use of the forces of the two countries available for air defense.[21]

NORAD is, in effect, a bilateral, integrated military organization responsible for defending Canada and the United States and their approaches—an area of 10.5 million square miles—against air attack. The essential import of NORAD, therefore, lies in the fact that Canada and the United States have placed their continental air defense forces under full operational control of one commander-in-chief (an American) and his deputy commander (a Canadian). The chain of command for the United States passes through the Joint Chiefs of Staff to the secretary of defense, to the president, and for Canada, through the Chief of Defence Staff to the minister of national defence, to the prime minister.

For operational purposes, Canada and the United States are regarded as a North American power grid, divided into geographic regions. NORAD's regional boundaries were redefined in 1975, which had the effect of placing all operations in Canadian airspace under the control of centers located in Canada and manned by Canadian personnel. NORAD consists of three component commands (i.e., commands that make forces available for NORAD operational control): (1) the Canadian Armed Forces Air Defence Command; (2) the U. S. Army Air Defense Command; and (3) the U.S. Air Force Aerospace Defense Command (which provides approximately 60 percent of NORAD's total personnel and equipment). However, the commander-in-chief of the Alaskan Command, which is a separate U.S. unified command, is also responsible to NORAD for the air defense of Alaska. In addition, the U.S. Navy contributes some personnel to the NORAD staff and makes some units available.

The Canadian contribution to NORAD lies in weaponry and surveillance functions. This is, of course, in addition to Canada's granting airspace and refueling rights to U.S. components in the event of an emergency. In addition, Canada makes major contributions in air-surveillance detection and identification, while it also supplies data on satellite traffic.

The focal point of NORAD is the Combat Operations Center (COC), the nerve center of the entire NORAD air system. The COC is located deep in the 9,565-foot Cheyenne Mountain, near Colorado Springs, and consists of a complex of eleven steel buildings covering 4.5 acres of tunnels and evacuated chambers. It is from here that the first warning of an air attack would come and from here that the control of the air battle would be directed. There is a hot line communication system connecting the COC with such points as the Canadian Armed Forces headquarters in Ottawa, the White House, the Pentagon, control posts overseas, and so on.

To summarize NORAD's activities, it operates radar posts that scan both the sky and space, squadrons of interceptors, ground-to-air missile batteries, and command posts that would direct the defense battle. More specifically (and at the risk of oversimplification), the NORAD mission can be divided into the functions of detection; determination of intent; and, in the case of attacking aircraft, destruction.

BILATERAL ECONOMIC COMMITTEES

There are three bilateral economic committees between the United States and Canada: the Ministerial Committee on Trade and Economic Affairs, the Balance of Payments

Committee, and the Committee on Trade Statistics. The first two are moribund, and the latter is active.[22]

The Ministerial Committee on Trade and Economic Affairs was established in November 1953. The suggestion for a joint committee was first forwarded during Prime Minister St. Laurent's visit to Washington on May 8, 1953. According to St. Laurent's report to the Commons on his meeting with President Eisenhower: "The matter did not go very far. . . . The President turned and said to the Secretary of State—'I want you and Mr. Pearson to look into that. . . .' " [23] Within six months an exchange of notes formally established the Ministerial Committee, appropriately occurring on the eve of President Eisenhower's November 13-15, 1953, visit to Ottawa. According to the exchange of notes, the committee has a threefold purpose: (1) "To consider matters affecting the harmonious economic relations between the two countries"; (2) "In particular, to exchange information and views on matters which might adversely affect" U.S.-Canadian trade; and (3) "To report to the respective Governments on such discussions in order that consideration may be given to measures deemed appropriate and necessary to improve economic relations and to encourage the flow of trade." [24] On the U.S. side, the committee formally consists of the secretaries of state, treasury, agriculture, and commerce, including other cabinet-rank officials "as the need arises." [25] On the Canadian side, members include the secretary of state for external affairs and the ministers of finance, trade, and commerce, and "either the Minister of Agriculture or the Minister of Fisheries, as appropriate," in addition to other needed cabinet-level officials.[26] According to the exchange of notes, the committee is to "meet at least once a year alternately in Washington and Ottawa."[27]

It should be noted that the Ministerial Committee on Trade and Economic Affairs was not intended to negotiate or conclude agreements. As the Canadian External Affairs minister remarked at the committee's last meeting, its discussions are intended "to help avoid future disagreements, and smooth the way for more formal negotiations which may follow" on specific problems.[28] However, since 1953 the Committee has only met thirteen times, usually on Canadian initiative, the last meeting taking place in Ottawa in November 1970. Significantly, this lapse between meetings is the longest in the committee's twenty-two-year history. This is especially noteworthy given the active U.S.-Canadian issues during this period, including trade, balance of payments, agriculture, anti-inflation measures, all areas in which the committee had been active in the past.[29] Indeed, the committee's not meeting is reminiscent of the Ministerial Committee on Defense's not convening during the difficult bilateral controversy concerning the Canadian acquisition of nuclear weapons. The committee is now in hiatus, its last public utterance being a pledge to maintain "close, continuing and frank consultation" and promising to meet again in Washington "at a date to be announced." [30] There are no plans for the committee to meet in the near future.

The Canada-U.S. Balance of Payments Committee was established in 1963 in an attempt to absorb problems generated by U.S. legislation concerning the balance-of-payments position. It was anticipated that meetings would be held semiannually at the official level. While quite active in the late 1960s until 1968, the last meeting of the committee was in June 1970. Indeed, given the evolving system of managed floating exchange rates, it is doubtful that the Balance of Payments Committee will be active in the future. The committee itself is not highly structured, and although it has a standard membership, if either the United States or Canada wants others to attend, they may. On the U.S. side it is chaired by the assistant secretary of the treasury, while other members at the civil service level include the Federal Reserve and the Department of Commerce. For Canada, the Finance Ministry, the Bank of Canada, and Statistics Canada are included.

The U.S.-Canada Trade Statistics Committee was established in 1971 to reconcile, harmonize, and monitor counterpart Canadian-U.S. trade statistics. Its creation was really the culmination of at least a twenty-year effort to reconcile Canadian-U.S. balance-of-payments trade statistics data. However, despite some success in narrowing the differences between Canadian-U.S. trade statistics, wide divergencies in reported statistics continued. Thus, at the June 1970 meeting of the Balance of Payments Committee it was proposed that officials in each country study the problem and determine the reasons for such wide divergencies in Canadian-U.S. trade statistics. The reported one-billion-dollar difference in Canadian-U.S. trade statistics for 1970 only reinforced the need for action on this matter.

The discrepancies in Canada-U.S. trade statistics data are the result of a number of factors. First, because of a lack of administrative control, exports in both countries tend to be undercounted. In this regard, private exporters frequently do not give correct export declarations to governmental authorities. Second, imports in both countries tend to be overvalued. That is, import values established for customs purposes often exceed the actual export valuation. It should be noted, however, that U.S. published import statistics are now based on the actual transaction value rather than on the customs value. Third, significant discrepancies between Canadian and U.S. trade statistics arose because of different classification techniques. For instance, until 1976 Canadian published trade statistics for the United States did not include Canadian exports to and imports from Puerto Rico; until 1973 figures for U.S. exports to Canada included shipments of grain and natural gas for subsequent transshipment; and last, U.S. import statistics for Canada include only those goods of Canadian origin and U.S. goods returned, while Canadian export and reexport statistics include goods of any origin delivered from Canada to the United States.

The mandate of the U.S.-Canada Trade Statistics Committee was to reduce these trade statistics discrepancies. In this, its assigned task was extremely important, for many of the Canadian-U.S. trading problems of the early 1970s were based on incorrect trade statistics data. Organizationally, the committee is cochaired by the chief economist of the U.S. Department of Commerce and the chief statistician of Statistics Canada. Serving as alternate cochairmen are the chief, Foreign Trade Division, U.S. Bureau of the Census, and the director, External Trade Division, Statistics Canada. Two task forces, one made up of officials from the Foreign Trade Division of the U.S. Bureau of the Census, the other made up of officials from the External Trade Division of Statistics Canada, do the basic technical work of the committee. The task forces themselves are very active, with ad hoc meetings and telephone communications occurring frequently. The formal committee is also active, with meetings usually taking place on an annual basis.

At the first meeting of the U.S.-Canada Trade Statistics Committee, in December 1971, it was agreed that "a trade reconciliation study will be carried out on the basis of an exchange of data on import and export trade at a very detailed commodity level, and that once harmonization has been achieved it will be necessary to monitor the counterpart statistics to prevent divergences from reoccuring." [31] That trade reconciliation study resulted in the development of a conceptual framework for the harmonization of Canadian-U.S. trade statistics. Based on 1970 data, the conceptual framework was published in a 1973 report entitled *The Reconciliation of U.S.-Canada Trade Statistics.*[32] Using rather complex formulas, the conceptual framework itself dealt with the timing of export and import transactions, the valuation of export and import transactions, and the definition of merchandise trade. Accordingly, subsequent years have seen the further use of this conceptual framework to harmonize Canadian-U.S. trade statistics. Indeed, now trade statistics are reconciled on a quarterly basis, and in the future it is likely that more computerized techniques will be used. Finally, if reduced discrepancies in counterpart Canadian-U.S. trade statistics are any indication, the U.S.-Canada Trade Statistics Committee has been a success.

BILATERAL COMMISSIONS AND THE INTERPARLIAMENTARY GROUP

There are six bilateral management commissions between Canada and the United States: the International Joint Commission, the International Boundary Commission, the International Pacific Halibut Commission, the International Pacific Salmon Fisheries Commission, the Great Lakes Fishery Commission, and the Roosevelt-Campobello International Park Commission. Of these six commissions, one is concerned with the equitable use of boundary waters and pollution abatement (the International Joint Commission); one with boundary maintenance (the International Boundary Commission); three with the conservation and preservation of fisheries (the International Pacific Halibut Commission, the International Pacific Salmon Fisheries Commission, the Great Lakes Fishery Commission); and one with the management of a park (Roosevelt Campobello International Park). Each of these commissions was established to handle issues which are of major importance to both Canada and the United States. Notably, the commissions attempt to resolve possible controversy or conflict between the two countries on a technical or scientific level before they escalate to a political level. Hence, decisions are based largely on scientific investigation and technical enterprise. It is useful to examine these six commissions individually, concentrating on their origins, organizational structures, and mandated functions. The Canada-U.S. Interparliamentary Group is also discussed in this section.

The International Joint Commission (IJC) was established under Article VII of the 1909 Boundary Waters Treaty and became operational in 1912. It grew out of public pressure for some method of adjudicating conflict over rights to boundary waters and waters crossing the boundary between Canada and the United States.

The mandate of the IJC involved four functions.[33] First, it has a very far-reaching arbitral function whereby it can definitively settle as an arbitral tribunal, without further recourse, any matter that the two governments agree to refer to it for this purpose. Although this power is technically not confined to boundary-water problems, it is, in effect, concerned only with pollution and water-quality considerations. It should be noted, furthermore, that this function of the IJC has never been invoked, nor does it seem likely that the IJC will serve as an arbitral tribunal in the future. The second function of the IJC is quasi-judicial in nature, whereby its authority is final in all matters involving the use and diversion of boundary waters or the obstruction of waters crossing the boundary. The third function of the IJC is investigatory in nature, whereby it serves as a fact-finding body. Finally, the fourth function of the IJC is to monitor compliance with its orders.

To perform these functions, the IJC consists of six commissioners, three appointed from each nation by the executive authority of the United States and Canada. One of the three is designated as chairman for his country and thus presides over meetings of the IJC held in that country. The IJC acts as a single body and makes its decisions on the basis of majority vote, although most votes represent a consensus of the group and are unanimous. While there are channels of communication between commissioners and their respective governments, individual commissioners are not representatives of their countries and are not under instruction but rather act in their own capacity much as judges do.[34] Over time, appointments to the commission have tended to be political in nature, frequently going to former officeholders, although in recent years several engineers and lawyers have been appointed.[35] Meeting semiannually and altering the sites between the two nations, the commission maintains a small staff in two offices in Washington and Ottawa. Recently, under powers given the IJC by the governments in the Great Lakes Water Quality Agreement of 1972, a regional office with special pollution-monitoring functions was opened in Windsor, Ontario. In addition, some of the important boundary waters have their own permanent boards of control which report to the International Joint Commission on surveillance of approved projects. Thus, there are some thirty subgroups of the commission, whose membership generally comes from officials of the states and provinces, and increasingly from the federal governments.

Current activities of the International Joint Commission include an examination of the effects of large variations in the levels of the Great Lakes. Under the Great Lakes Water Quality Agreement, the commission has monitored pollution levels and coordinates programs prescribed by the agreement to limit and reduce pollution. The Richelieu-Champlain issue and the Garrison Dam project have also been matters of concern to the IJC, as has pollution surveillance on many of the cross-boundary rivers.

The International Boundary Commission is the second Canada-U.S. commission. Having by treaty established the boundary line between Canada and the United States over a period of time from 1783 to 1903, the United States and Britain, acting for Canada, signed a series of treaties in 1903, 1906, 1908, and 1925 providing for the joint survey and demarcation of the boundary line.[36] Under Article I of the

Canada-U.S. 1908 International Boundary Demarcation
Treaty, the task of this survey and demarcation was entrusted
to the International Boundary Commission with the exception that the boundary in the Great Lakes and the St.
Lawrence River was administered by the International Waterways Commission (which was succeeded by the International Joint Commission). Under the original treaties the first
task of the Boundary Commission was to survey the entire
length of the boundary, establish new or repair markers for
the boundary on land and sea, and prepare charts of the
boundary. Upon receiving the survey, the two governments
agreed in another treaty, signed in February 1925, to extend
the mandate of the International Boundary Commission to
cover the constant maintenance of the boundary and its
markers.

The International Boundary Commission consists of two
commissioners, one appointed by the executive of each
country. The treaties specified that the commissioners should
be "scientific experts" or "expert geographers or surveyors"
and that they have a technical staff to assist them in their
work. The work of the commission in maintaining the
boundary requires that the boundary be entirely surveyed
once every ten years. Thus, the commission has a system
whereby 10 percent of the boundary is covered each year
when markers are repaired or replaced. In addition, the
International Boundary Commission is formally empowered
to determine the locations of specific boundary points in the
settlement of boundary questions that might arise between
Canada and the United States. Finally, the commission,
which meets annually alternating between Washington and
Ottawa, is frequently called upon by customs and immigration officials to make precise surveys of the boundary
required in particular cases being handled by those agencies.

The International Pacific Halibut Commission was created
by the Convention for the Preservation of the Halibut

Fishery in the North Pacific. It was the first formal treaty signed by Canada without the participation of Great Britain and thus marked an important step in the emergence of Canada as an independent entity. Ratified in 1923, the treaty was in response to a growing consensus in both the U.S. and the Canadian fishing industries that some method of conservation was needed to protect the long-term viability of halibut fishing in the Pacific Ocean. On the basis of its studies and recommendations, the authority of the commission was slowly enhanced through two subsequent Canada-U.S. conventions adopted in 1930 and 1937. Following World War II, uncertain of its authority to set adjustable seasons, the commission recommended the negotiation of another convention. A new convention was signed in 1953, which changed its name from the International Fisheries Commission to the International Pacific Halibut Commission.[37]

At the present time the commission consists of six members, three from each country. The United States has a requirement that one of its three commissioners will be from Alaska. Current practice is for one commissioner from each country to be an official of the respective federal fisheries agencies; one to be a fisherman; and one to be a representative of the fishing industry, either a buyer or a processor. The commissioners over time have had long tenures, the average being nine years, giving the commission a stability that has enhanced its work. In the past the commission met annually on a three-year cycle, with two meetings in Seattle, the seat of the commission's permanent staff, and the third meeting in either Alaska or Canada. At the 1974 annual meeting it was agreed that the meetings in the future would alternate between sites in the United States and Canada. The commission itself appoints a director of investigation, who is in charge of the permanent staff of the commission, which conducts the scientific investigations into the life of the halibut, needed to arrive at the regulations which the commission is empowered to enact. The commission then approves the regulations which the scientific staff recommends, and submits them to the U.S. and Canadian governments. Enforcement of these regulations is carried out by the various agencies of both governments throughout the areas, on behalf of the commission, and the convention requires that all vessels in the area cooperate with the commission and its staff in the conduct of its scientific inquiries.[38] The expenses of the commissioners themselves are paid by the respective governments, and the joint expenses of the commission and its staff are divided equally between the two governments.[39]

The International Pacific Salmon Fisheries Commission, headquartered in New Westminster, British Columbia, was formed on the basis of the Sockeye Salmon Convention, which was signed in 1929 and ratified in 1937. The commission began operations in 1937 by undertaking an eight-year-period study of spawning runs. After the investigation period, the commission, having consulted their advisory board, began the practice of annual recommendations for regulations in the salmon fishery. In December 1956 the two governments signed an additional protocol to the 1937 convention authorizing the commission to conduct studies and then devise a program for the maintenance of pink salmon fisheries in addition to the sockeye.

The International Pacific Salmon Commission consists of three members from each country appointed by the president of the United States and the prime minister of Canada, respectively. The six are officials of government agencies concerned with fish on either the federal or state/provincial level or important local figures. Their tenure of office has generally been quite long, particularly on the Canadian side where two of the earliest appointments served almost thirty years. Commission meetings occur several times a year, usually in the summer months where adjustments of regulations or special problems are considered. In addition, the commission holds regular meetings with its advisory board, which consists of representatives of the fishing industry who informally examine all proposed regulations and recommendations. Several meetings concerning administrative matters are held, and at least one annual meeting is held with officials of the two federal governments on matters of major concern in enforcement and the special recommendations of the commission such as those over the hydroelectric projects. Finally, there is usually a large public meeting at the end of the year in which the annual report is presented.

The commission's primary activities are to restore, maintain, and extend the fisheries and to do this by regulating seasons, catches, and equipment so that the portion of fish caught each year is equal for the two countries. The commission's professional staff, consisting of a director and approximately forty individuals, is also authorized to carry on studies of the natural history of the area and of salmon as well as to carry on breeding or culturing experiments to strengthen spawning, and thus the fishery.[40]

The Great Lakes Fisheries Commission was created by the Convention on Great Lakes Fisheries signed by the United States and Canada on September 10, 1954. Instruments of ratification were exchanged and the convention came into force in 1955, but it was not until April 1956 that the Great Lakes Fisheries Commission had its first meeting. The commission replaced several temporary boards and commissions which had been founded to study the problems of the Lakes individually or as a group since 1893.[41]

Most of the work of the commission was taken up with sea lamprey control for the first ten years of its operation, as is evidenced in the budgetary allocations, which reached almost $1,500,000 for control measures as opposed to less than $50,000 for administration and all other projects. In 1965 the commission passed amendments to its rules of procedure, expanding the scope of its operations. Not only did it authorize the appointment of a commission official who would concern himself particularly with the restoration of fish species in the Lakes, it also agreed to the formation of several commission committees. Whereas prior to 1965 the commission was assisted by scientific advisors who participated ad hoc, in that year the advisors were organized into the present committees: Management and Research and its subordinate Lake committees, Sea Lamprey Control and Research, and Finance and Administration.

The original Convention of Great Lakes Fisheries had established a, commission of six members, three from each nation, and under the 1965 new rules of procedure, this was expanded to eight, with four from each nation. The four delegates from each nation are grouped together in national sections, and each section has one vote, thus requiring that all decisions be unanimous, with the agreement of both Canada and the United States. The officers of the commission are an alternating chairman and vice chairman, who must come from different countries and are elected for two-year terms. Those appointed to the commission have generally been federal or state/provincial officials working in the area of fisheries, although at times local community officials have been appointed. The commission can make recommendations only; it has no regulatory power. The activities of the commission today continue to concentrate on sea lamprey control and fish population restoration.

The Roosevelt Campobello International Park Commission was created in an agreement signed by President Lyndon B. Johnson and Prime Minister Lester B. Pearson in January 1964. Providing for joint maintenance of President Franklin Roosevelt's summer residence, the agreement was approved by the Congress of the United States and the Parliament of Canada, and the commission met for the first time in August

1964. The offer of the land to both nations had been made by the Hammer family to Prime Minister Pearson and President John F. Kennedy in May 1963. The park was formally dedicated in 1964 and during the next season was opened to visitors, the number of which has steadily increased over the years. The commission has hired a staff for the park, has arranged for general maintenance on a regular basis, and has acquired additional properties to fill out the park site around the Roosevelt land. The Roosevelt cottage has been set up as a museum, and other buildings have been constructed or planned for the area. The first completed was a visitors' center, which was opened by Queen Elizabeth in July 1967 and for which the commission had planned a number of activites, including films on the life of President Roosevelt. A large parking area and guest house for a limited number of visitors were the next projects, including plans for a convention center.

The Roosevelt Campobello International Park Commission consists of three commissioners appointed by each government, with the requirement that in appointing one of the commissioners the federal government must consult the state of Maine and the province of New Brunswick, respectively. The commission has a chairman and a vice chairman, one from each country, who are elected for a term of two years. The agreement creating the commission calls for an executive secretary of the park and such a staff as the commission shall require to work on the island. The commission itself usually meets three times a year, with one meeting being held in the park during the summer.[42]

The Canada-United States Interparliamentary Group was founded in 1959 under the authority of resolutions of the Canadian Parliament and the U.S. Congress. It generally consists of twenty-four representatives from the legislature of each country. However, exact totals vary because other commitments prevent the attendance of some members, and other parliamentarians will attend even though they are not formally part of the delegation. The composition of the delegation differs in each country because of the different constitutional systems. In Canada the Speakers of the House of Commons and the Senate generally lead the delegation, which is divided in a ratio of three to one in favor of members of the House of Commons. The rest of the seats on the delegation are allocated to the parties in a way which corresponds to the strength of the parties in each House. Cabinet members are usually not part of the delegation, although leaders of the official opposition frequently are. In the United States the delegation is equally divided between the two Houses of Congress, although the work load of senators makes it difficult to fill the delegation from their Chamber and achieve their regular attendance. The chairman of each side of the U.S. delegation is usually a member of the House International Relations Committee and the Senate Foreign Relations Committee. Assignment to the group is generally on the basis of expressed interest, and the appointments are made by the leadership.[43]

The meetings themselves are organized into two or three committees on various bilateral issues. These committees are chaired by the leaders of the delegation which is host to the particular meeting, and they report to a plenary session of the group, which is the core of the annual meeting. Thus, in Canada the Speakers of the Senate and House of Commons are the chairmen, whereas in the United States the leaders of the House and Senate delegations serve as chairmen for the committees of the group.[44] Between meetings there is a steering group in each legislature whose basic function is to arrange for and plan upcoming meetings of the group. The steering group in both countries consists of the leaders of the delegations at the last meeting and seven other members, who are then the core of the delegation to the upcoming meeting and generally can be said to be those who keep most apprised of bilateral issues. The steering groups are serviced by the staffs of the U.S. Senate Foreign Relations Committee and the House International Relations Committee and the Canadian House of Commons Committee on External Affairs and National Defence and the Senate Committee on Foreign Affairs, who also act as secretariat for the annual meetings themselves.

The rules agreed upon at the January 1959 organizational meeting have, with few changes, been the basis for the operation of the Interparliamentary Group throughout its existence. It was agreed at that time that the group would be "informal" and "transient," in that its meetings would be off-the-record discussions and that, aside from these regular meetings, it would have no ongoing existence through a staff.[45] To allow for the greatest freedom of discussion among the representatives of the two legislatures, the business meetings of the interparliamentary group are held off the record and are closed to the press. Only parliamentarians and a limited staff attend the meetings, although frequently the group will meet with the president or prime minister and other government officials in Washington or Ottawa. The tenor of the discussions at each meeting is reported in a press release, which is also the basis for the annual report to the Congress and Parliament. Any member of the group can report individually to the press on the meetings, but he cannot directly quote any other member. No votes are taken at the meetings; the discussions are not binding.[46]

SUMMATION AND ASSESSMENT

What conclusions can be drawn from this network of bilateral Canada-U.S. organizations? Historically, the twentieth century has witnessed an increasing utilization of bilateral organizations as a technique of regional management. As the examination of the individual organizations has shown, these organizations have taken four different forms: committees, an integrated military command, commissions, and an interparliamentary group. The commissions have proven the most useful and enduring organizational technique, although their very relevance and effectiveness is grounded in the fact that they deal essentially with rather undramatic and easily depoliticized technical matters. Of these commissions, the International Joint Commission remains a monument to successful regional management, but even here the expectations of a quasi-judicial body have been eroded in the face of an increasingly technical and investigatory IJC role.

The record of the joint Canada-U.S. committees is less defined and less successful as an organizational technique. Clearly, the Permanent Joint Board of Defence has played an instrumental role in the evolution of Canada-U.S. defense relations, but the salience of this committee is an exception rather than a rule. Of the different types of committees, the military organizations have proven to be more extensive and active than the economic committees. This reflects both the less competitive and conflictual nature of military issues and the activity of transborder coalitions of Canadian and U.S. military personnel, whose interactions have been institutionalized through formal committee structures. The integrated military command structure of NORAD, which has evolved through four renewal agreements, has been useful and adaptable, but it continues to fight its battle against technological obsolescence. The Canada-U.S. Interparliamentary Group, created with the conviction that a periodic meeting of legislators would further reciprocal understanding, continues to function actively, thereby fulfilling its mandate.

If the function of bilateral organizations in the Canada-U.S. context is essentially a managerial one, at the same time these organizations could play a significant role in terms of furthering political integration between Canada and the United States. A useful formulation is provided by Nye in his book, *Peace in Parts,* in which "institutional integration" is regarded as a component of political integration, and consists of two dimensions—bureaucratic and jurisdictional.[47] That is, in assessing whether there is integrative growth, one looks first at the strength of the central institutions to see if there has been an increase in bureaucratic resources of budget and administrative staff.[48] Second, one examines the jurisdictional or legal aspect to determine the extent to which central institutions have gained supranational autonomy from direct control by the member states.[49]

Applying the Nye formulation to the Canada-U.S. organizational experience, it can be seen that there has been no significant increase in integration. Indeed, as the era analysis of the bilateral organizations has shown, there has been a decreasing usage of, and governmental commitment to, joint organizations as a technique of issue resolution since the 1960s. Apart from attempts to fund and staff existing responsibilities, there has been no significant increase in the bureaucratic resources allocated to the bilateral organizations. Moreover, there has been no significant jurisdictional increase in supranational autonomy on the part of the organizations. In fact, as has been noted, the most potentially supranational organization, the International Joint Commission, has tended to move away from its intended purpose of serving as a quasi-judicial body toward a function that has been increasingly technical and investigatory.

Notwithstanding the absence of significant integrative growth, has there been any spillover in which the creation of a bilateral organization in one area somehow spills over into another area whereby an additional joint organization is created? While some authors have suggested that there has been little spillover except in the regulatory commissions,[50] the case may not be as clear-cut as this. That is, there is at least some evidence to suggest that Canadian and U.S. officials consciously used one organization as a model in the creation of additional organizations in different policy areas. The International Joint Commission seems to have served as a model for the creation of the Permanent Joint Board on Defence, which in turn served as an organizational model for the creation of the World War II Canada-U.S. economic committees.

For example, Canadian Defence Minister Brooke Claxton could observe: "The Boundary Waters Treaty of 1909 provided for the International Joint Commission of three representatives of each country to deal with all the boundary disputes between the two nations. In setting up the Permanent Joint Board on Defence, your President and our Prime Minister were thinking of the composition and successful operation of that Commission." [51] In the same sense the relationship between the PJBD and the World War II joint Canada-U.S. economic committees (active from 1941 to 1944) was assessed by Canadian Deputy Minister of Finance W. C. Clark. In 1941 Mr. Clark claimed that the joint economic committees were designed "in many respects" as a "parallel in the field of economic co-operation to the Joint Board on Defence." [52]

An even clearer example of using an organization as a model can be found in an examination of the exchange of notes establishing the two Canada-U.S. ministerial level committees. The Joint Cabinet Committee on Trade and Economic Affairs was created in 1953, and the Cabinet Committee on Joint Defence was created in 1958. The language establishing the two committees, the delineation of the purpose and procedures of the two committees, and the description of their functions are almost identical. Clearly the economic attempt at organizational accommodation was replicated five years later when there was a corresponding need for organizational accommodation in the strategic sector.

What about the potential for future organizational integration in the case of Canada and the United States? Such an assessment must be grounded in an examination of those factors responsible for the establishment and growth of bilateral organizations. While several considerations come to mind, four interrelated factors can be identified as being particularly salient. First and most obvious is the degree of basic governmental commitment to increased institutionalization. Without an intergovernmental commitment, new organizations will not be established, and existing organizations will fall into disuse. In the Canada-U.S. context, this can be seen in a comparison of the organizational activity in the 1950s with the post-1970 period. It should also be noted that an intergovernmental commitment to bilateral organizations goes beyond the desire to establish and fund an organization, to include the degree of supranationality which officials wish to confer upon it. Here the evidence is clear that Canadian and U.S. officials have consistently rejected any major degree of bilateral organizational supranationality.

A second factor affecting organizational growth in the case of Canada and the United States concerns the hierarchical level of officials who constitute the membership of the organization. Here one need only look at the two ministerial committees to see that their high level cabinet membership precluded not only organizational growth but also the committees' sustained policy relevance. Quite simply, it is naive to assume that ministerial level officials, with diverse interests and work loads, could or would meet regularly on a binational basis to review the state of the Canada-U.S. relationship. Moreover, it is precisely at those crisis points in which a cabinet-level meeting might be useful in resolving difficulties that a cabinet-level meeting is politically unfeasible from the standpoint of the two national governments. It is, for example, no accident that the Cabinet Committee on Joint Defence did not meet during the most intense and abrasive period of the Canada-U.S. nuclear weapons controversy. Indeed, when the cabinet committee finally did meet, it was only after a change in the Canadian government and only after the controversy had abated.

A third factor affecting organizational growth concerns the policy or issue area in which the organization is operating. A conventional hypothesis, perhaps most succinctly expressed by Nye, is that "institutional growth and extension of authority are more likely in areas that are technical and politically unimportant and where the existence of institutional authority has little impact on critical national or regional interests." [53] Certainly this hypothesis holds in the case of Canada and the United States. If integration is measured by degree of permanency of staff and resources, and degree of joint decision-making, one study of the Canada-U.S. case shows that organizations having the highest degree of integration "are designed to cope with problems arising directly from geographical contiguity: border monuments and parks, boundary waters, fisheries, pollution, and to a lesser extent, defence." [54] In contradistinction, those bilateral organizations having the least integrative features "are concerned with issue areas and policy sectors where interests seem to diverge strongly along national lines" [55] (including, e.g., trade and balance-of-payments matters). Finally, in issue areas in which there is virtually no area of shared interest, there is no organizational growth at all, but rather the utilization of such other resolutive techniques as treaties and ad hoc negotiations.[56]

In conclusion, it should be noted that the utilization of the Canada-U.S. joint organizations has not replaced existing channels of transborder issue resolution, nor were they meant to do so. If the progenitors of these joint organizations had excessive expectations about their usefulness in regional management, the passage of time has both dampened this original enthusiasm and documented the very real, if somewhat more modest, contributions these organizations can make.

NOTES

1. See Charles Pentland, *The Canadian Dilemma* (Paris: published for the Atlantic Institute for International Affairs by Saxon House, 1973), p. xi.

2. Quoted in Donald M. Page, "Canada as an Exponent of North American Idealism," *The American Review of Canadian Studies, Vol. III, No. 2 (Autumn 1973), p. 37.*

3. J.W. Pickersgill, *The Mackenzie King Record,* vol. I (Toronto: University of Toronto Press, 1960), p. 433.

4. Brooke Claxton, "Canadian-U.S. Cooperation: A Lesson of Peace to All Nations," Speech Ogdensburg, New York, August 17, 1948, SS48/42.

5. Ibid.

6. A useful, general, but formalized definition of an organization is "a social system that has an unequivocal collective identity, an exact roster of members, a program of activity, and procedures for replacing members." Theodore Caplow, *Principles of Organization* (New York: Harcourt, Brace and World, 1964), p. 1.

7. This committee has been replaced by a continuing board under the auspices of the International Joint Commission. Nevertheless, the committee was rather unusual as it was created under the North Atlantic Treaty Organization's (NATO) Committee on the Challenges of Modern Society.

8. The White House press conference of Arthur A. Hartman, assistant secretary of state for European affairs, the Briefing Room, December 4, 1974, 5:12 P.M., EST, Office of the White House Press Secretary.

9. Office of the White House Press Secretary, the White House.

10. U.S. Department of State, unclassified incoming telegram, action copy, from U.S. Embassy, Ottawa, to secretary of state, Washington (85277).

11. For a discussion of the differences between commissions and committees, see Don C. Piper "The Role of Intergovernmental Machinery in Canadian-American Relations," *The South Atlantic Quarterly,* Vol. LXII, No. 1 (Autumn 1963), pp. 551-74.

12. There was an additional joint organization, the Canada-U.S. Industrial Mobilization Planning Committee, but it has not met for over twenty years. Originating in Canadian-U.S. discussions in June 1948, the committee was established by an exchange of notes on April 12, 1949. Its

mission was to "exchange information" and "consider recommendations" with a view to the coordination of the plans of the United States and Canada for industrial mobilization. In addition, it was responsible for cooperation with the Permanent Joint Board on Defence on mobilization matters. The Canadian committee members were the minister of trade and commerce and the chairman of the Industrial Defence Board; the U.S. members were the chairman of the National Security Resources Board and the chairman of the Munitions Board. The committee held its first meeting in Washington on June 1, 1949. Largely organizational in nature, a number of subcommittees were established to examine specific production and supply questions. The Industrial Mobilization Planning Committee held its second meeting on August 8, 1950, in Ottawa, where it· reviewed the reports of the subcommittees, while recommending that studies be made of the basic Canadian and U.S. industrial programs including the necessary steps to meet production and supply requirements that these plans called for. Related to these studies was the question of regulations concerning priorities, allocations, and export controls. To assist in this undertaking, it was decided to define a set of principles which would define and· motivate joint Canadian-U.S. utilization of materials and resources. This culminated in the October 20, 1950, Canadian-U.S. exchange of notes which formalized the resulting "Statement of Principles for Economic Cooperation" between the two nations. The committee met again on October 8, 1953 in Washington, and reaffirmed the October 1950 Principles for Economic Cooperation. This summary is based upon: United Nations Treaty Series, Vol. 206, No. 2789, (1955), pp. 241-47; "Joint Canada-U.S. Industrial Mobilization Planning Committee," *External Affairs Bulletin* (Ottawa: Department of External Affairs, January 1951), pp. 21-22; and "Canadian-U.S. Economic Cooperation Review," *External Affairs Bulletin* (Ottawa: Department of External Affairs, November 1953), pp. 325-26.

13. "U.S.-Canadian PJBD to Continue Collaboration for Security Purposes-Released to the Press February 12", *Department of State Bulletin*, XVI, No. 399 (February 23, 1947), p. 361; *Canada Treaty Series*, 1947, No. 43. This statement of defense collaboration remains in effect.

14. General Charles Foulkes, "The Complications of Continental Defence," Livingston T. Merchant, ed. in *Neighbors Taken for Granted: Canada and the United States* (New York: Praeger, 1966), p. 117. The feasibility of transferring all the Permanent Joint Board on Defence's planning functions to the NATO organization was discussed but was decided against for the following reasons: first, the United States, while stressing the permanent nature of the Permanent Board, emphasized that NATO was established through a twenty year treaty. Second, while NATO concerned the Atlantic area and not the Pacific, the Permanent Board had already made Canadian-U.S. defense arrangements concerning the Pacific area. Third, the United States was hesitant to give the European partners

Canada's degree of access to intelligence and research and development data. Fourth, the United States felt that if Canadian-U.S. air defense was included in NATO, pressures concerning the emphasis of European defense at the expense of North American defense might be generated through the revealing of the actual extent and scope of North American defense to the European allies. Finally, in that the Canadian-U.S. air defense was so intimately involved in the protection of the U.S. strategic Air Force, the United States was opposed to air-defense inclusion in NATO with the consequent possibility of a veto or multilateral control regarding its use. (Ibid., pp. 117-118.) In 1952 the NATO Council decided to establish integrated commands under supreme commanders in place of the system of regional planning groups, and again the question of integration of North American defense planning into NATO arose, was discussed, but was rejected "when it was realized that the introduction of the European pattern command system would no doubt entail the appointment of an over-all U.S. commander for all defense planning in both the U.S. and Canada." (Ibid., p. 119.) The Canada-U.S. Regional Planning Group was therefore continued in lieu of an integrated command like that of Allied Command Atlantic.

15. United Nations Treaty Series, Vol. 325, No. 4792 (1959), p. 250. The cabinet committee came into force on September 2, 1958, by the exchange of notes.

16. TIAS 6325, "Civil Emergency Planning Agreement Between the U.S.A. and Canada," effected by exchange of notes signed at Ottawa, August 8, 1967.

17. This discussion of the committees' organizational structure is based upon William Willoughby's draft manuscript entitled "Cooperation in Civil Defence and Emergency Preparedness."

18. Department of Defence Production, Ottawa, Production Sharing Handbook: Canada-U.S. Defence Production Sharing, 4th ed. (1967), pp. 1-2.

19. On the U.S. side were the Treasury and Commerce Departments, and on the Canadian side were the Department of External Affairs and the Treasury Board Secretariat.

20. This section on NORAD is excerpted from: Roger F. Swanson, "NORAD: Origins and Operations of Canada's Ambivalent Symbol," International Perspectives (November/December 1972).

21. "Canada and U.S. Renew NORAD Pact," Canada Weekly, Vol.III, No. 22, (May 28, 1975), p. 4.

22. In addition to the above three committees, there was a short-lived Technical Committee in Agricultural Marketing and Trade Problems which was established at the June 1967 meeting of the Canada-U.S. Ministerial Committee on Trade and Economic Affairs. Holding its first meeting in November 1967 and consisting of senior U.S. and Canadian agriculture and trade officials, its purpose was to consider matters of trade

in agricultural products with the anticipation of meeting in the spring and fall of each year. The Technical Committee issued no communiqués; indeed, its creation was not even mentioned in the press releases following the Ministerial Committee meeting at which it was established. Nor was its death dignified with a public announcement when the Ministerial Committee at its November 1970 meeting opted for an "agricultural trade consultation procedure" rather than a formal committee structure. One sentence in the communiqué emanating from the November meeting addresses itself to this: "The members also reviewed ways of dealing with problems in crossborder trade in certain agricultural commodities and noted that agreement had been reached on establishment of a new consultative procedure in this regard." This procedure is now in use when either the United States or Canada takes short-term protective action. It has been used, for example, when Canada in effect put a duty on strawberries, and the United States received concessions on cranberries in return. The procedure is used mainly for disputes involving eggs, fruits, vegetables, and poultry. It has no formal name, and while the United States considers it an official procedure, Canada is reluctant to say it has a formal status. It may be invoked by either side; there are no communiqués issued; and it generally consists of representatives from the U.S. Department of Agriculture and the Canadian Department of Industry, Trade and Commerce, with participation by other agencies, especially the U.S. State Department and the president's special trade representative, and Canada's Department of External Affairs.

23. *Canadian House of Commons Debates* May 9, 1953, pp. 5055-57, 63, as quoted in Roger Frank Swanson, *Canadian-American Summit Diplomacy 1923-1973* (Toronto: McClelland and Stewart, 1975).

24. For the November 12, 1953 exchange of notes, see 5 U.S.T. 314.

25. Ibid.

26. Ibid.

27. Ibid.

28. Ibid., pp. 434, 436.

29. See Peter Buckley, "Top Level Trade Talks Left in the Air," *Winnipeg Free Press*, August 27, 1973, p. 6.

30. *External Affairs Bulletin*, op. cit., p. 438.

31. Summary Statement of Results of the First Meeting of the U.S.-Canadian Trade Statistics Committee, Monday, December 13, 1971.

32. A report by the U.S.-Canada Trade Statistics Committee, published jointly by the United States and Canada.

33. See International Joint Commission, United States and Canada, "Rules of Procedure and Text of Treaty," Ottawa, Canada, and Washington, D.C, 1965. See also Don C. Piper, op. cit., p. 553.

34. International Joint Commission, United States and Canada, pamphlet of the U.S. Department of State, January 1974.

35. On appointments to the IJC, see William R. Willoughby, "The

Appointment and Removal of Members of the International Joint Commission," *Canadian Public Administration* (Fall 1969), pp. 411 ff.

36. This section is based upon House of Commons, Canada, Committee on External Affairs and National Defence, Appendix A. "Joint Canadian United States Institutions" (November 20, 1969), p.355. See also James H. Van Wagenen, "International Boundary Commission United States and Canada," mimeographed document obtained from International Boundary Commission.

37. This history is compiled from F. Heward Bell, "Agreements, Conventions and Treaties between Canada and the United States of America with respect to the Pacific Halibut Fishery," Report of the International Pacific Halibut Commission, Number 50, Seattle, Washington: International Pacific Halibut Commission, 1969, pp. 5-22.

38. International Pacific Halibut Commission, *Annual Report 1973* (Seattle, Washington: International Pacific Halibut Commission, 1974), p. 25.

39. Bell, op. cit., p. 79-80.

40. International Pacific Salmon Fisheries Commission *Annual Report* 1971, 1972, 1973. New Westminster, British Columbia: International Pacific Salmon Fisheries Commission, pp. 9, 6, 4.

41. *Annual Report*, Great Lakes Fishery Commission, 1956 (Ann Arbor, Michigan, 1957).

42. Taken from the annual reports of the Roosevelt Campobello International Park to the secretary of state of the United States and the secretary of state for external affairs of Canada from 1964 to 1972 as well as the agreement between the government of the United States and Canada relating to the establishment of the Roosevelt Campolbello International Park.

43. Matthew J. Abrams, *The Canada-United States Interparliamentary Group* (Ottawa: Parliamentary Center for Foreign Affairs and Foreign Trade, 1973) p. 7.

44. Ibid., pp. 27 ff.

45. Ibid., p. 19.

46. Summary Report of the First Meeting of the Canada-United States Interparliamentary Group (Washington, D.C.: U.S. Government Printing Office, 1964).

47. J.S. Nye, *Peace in Parts: Integration and Conflict in Regional Organization* (Boston: Little, Brown and Company, 1968), p. 37. The second component of political integration is "policy integration," which he refers to as "interdependence in policy formation." The third component is "attitudinal integration," which Nye defines as a "sense of mutual identity and obligation." This threefold distinction is useful in emphasizing that organizational or institutional integration is but one component of political integration.

48. Ibid., p. 38.

49. Ibid.

50. Holsti and Levy, "Bilateral Institutions and Transgovernmental Relations Between Canada and the United States," op. cit., p. 879.

51. Brooke Claxton, "Canadian-U.S. Co-operation—A Lesson of Peace to All Nations," Ogdensburg, New York, August 17, 1948, op. cit.

52. W.C. Clark, "From the Canadian Point of View," in Reginald G. Trotter and Albert B. Corey, eds., *Conference on Canadian-American Affairs* (Toronto: Oxford University Press, 1941), p. 71.

53. Nye, op. cit., pp. 23-4.

54. Holsti and Levy, op. cit., p. 880.

55. Ibid.

56. A fourth factor affecting organizational growth concerns the temporal point in which the organization was established. This has been creatively identified in the case of Canada and the United States by Holsti and Levy. (Ibid., p. 881.) Indeed, in their study, these two authors maintain that "An important key to institutional growth, therefore, may not be so much the type of issue area or the extent to which institutions handle political matters, but the degree to which basic principles governing allocation of costs, rewards, and responsibilities between the two countries have been worked out prior to the launching of institutions." They cite as evidence the 1909 Canada-U.S. Boundary Waters Treaty which defines fundamental rules that have guided issue resolution since 1909. The significant factor here is therefore the fact that the treaty ground rules and the subsequent IJC were established before the most serious problems arose. This was not the case in other issue areas in the Canada-U.S. context in that ground rules and organizational structures were created after the most serious problems arose.

V

INTERGOVERNMENTAL PERSPECTIVES EXTENDED: TRANSNATIONAL AND TRANSGOVERNMENTAL ACTORS *

The preceding chapters in this book have dealt with intergovernmental perspectives on the Canada-U.S. relationship. They have concentrated on U.S. and Canadian governmental actors who are responsible for the management of the bilateral relationship. The question at this point is: How do these governmental actors come together in transborder dealings? The first part of this chapter answers this question by identifying pure intergovernmental transactions. This term simply refers to those transborder dealings which involve only governmental actors. Because we know so little about how these dealings occur, this section examines pure intergovernmental transactions as a three-stage phenomenon: preprocess, process, and postprocess. To illustrate what a pure intergovernmental transaction looks like, the issue of

* This chapter was originally published as an article entitled "An Analytical Assessment of the U.S.-Canadian Issue Area," which appeared in *International Organization*, Vol. XXVIII, No. 4 (Autumn 1974), pp. 781-802.

the U.S. government closing a military base in Canada is frozen and disaggregated.

The actual Canada-U.S. relationship is of course much more complex than this formulation suggests in that the relationship includes not only governmental actors but also other types of actors. In fact, two classes of actors can be identified in addition to governmental actors.[1] There are transnational actors, which consist of all nongovernmental actors involved in transborder dealings, ranging from corporations to labor unions. In addition, there are transgovernmental actors, which include those governmental actors involved in transborder dealings who "go it alone" by departing from regular routines of their organizations. In the most general sense, therefore, we have to consider the activities of three classes of actors in looking at the Canada-U.S. relationship—governmental, transnational, and transgovernental.

These classes of actors have implications for the types of transborder dealings that occur in the context of the Canada-U.S. relationship. We are not dealing just with pure intergovernmental transactions (e.g., transactions involving only governmental actors). The second part of this chapter therefore identifies and examines the dynamics of mixed transactions, which in effect consist of intergovernmental dealings involving transnational or transgovernmental actors who participate in the dealings but do not essentially alter the outcomes. More specifically, this section examines mixed transactions by assessing the utility of transnational and transgovernmental activites.

Finally, having identified pure and mixed transactions, we have to absorb the fact that the involvement of transnational or transgovernmental actors in intergovernmental transactions (or the reverse) could significantly alter the outcomes of the transactions themselves. The third part of this chapter therefore identifies and examines the dynamics of transformative transactions, which refer to transborder dealings in which the activities of new actors actually alter or transform the transaction, for example, from a transnational one to an intergovernmental one.

Section four of this chapter delineates those factors that encourage transnational and transgovernmental activity, and section five assesses the significance of this activity. Those factors militating against transnational and transgovernmental activity are examined, as are the costs and benefits of such activity. The concluding section of this chapter presents a summation and assessment by looking at the definitional problems involved in this rather complex phenomenon known as the Canada-U.S. relationship.

In effect, this chapter develops a paradigm, which is, of course, but one way of approaching what are conventionally regarded as the relations between nations. Throughout this chapter, the Canada-U.S. defense issue area is used to test the paradigm, which is also applicable to other bilateral and multilateral transborder dealings in all issue areas. This wider applicability lies in the analytical properties of the paradigm, which permits empirically grounded consideration both of differences between different issue areas and of the activities of actor combinations within these areas. It should be added that the illustrative defense case studies and examples used throughout this chapter have been intentionally selected to cover a maximum historical time span while drawing upon easily available primary and secondary sources.

PURE INTERGOVERNMENTAL TRANSACTIONS AS A THREE-STAGE ISSUE FLOW

If a pure intergovernmental transaction refers to Canada-U.S. issue flows in which there is no transnational or transgovernmental activity, the question is: What do such flows look like? It is analytically useful to regard such flows as a three-stage sequence of interactions occuring within each government and between the two governments. The preprocess stage consists of those activities and events that require a Canada-U.S.-decision in the first place. Organizationally, this stage involves only the activities within the government initiating the flow and ends when there is a formal trans- border contact with officials of the second government. At this stage, officials of the initiating government discuss what their government's position should be and what is negotiable (definition of conceptual parameters) while also deciding upon those channels through which the issue will be pro- cessed (definition of organizational parameters). The process stage begins when officials of the first government formally begin negotiations with officials of the second government and ends when the issue is perceived as being essentially resolved by the participating actors.[2] Organizationally, this process stage involves interactions within each government and transborder interactions between the two governments. At this stage the issue is resolved, but within the context of largely preestablished conceptual and organizational parameters. The postprocess stage consists of those activ- ities taken to implement the resolution reached in the process stage. Organizationally it involves interactions within each government and transborder interactions and consists of attempts to expedite the implementation of the issue resolution.

To illustrate what a pure intergovernmental issue flow, with its three stage sequence, is like, an actual issue has been frozen and disaggregated—a U.S. base closing in Canada in which the United States was the initiator of the issue. Because of severe budgetary pressures, the United States decided to execute worldwide personnel and base reductions involving thirty actions overseas and three hundred in North America, of which only Base X in Canada was involved. The preprocess stage of this base closing issue flow organiza- tionally involved the following steps:

(1) A middle-level official of the Plans and Policy
     Division of the Air Force (Department of Defense)
     informally notified a middle-level official in the
     Directorate for European and NATO Affairs (Of-
     fice of the Assistant Secretary of Defense for
     International Security Affairs) that the military was
     planning a cutback including U.S. military person-
     nel and Canadian civilian employees at Canadian
     Base X.

(2) This second official consulted with an official of the
     Plans and Policy Directorate, Western Hemisphere
     (Joint Staff, Joint Chiefs of Staff, Department of
     Defense) and an official of the Office of Canadian
     Affairs (Bureau of European Affairs, Department of
     State) regarding the most appropriate means of
     consulting with the government of Canada

This preprocess stage formally occurred entirely within the
U.S. government. A general decision to close 330 bases
catalyzed those U.S. officials responsible for Canada-U.S.
defense relations. These officials discussed channels through
which the issue would be processed, and coalitions within the
U.S. government were formed in an attempt to decide what
the U.S. position should be and what was negotiable
concerning anticipated Canadian reactions. Organizationally
the U.S. actor expansion was noteworthy in this preprocess
stage. The first step occurred entirely within two organizational units of the Department of Defense, while step two
expanded to a third Defense Department unit and included
a unit in the State Department.

The process stage of this issue flow organizationally
involved the following steps:

(1) A middle-level Foreign Service officer of the Office
     of Canadian Affairs approached the counsellor for

political-military affairs in the Canadian Embassy, outlining the overall issue and requesting at what level the Canadians would like to discuss it.

(2) As a result, the minister of the Canadian Embassy met with the following U.S. officials: director, Directorate for European and NATO Affairs; director, Office of Canadian Affairs; chief, Plans and Policy Directorate; an official from the Office of the Assistant Secretary of Defense for Public Affairs; and an official of the Plans and Policy Division of the Air Force. The Canadian minister was briefed on U.S. intentions, and the U.S. officials requested Canadian concurrence regarding press-release policy. The minister of the Canadian Embassy requested time to discuss the issue with relevant Canadian officials, including local officials in the Base X area.

(3) Internal Canadian government discussions followed, involving ministers of five Canadian government departments: Defense, External Affairs, Transport, Supply and Services, and Manpower and Immigration. Local officials were also consulted.

(4) The Canadian ambassador made requests regarding severance conditions for Base X Canadian personnel and met with U.S. officials at the level of assistant secretary of defense for international security affairs.

(5) The U.S. officials reviewed the issue completely and received approval at the Secretary of defense level to agree to certain of the Canadian requests. The U.S. position was returned through the assistant secretary of defense level.

(6) After the Canadian ambassador consulted with his government, the counselor of the embassy tele-

> phoned his government's concurrence in the press
> release policy and registered no objection to the
> U.S. position

This process stage involved both interactions within each government and transborder interactions between the two governments. Steps one and two consisted of the presentation of the U.S. position to the Canadian Embassy (transborder). Again, the actor expansion was noteworthy, both organizationally and functionally. Step one involved a middle level of the State Department and the Canadian counselor: step two involved the Canadian minister and high-level U.S. officials representing four organizational units of the Defense Department and one unit of the State Department. Step three consisted of the Canadian formulation of its position and included very high-level discussions involving ministers of five government departments as well as local officials. Step four consisted of the Canadian presentation of its position to U.S. officials (transborder). Step five consisted of U.S. consideration and reply to the Canadian position (transborder); and step six involved Canadian consideration of the U.S. position and resolution of the issue (transborder).

The postprocess *stage* of this issue flow organizationally involved the following step:

> At Base X, the U.S. base commander, the nearest U.S.
> consul general, local officials, and representatives of the
> five Canadian government departments began planning
> to alleviate economic problems and to investigate possi-
> ble Canadian use of part of Base X facilities.

Hence, the postprocess stage involved U.S. and Canadian officials meeting to facilitate the implementation of the agreement reached in the process stage.

MIXED TRANSACTIONS: THE UTILITY OF TRANSNATIONAL AND TRANSGOVERNMENTAL ACTIVITY IN INTERGOVERNMENTAL FLOWS

Mixed transactions refer to intergovernmental flows involving transnational or transgovernmental activity that does not essentially alter the outcome of the flows themselves. That is, those decisions involved in intergovernmental issue flows are not significantly affected by, or dependent upon, this transnational or transgovernmental activity.

The question as this point is: What is the utility of transnational and transgovernmental activity for those actors engaged in it? It can be hypothesized that its usefulness is dependent upon the stage in which it occurs in an intergovernmental flow. Three distinct types of this activity can be isolated. (1) Formulative transnational or transgovernmental activity occurs in the preprocess stage when actors interject their position into another government's decision-making before formal transborder contact is made. This interjection, which can create transborder coalitions, can be initiated by the actors themselves, or their participation can be invited by the actors of the other government. Such interjection enables actors to participate in another government's decision-making before the procedures and positions of the latter government have coalesced. However, because the preprocess stage formally occurs entirely within a single government, it may be difficult for external actors to determine who is responsible for dealing with the issue. Moreover, it may be counterproductive for these external actors to become involved in the internal affairs of another government. (2) Resolutive transnational or transgovernmental activity occurs in the process stage. Too late to define the conceptual and organizational framework of the issue flow, bureaucratic coalitions within each government line up with their transborder counterparts to maximize their positions and influence the outcome of the issue flow in a manner satisfactory to them. (3) Facilitative activity occurs too late to form transborder coalitions to influence issue outcomes. It is, however, still possible for transborder actors and coalitions to facilitate the implementation in a manner favorable to them. Both resolutive and facilitative activities are easier to undertake than formulative activities because the actors responsible for the issue are now clearly delineated through transborder contacts which are themselves both legitimized and regularized through formal negotiating procedures. All three types of transnational and transgovernmental activity are particularly useful in that they enable actors to receive external support vis-à-vis internal bureaucratic coalitions.

An illustrative case of formulative transgovernmental activity occured in the autumn of 1973, when the Canadian defence minister announced a five-year financing formula for Canadian defense expenditures. These budgetary arrangements prompted Canadian defense officials to decide to close three Pine Tree Line radar stations in order to increase procurement flexibility in other areas. This decision was viewed as affecting U.S. defense interests.

(1)   In September U.S. defense officials held meetings with their Canadian counterparts in Ottawa. During one of these meetings, Canadian officials explained their intention and reasons for terminating the three radars. They then presented the U.S. officials with the draft of a diplomatic note concerning the closings that they intended formally to submit to the U.S. government. The Canadian officials requested that the U.S. officials (who would also process the formal note in Washington) read the draft note and discuss revisions with them before departing.

(2) This first stage would then be followed by the
     Canadian government sending a formal diplomatic
     note to the U.S. government, incorporating the
     suggestions of the U.S. officials.

The utility of this formulative transgovernmental activity to
both governments is significant. By inviting U.S. officials to
become involved in their preprocess stage internal discussions, Canadian officials, who initiated the flow, could test
U.S. responsiveness to their position and absorb U.S. reservations before formal negotiations began. The advantage to
U.S. officials consisted of their participation in the definition
of the Canadian bargaining position and procedures before
they had coalesced.

An illustration of resolutive activity occurred in January
1963 and deals with Canadian acquisition of nuclear war-
heads which the U.S. and Canada had been formally
discussing for some time.[3] Retiring as the Supreme Allied
Commander Europe (SACEUR), Gen. Lauris Norstad took
his leave by visiting the NATO capitals.[4]

(1) in Ottawa, Norstad first called on the governor
     general. Although Prime Minister Diefenbaker was
     in Ottawa, he did not meet with the general.
     Associate Minister of Defence Pierre Sevigny acted
     as the general's host.
(2) During a press conference on January 3, 1963,
     Norstad asserted that contrary to the Canadian
     government's official position Canada was commit-
     ted to the acquisition of nuclear weapons within
     NATO, that the commitment had not been
     fulfilled, and that a prerequisite for both the
     emergency nuclear arms equipping of Canada's air
     division in NATO and the nuclear training of this

division was a bilateral agreement with the United
States.

Norstad was the first top-level NATO officer to take this
position publicly. The impact of his press conference stemmed entirely from his NATO organizational role. His opinion of Canada's commitment therefore carried great weight
in influencing Canadian opinion; and the fact that it was
expressed on Canadian soil interjected it into the mainstream
of the increasingly agitated Canadian public debate. This
then tended to fortify the U.S. position on the Canadian
acquisition of nuclear weapons and armed those Canadians
who opposed the government's policy. The general's action
illustrates resolutive activity in that it constituted an attempt
to influence the conclusion of the Canadian nuclear debate
during the process stage in a manner satisfactory to the
organization with which he was associated.

An illustration of facilitative transgovernmental activity
occurred in June 1942.[5] U.S. officials concerned about the
Japanese threat to the Aleutian Islands held discussions with
Canadian officials in which it was agreed that the Royal
Canadian Air Force (RCAF) would provide immediate air
reinforcements for Alaska. Although agreement was reached,
the actual measures undertaken by the Canadian authorities
were regarded as being insufficient by U.S. officials.

(1) To facilitate Canadian action on the U.S.-Cana-
dian agreement, Lieutenant General Stanley D.
Embick, the U.S. Army member of the PJBD,
telephoned Air Commodore F. V. Heakes, the
RCAF member of the board. Embick, citing the
formal joint war plan, requested that Heakes
expedite matters to accelerate Canadian action.

(2) Heakes agreed with Embick, interjected his request

> into the Canadian military decision-making process, and two RCAF squadrons were immediately ordered to move to Yakutat by the chief of the Canadian Air Staff.

Notwithstanding the fact that the PJBD is an advisory body, this is an illustration of an executive action performed by a member of the board acting transgovernmentally. Indeed, although the issue had been resolved, further activity was deemed necessary in the postprocess stage to facilitate the implementation of the agreement.

TRANSFORMATIVE TRANSACTIONS

Given transnational and transgovernmental activity in intergovernmental flows (mixed transactions), can transnational or transgovernmental actors performing this activity predominate, and if so, what happens to the flows themselves? It is indeed possible that at some stage in an intergovernmental flow, governmental activity is absorbed or superseded by transnational or transgovernmental activity. The flow is therefore transformed from an intergovernmental one into a transnational one (transnationalization) or a transgovernmental one (transgovernmentalization). However, more important in the U.S.-Canadian defense issue area is the reverse variation—the transformation of a transnational or transgovernmental flow into an intergovernmental one (intergovernmentalization). All three forms are subsumed under the term "transformative transactions," referring to flows in which new actors become involved and predominate in the sense that they significantly affect the decisions made in, and hence the outcomes of, the flows themselves. It must be emphasized that discussions of actor predominance refer both to replacing one actor with another, and to the same actor starting out in one role and later switching to another role.

A case of intergovernmentalization occurred in 1943 with the Canadian decision to use its forces in the U.S. campaign against the Japanese in the Aleutian Islands.[6] On April 19, Gen. John deWitt (commanding general of the U.S. Western Defense Command) visited Maj. Gen. G.R. Pearkes (Canadian GOC Pacific Command) in Vancouver. They discussed the feasibility of a combined U.S.-Canadian attack on the Japanese enclave at Kiska. Pearkes's report to his superiors did not mention possible Canadian participation.

(1) On May 8 Maj. Gen. Maurice Pope (chairman, Canadian Joint Staff mission in Washington, Canadian member of the PJBD, and liaison between the Canadian War Committee in Ottawa and the Combined Chiefs of Staff in Washington) discussed the matter with J.D.Hickerson (U.S. State Department officer and secretary of the U.S. section of the PJBD).Pope reported this conversation to Lieutenant General Stuart in Ottawa (chief of the Canadian General Staff), and on May 12 Stuart authorized Pope to discuss the project with Gen. George Marshall (chief of STAFF, U.S. Army). However, in his message to Pope, Stuart acknowledged that the minister of national defence (Ralston) had not yet been consulted in the matter.

(2) Pope met with Marshal and on May 24 learned that U.S. officers were pleased with the prospect of Canadian forces participating. Marshall also authorized deWitt to meet with Pearkes to establish plans and procedures.

(3) The War Committee of the Canadian cabinet learned of the plans at this point. Prime Minister

King was upset that his military officers had negotiated with their U.S. counterparts before higher-level Canadian officials knew fully what was being proposed. On May 28 King and Ralston learned that Canadian forces (eighteen officers who were going as observers) were en route. King was distressed about this Canadian involvement occurring without his knowledge and without a request from the U.S. Combined Chiefs of Staff. He insisted that an invitation would have to come from either the president or the U.S. Secretary of War (Stimson).

(4) In Washington, Pope informed Hickerson that Canada wanted an invitation from the secretary of war to the minister of national defence. Pope then visited the U.S. deputy chief of staff, notifying him of the request. A letter from Stimson to Ralston followed: After consideration in a May 31 Canadian cabinet meeting, it was approved in principle that Canadians would join U.S. forces only a day before the invading force was dispatched.

This flow was initiated by transgovernmental actors acting independently of higher-level governmental authorities. King noted in his diary that he "objected strongly to our Chiefs of Staff and others of the High Command in Canada negotiating with corresponding numbers in the U.S. before the Minister had a full knowledge of what was proposed, the War Committee included, and most of all, myself as Prime Minister." However, the flow was transformed into an intergovernmental flow through a high-level authorization insisted upon by the prime minister himself. Again, to quote King: "It was finally agreed that the communication would have to come from either the President to myself, or Stimson to Ralston, to get matters on Ministerial level and out simply of the military level; indeed this whole thing has worked from the bottom up instead of from the top down . . ." In short, the transgovernmental actors in the flow could not maintain their predominance because the final decision to proceed rested with higher-level governmental actors. Indeed, the actor risks involved in such transgovernmental activity are evident in King's assessment: "I would have insisted on a cancellation of the whole thing, were it not that . . . to have cut if off would have raised a serious situation regarding relations to U.S. and Canadian armies on the Pacific, and probably involve Stuart's resignation." [7] After the authorization of this transaction through the Stimson-Ralston correspondence, the transgovernmental actors themselves switched roles by becoming governmental actors in performing activities which now had been formally legitimized.

It should be noted that the implementation of King's requirement for a higher-level formal decision was not an easy request because it involved U.S. organizational SOPs. Given different SOPs on both higher and lower levels and civilian-military control as well as the jealousy with which the U.S. organizational units guarded themselves from intrusion by other units, difficulties arose on the U.S. side. Pope is quoted as saying that when he told Hickerson the Canadian government wanted an invitation from the secretary to the minister to collaborate, Hickerson "laughingly told me to forget whatever Calvinistic tendencies there might be in my system and not to set out in an attempt to reform U.S. army procedure." [8] The U.S. deputy chief of staff who finally approved the communication was at first "hostile" but finally agreed that there was "no reason why Mr. Stimson should not address a general invitation to Mr. Ralston provided all details were settled through the military channel," adding that he did "not want this approach to Canada to go anywhere near the State Department." [9]

FACTORS ENCOURAGING TRANSNATIONAL AND TRANSGOVERNMENTAL ACTIVITY

Having identified pure, mixed, and transformative transactions, it is useful to examine those factors which tend to encourage transnational and transgovernmental activity. It may be hypothesized that there are five interrelated attributes of the defense issue area that encourage this activity: (1) U.S. and Canadian procedural predilection for an informal defense relationship; (2) the relatively small number of actors involved; (3) the multiple roles of these actors; (4) the transborder professional identifications of these actors; and (5) the technological content of defense issues. The first factor is reflected rhetorically in a cautious juxtaposition of U.S.-Canadian similiarities against the Canadian desire to maintain a separate national existence. Procedurally this is expressed in "special" as opposed to *comme les autres* decisional techniques. It is therefore not surprising that the U.S.-Canadian defense relationship is characterized by a marked absence of comprehensive joint agreements. Apart from the North Atlantic Treaty, there is no single formal agreement defining reciprocal strategic expectations and obligations. Indeed, the most definitive and comprehensive pledge of bilateral defense commitments remains that of the Roosevelt-King statements of 1938.[10] The August 1940 Ogdensburg Declaration, regarded as the genesis of the contemporary defense relationship, was not a declaration but a six-sentence, unsigned press release issued by King and Roosevelt. The April 1941 Hyde Park Agreement, generally viewed as the economic counterpart of the Ogdensburg Declaration, was more specific in delineating its objectives, but made no organizational provisions for its implementation. Even the NORAD agreements (1958, 1968, 1973) have never defined specific U.S. and Canadian forces and facility-level contributions, leaving these matters as an item of continuing negotiations. This informality, which is a response to the domestic exigencies of the United States, and more especially of Canada, has permitted flexible reactions to both international and national vagaries. However, it has encouraged transnational and transgovernmental activity by leaving undefined and unsystematized the organizational roles of the defense actors and the scope of the defense relationship, whether in terms of crisis response, personnel and matériel commitments, or procedural and consulative matters.

A revealing example of this procedural informality occurred on October 28, 1946, when President Truman met with Prime Minister King in Washington to discuss joint defense. Immediately thereafter King recounted the meeting to Canadian Ambassador Designate Hume Wrong. Wrong sent a telegram summarizing the meeting to Lester Pearson, under secretary of state for external affairs in Ottawa. In a conversation with U.S. Ambassador Ray Atherton, Pearson recounted the Truman-King meeting in detail. Atherton then reported its content in a dispatch to J. Graham Parsons, assistant chief of the State Department's Division of Commonwealth Affairs, who recorded it in a top-secret memorandum. This memorandum served as the State Department's record of the Truman-King meeting, a record the department obtained from Canadian sources.[11]

The second factor encouraging transnational and transgovernmental activity in the defense issue area is the relatively small number of actors involved. There are some seventy-five major defense actors in the United States and Canada who are professional experts in their respective fields, know one another personally, and meet in fairly regular sessions. This small transborder defense cluster expedites the resolution of defense issues along informal, personalized lines. The attitudinal impact of this small number of actors is manifested, as a U.S. official recently observed to this author, in a profound transborder "sense of membership."

A third factor concerns the multiple roles of the actors in the defense cluster. For example, the joint U.S.-Canadian Military Cooperation Committee (MCC) and the Regional Planning Group on NATO (RPG/NATO) have essentially identical membership and the same working teams and subcommittees. In addition, the MCC normally meets in combined session immediately prior to the Permanent Joint Board on Defense (PJBD), a sequence which furthers the interactions of these two joint organizations. (The PJBD is both civilian and military, whereas the MCC and RPG/NATO are strictly military.) Members of the working teams of the MCC and RPG/NATO also serve as military assistants to the PJBD. The fact that membership on any of the joint U.S.-Canadian defense organizations is part-time also encourages these multiple roles. Thus, officials of both the Canadian affairs offices of the Pentagon (Directorate for European and NATO Affairs) and the State Department (Office of Canadian Affairs) assist in the preparation of PJBD agendas and attend the meetings in addition to their regular functions. It is also important to note that these multiple roles are sequential for specific actors. For example, Canadian Gen. Maurice A. Pope, appointed to the PJBD in 1941, remained on this body as he professionally advanced in the following sequence: assistant chief of the general staff, vice chief of the general staff, representative of the cabinet War Committee in Washington and chairman of the Joint Staff, and the prime minister's military staff officer and military secretary to the War Committee.

In short, the import of these multiple roles as they encourage transnational and transgovernmental activity should not be underestimated. Hence, one relatively recent case involved a U.S. military officer who was a member of one of the joint U.S.-Canadian defense organizations. To help meet a U.S. shortage of barbed wire needed for the protection of village-manned self-defense forces in Vietnam, the U.S. officer, acting in his service rather than in joint organizational capacity, telephoned his Canadian organizational counterpart about getting the wire from plentiful Canadian sources. The Canadian official, then, acting in his service capacity, helped acquire the wire for the United States.

The fourth factor encouraging transnational and transgovernmental activity is the presence of transborder defense coalitions in which professional identifications tend to take precedence over national identifications within the dynamics of issue flows. In the PJBD during World War II, an observer asserts that "divisions of opinion seldom occurred on strictly national grounds" but that generally "the cleavage was along service lines." [12] Another observer adds that "on one issue, Canadian and United States army officers might be found united in argument with Canadian and United States naval officers; or the service members of both nations might find themselves on the opposite side of a discussion from the civilian members." [13] These transborder coalitions have continued, notwithstanding the Canadian armed forces unification and the difficulties between the Nixon and Trudeau governments. Thus, the following transborder coalitions can be said to be relatively active: air-air, navy-maritime, army-land, State Department-Department of External Affairs, Department of Defense-Department of National Defence and officials involved in defense-production sharing.

To abstract a current example concerning a procurement issue, the Canadian cabinet approved a Department of National Defence proposal to replace the aging Argus CP-107 aircraft with a long-range patrol aircraft for antisubmarine warfare. Given cabinet concern with the replacement's multiple role capability, the three leading candidates were an adapted version of the U.S. Boeing 707, the U.S. Lockheed P-3 ASW aircraft currently in service with the U.S. Navy, and the more specialized UK Nimrod, currently in service with the Royal Air Force. Canadian maritime force officials agreed with U.S. naval officials that the Canadian purchase of the P-3 would be mutually desirable for professional and budgetary reasons. Defense Department officials responsible for the defense-production-sharing agreements (DPSA) informally stated to their Canadian counterparts the importance of purchasing a U.S. model, and in view of a cumulative U.S. DPSA $500 million deficit, they expressed reservations about DPSA's continuance should this not be done. U.S. Treasury officials strongly concurred. After a cursory study requested by the Department of Defense, systems analysts who are aware of Ottawa's concern with the larger political and economic aspects arrived at neutral conclusions between the two U.S. alternatives. Canadian officials of several departments then decided to institute a fly-off between the alternative models, the result being the selection of Lockheed P-3.

The fifth factor concerns the technological content of defense issues, which tends to decrease national barriers and increase specialized transborder collaboration. This goes quite beyond the U.S.-Canadian defense-production-sharing agreements to include a broader economic-scientific relationship.[14] Seven facets can be discerned: supportive economic activity (e.g., World War II complementarity in agriculture and taxation); collaboration in atomic energy; exchange of defense-related scientific data; military standardization (e.g., sharing of matériel and parts); collaborative applied research; collaborative development; and collaboration in defense procurement. The significance of this technological content is evident in reviewing U.S.-Canadian economic cooperation related to defense matters during World War II.[15] The rationale for this cooperation was twofold—to accelerate the acquisition of military matériel and to alleviate the pressure on Canadian foreign exchange early in the war. The import of this cooperation did not escape Prime Minister King, who observed that the Hyde Park Agreement "constitutes an acceptance of the economic interdependence of Canada and the U.S.," having a "permanent significance," and involving "nothing less than a common plan of the economic defense of the western hemisphere." [16] King's assessment was not hyperbolic, for World War II collaboration resulted in an unprecedented coordination of the U.S. and Canadian economies and in "the almost complete erasure of national boundaries for certain purposes." [17] For example, the Combined Production and Resources Board recommended that a proposed war plant in Canada not be constructed because U.S. productive facilities were already sufficient for U.S. and Canadian needs; the Combined Food Board reduced competitive bidding on foodstuffs that were shortage items; a 1942 U.S.-Canadian agreement facilitated the transborder movement of agricultural labor and machinery, and according to a May 1942 U.S. executive order, emergency purchases of war matériel could be imported without duty. Moreover, three major joint agreements were concluded regarding exemption of military construction from taxation.[18]

This wartime collaborative environment encouraged transnational and transgovernmental activity. One author has noted that the "informal and direct methods used by the nondiplomatic missions raised certain issues concerning the control and synthesis of external policies." [19] Indeed, important agreements were sometimes "made quite informally, almost by word of mouth and outside the normal channels of diplomatic intercourse"; and even though the departmental representatives were "supposedly dealing only with matters of a technical nature," the fact remained that "some of the decisions taken bordered on high policy, especially in matters relating to war procurement and production." [20]

THE SIGNIFICANCE OF TRANSNATIONAL AND TRANSGOVERNMENTAL ACTIVITY

In view of those factors encouraging transnational and transgovernmental activity in the defense issue area, one might conclude that even a casual projection would have to emphasize a continuing if not increasing transnational and transgovernmental content. However, such a conclusion would disregard the major factor militating against this activity. Of all the issue areas, that of defense involves matters of especially high national policy in conjunction with a government's insistence of maximum secrecy and maneuverability of action. In a more general sense, the extent to which transnational and transgovernmental activity is permitted by authoritative actors is dependent upon two facets of actor behavior: their tolerance level concerning this activity and their decisional resources in monitoring and controlling it. This is essentially a question of the extent to which actors, at all organizational levels, attempt and are able to maintain a central role in making those decisions determining the outcome of a given issue. It can be speculated that most authoritative actors have a bias against unintegrated activity to the extent that it involves a loss of their decisional centrality.

In the defense issue area, this transgovernmental activity can involve the most basic constitutional considerations of the two governments—the parameters set by civilian control of the military. Transnational activity is also sensitive, but here there is a tradition of harnessing these actors. For example, the chairman of the 1917 Canadian war mission to the United States was Lloyd Harris, director of Massey-Harris. The prevalence of "dollar-a-year" men in the Canadian government defense production effort during World

War II and the career patterns of many corporation executives are in keeping with this tradition.

Notwithstanding the fact that most authoritative actors have a bias against unintegrated activity, they tend to utilize such activity themselves when they see it as being operationally effective, while simultaneously disavowing that it is unintegrated. And they may have a point, for while their organizational responsibilities are generally quite clearly defined, their operational roles are to a great extent self-determined and self-fulfilling. An actor's decisional resources in monitoring unintegrated activity are especially complex, for those capabilities enabling an actor to make a decision depend upon *inter alia* the extent to which he plays a central role within his organizational unit and the extent to which his organizational unit plays a central role within the overall organization and sets of organizations.

The unknown factor regarding transnational and transgovernmental activity in all issue areas concerns shifts in overall organizational and governmental priorities. For example, defense matters in the United States have constituted the high-priority item throughout the cold war, but current indications are that economic preoccupations have assumed the importance heretofore reserved for defense matters. Certainly such shifts are a major factor affecting transnational and transgovernmental activity, but how and to what extent we do not know. Indeed, we have not established the interrelationships among the priority level of an issue, the amount of activity within a government and between governments in conjunction with the priority level, and the degree of transnational and transgovernmental activity with respect to priority and amount. Nor have we examined in the context of transnational and transgovernmental relations, the impact of shifts of governmental priorities on the dynamics of politicization (i.e., issues being raised from functional to political levels), and depoliticization. Nor have we rigorously considered the possibility that there might be entirely different decisional flows among the different issue areas, and within an issue area concerning the actor level at which an issue is processed.[21]

The assessment of decisional cost benefits of transnational and transgovernmental activity is especially difficult. Suffice it to say that any assessment must take into account four considerations. Such assessments ultimately depend upon the referent (i.e., is it being assessed from the standpoint of the United States, Canada, or the United States and Canada?). Second, it must be acknowledged that the decisional motivations for pursuing congruent policies might be based on different if not contradictory interests and that the cost benefits accruing to both governments are not necessarily of the same type. Third, caution must be exercised with respect to the superimposition of present preoccupations in evaluating past transactions. Finally, caution must be exercised concerning presuppositions that bargaining situations are inherently those in which one actor's gain is the other's loss.

An illustrative example of both the shift in issue priorities and the resultant assessment of cost benefits concerns the U.S.-Canadian defense-production-sharing agreements.[22] Certainly the advantages Canada obtained in the 1959 agreement were noteworthy—significant exemptions from the "Buy America Act" and regular U.S. customs duties. However, the 1959 arrangements were altered as early as 1963 when it was agreed in principle that in the long run there should be a "general balance" in the transborder defense trade. It was this understanding that caused current difficulties, given a cumulative U.S. $500 million deficit with Canada on the transborder defense trade. What appears to have happened is that the U.S. assessment of the cost benefits stemming from the agreements have shifted as a result of an overall shift in U.S. governmental priorities. That is, when U.S. priorities shifted from strategic to economic, the U.S. criterion of the agreements became largely that of the effect on the balance of payments. Heretofore the United States was willing to endure what it saw as an increasing deficit with Canada due to such strategically important factors as the maintenance of a Canadian defense industry in conjunction with joint military collaboration, and the acquisition of Canadian defense matériel for use in the Vietnam conflict. Hence, the U.S. reexamination of the agreements resulted from the shift in overall governmental priorities between strategic and economic factors.

The Canadian assessment of the cost benefits of the overall defense relationship includes to a very great extent political criteria in terms of the U.S. impact on Canadian territorial and conceptual sovereignty. Indeed, the Canadian concern about the U.S. impact, which is essentially attributable to bilateral isolation and disparity, adds a major political dimension concerning the Canadian assessment of both U.S. defense activities in Canada and the effect of Canada's involvement with the United States on Canadian independence of external action. However, the case can be made that the U.S.-Canadian defense relationship operates, not in spite of different evaluative criteria, but because of them. That is, it may be because of these differing U.S. and Canadian perceptions of the defense links being formed, and the dissimilar U.S. and Canadian cost benefits generated, that the defense linkage is often possible in the first place. However, these same differences may simultaneously limit its longevity as the international situation changes. If this speculation is substantiated, it would suggest the U.S.-Canadian defense relationship is bilaterally dysfunctional. It could be that which makes the defense relationship functionally useful for the United States and Canada, respectively (in enabling both nations, especially Canada, to register and pursue their self-definition of national needs), resulting in a defense involvement that is bilaterally dysfunctional in the sense that differing decisional motivations and subsequent dissimilar benefits ensure fundamental future U.S. and Canadian disagreement.

The implications of this speculation are important concerning transnational and transgovernmental activity in analyses of the extent to which the U.S.-Canadian defense relationship is an integrative process, especially in terms of its irreversibility. For example, this speculation might suggest that the linkages will not pass an irreversible point in terms of an integrative process, notwithstanding transnational and transgovernmental activity. On the contrary, it could be that the differing perceptions and subsequent cost benefits ensure future disagreements that tend to arrest integrative dynamics precisely because these disagreements are grounded in the nature of the defense relationship itself.

This situation, of course, points to the need for rigorous empirical investigation of an organizational and governmental unit's disassociation possibilities and costs as the originally different but convergent forces furthering integration lessen. It may also be noted that the problem with any alliance is that as those congruent threat perceptions that create and sustain it diminish the alliance becomes less cohesive. But, if, rather than congruent threat perceptions perpetuating an alliance, there are fundamentally different assumed payoffs, alliance cohesiveness is a priori subject to lesser-order disturbances than those that stem from a perceived diminution of the external threat. Obviously this is not an either/or situation, since all alliances involve both military and nonmilitary payoffs. However, the U.S.-Canadian defense relationship, because of its bilateral isolation and disparity, might be especially characterized by a dichotomous payoff structure.

SUMMATION AND ASSESSMENT

In summation, this chapter identified three general classes of actors active in the Canada-U.S. relationship: intergovernmental, referring to governmental actors active in transborder dealings; transnational, referring to nongovernmental actors; and transgovernmental, referring to governmental actors who act on their own independently of organizational routines. This chapter then discussed the threefold nature of transborder transactions: pure intergovernmental, involving only governmental actors; mixed transactions, involving actors in addition to governmental ones but who do not alter the outcome of the flows; and transformative transactions, involving flows in which the activities of new actors significantly alter the outcome of the flows. Finally, this chapter identified those factors which encourage and discourage transnational and transgovernmental activity and assessed the cost benefits of these activities. The paradigm developed in this chapter is applied to the defense issue area, and the most immediate need is of course to test it by applying it to such other areas as the economic sector.

It should be noted that this chapter has concentrated on transgovernmental as opposed to transnational transactions, since the transgovernmental dimension has been most neglected in world polity analyses and appears to be rather more relevant to this issue area than the transnational one. Although analyses of political organization incorporate the transgovernmental dimension in theory, they tend to confine this dimension to the nonempirical use of a few examples, themselves often questionable because they are not grounded in the structural milieu in which they occur. This is not surprising. Because the units of analysis of transnational transactions are defined according to an actor's formal position, all an analyst has to do is identify nongovernmental actors involved in transborder dealings. For transgovernmental transactions, however, the analyst has to use a definition based not on position but on role. Not any subgovernmental transborder actor is by definition transgovernmental, but only those that act independently in international relations. Since it is often difficult to determine when an actor is acting independently in international relations, analysts are tempted to apply the position-based definition to transgovernmental transactions and inaccurately to regard all subgovernmental transborder dealings and informal contacts as transgovernmental.[23]

Another point of clarification is also definitional in nature. Transgovernmental relations can be defined as transborder subgovernmental transactions not controlled or closely guided by the policies of cabinets or chief executives. However, an analyst using this definition cannot identify the unit of analysis without first identifying what a government policy is at a given point. Notwithstanding advantages in such an approach, "policy identification" would seem to have limitations concerning its empirical application. These limitations stem from the level of generality in which executives so often formulate and articulate policy, the fact that so many functional U.S.-Canada dealings at the core of the relationship are processed entirely by lower-level action officers who receive no higher-level guidelines, and the contextual elusiveness of fluid shifts of bargaining positions and overall issue priorities.

This chapter identifies transgovernmental transactions by looking at role deviation rather than at departure from government policy. The role in question is organizational in nature; indeed, it is less a role in a social-psychological sense than it is an operation or function in an organizational sense. Transgovernmental relations are therefore defined by this author as those transborder dealings in which there is a departure on the part of one or more governmental officials from the SOPs of the organizational units which encompass them. Quite simply, they are organizationally unintegrated governmental points of contact across national boundaries. These SOPs, by which transgovernmental relations are identified, are not only relatively easy to isolate but are also useful analytically. For example, if one is interested in the effect of transgovernmental transactions on the erosion of overall governmental authority, analyses would seem to be more usefully directed at the SOPs and activities that constitute issue flows than at governmental policies. Moreover, the use of SOPs as a definitional base includes the significant possibility of chief executives themselves acting as transgovernmental actors.[24] For example, it is legitimate and useful to ask if Prime Minister Diefenbaker was not himself a transgovernmental actor during the 1957-58 establishment of NORAD. This question can be answered by looking, not at the policies of the Diefenbaker government, but at the SOPs of the Canadian parliamentary system. Thus, if the Canadian processing of the North Atlantic Treaty is taken as a representative model of Canadian SOPs in such matters, Diefenbaker could be considered a transgovernmental actor.[25] In contrast, those who use cabinet and executive policies as a definitional base in identifying transgovernmental relations permit only lower-level bureaucracies to depart from these policies and hence be considered transgovernmental actors.

It is perhaps useful to place the paradigm developed in this chapter in the context of the formative work done concerning transnational relations. The Nye and Keohane formulation, which appeared in the Autumn 1974 issue of *International Organization*, was instrumental in orienting attention toward aspects of global interactions that were often missed in traditional state-centric perspectives.[26] The Nye-Keohane formulation had two major dimensions: "interstate interactions," which constitutes the state-centric view of global interactions as being almost entirely initiated and sustained by governments of nation states; and "transnational interactions," which includes in the broadest sense "all of world politics that is not taken into account by the state-centric paradigm." These transnational interactions are then subdivided into two categories—"transnational," referring to interactions "when at least one actor is not an agent of a government or an international organization"; and "transgovernmental," referring to interactions between governmental subunits in which there is a deviation "from formally prescribed roles." This is a most useful formulation, and it is to it that this author is initially indebted. However, as has been seen, the Nye-Keohane formulation has been modified and extended by the author in several ways.

To go beyond the concepts developed in this chapter, we are in the most basic sense dealing with three types of transborder dealings, each of which has its own subsets: pure, mixed, and transformative transactions. Pure transactions are those transborder flows in which all the actors are of the same type. There are three categories: (1) pure transgovernmental, involving purely governmental actors acting in accordance with their organizational mandates (but including non-governmental actors whose activities are entirely integrated into the organizational interfaces of the mandates of the governmental actors); (2) pure transnational, involving purely nongovernmental actors; and (3) pure transgovernmental, involving purely governmental actors acting outside their organizational mandates.

Mixed transactions are those transborder flows involving more than one type of actor but in which the new actor(s) does not predominate. There are two categories. The first is intergovernmental, involving, in addition to predominate governmental actors acting within their mandates, transnational and/or transgovernmental actors. Thus, any flow involving governmental actors acting within their mandates at any point and at any level, regardless of salience, is considered a mixed transgovernmental flow. The second category of mixed transactions is transnational/transgovernmental, involving a combination of transnational and transgovernmental actors, but without any governmental actors.

Transformative transactions are those transborder flows in which new actors become involved and predominate in the sense that they significantly affect the decisions made in, and the outcomes of, the flows themselves. The flow can therefore be transformed from an intergovernmental one into a transnational one (transnationalization) or a transgovernmental one (transgovernmentalization). Alternatively, a transnational or transgovernmental flow can be transformed into an intergovernmental one (intergovernmentalization).

Given the importance of holding the intergovernmental dimension as an analytical referent, the definition of intergovernmental relations is expanded to include situations in which one actor is governmental and the other(s) transnational or transgovernmental. The alternative of defining such mixed transactions as transnational or transgovernmental would definitionally preclude their consideration as part of an intergovernmental flow, with attendant analytical constraints.

The advantages of holding an expanded intergovernmental category are threefold. It permits direct examination of: (1) transnational and transgovernmental activity in governmental decision-making processes (i.e., especially the dynamics of transformative transactions); (2) the decisional cost benefits of this activity in these processes (i.e., the very utility of this activity in intergovernmental flows); and (3) the entire question of governmental erosion and control concerning this activity (i.e., the extent to which governmental decision-making processes mitigate for or against this activity in conjunction with the need for, and feasibility of, governmental control mechanisms). It might be noted that this author's

use of this expanded intergovernmental category is not
without its costs, for it does not permit direct examination of
the pure transnational, pure transgovernmental, or mixed
transnational/transgovernmental categories. However, these
are limited categories, for there would seem to be relatively
few transborder sequences of major import concerning loss of
governmental control in which governmental actors would
not formally attempt to monitor and control the activities in
these sequences by interjecting themselves into the flows.
This interjection by governmental actors would at least
consist of formally notifying these actors of the relevance to
their activities of the appropriate governmental parameters,
if not legal frameworks. This notification would thus definitionally shift the pure transnational, pure transgovernmental,
or mixed transnational/transgovernmental flows to the mixed
intergovernmental category because the governmental actors
become formally involved in the flows. Even in those limited
instances in which there is no formal governmental interjection in some form, examinations of pure transgovernmental
or mixed transnational/transgovernmental flows still requires
the use of mandated governmental activities as a definitional
base against which the fact of organizational deviation can be
verified as a prelude to categorization.

In considering alternative approaches to the study of the
Canada-U.S. relationship, it is important to note that the
ultimate criterion of the effectiveness of an analytical perspective is a researchable specificity rather than a heuristic
inclusiveness. The full potential of any approach will be clear
when it is used to address precisely the structural interrelationships among actors, their organizational milieus, and the
concomitant SOPs through which issue flows are processed.[27]

NOTES

1. See Robert O. Keohane and Joseph S. Nye, Jr., eds., "Transnational Relations and World Politics," *International Organization*, Vol, XXV, No. 3 (Summer 1971), p. 753.

2. It should be noted that the definitional base has been shifted somewhat (from a behaviorally oriented to a perceptually oriented referent) between the determination of the preprocess/process stage boundary and the process/postprocess stage boundary. The alternative of preserving definitional symmetry by using a behaviorally oriented referent to determine the boundaries of both stages would shift analytical emphasis away from the significant questions regarding the differences between issue resolution and implementation, and the concomitant differing utility of transgovernmental and transnational activity in the resolutive and implementative phases. Despite the loss if one invoked this alternative, it should not be discarded as a conceptual possibility. However, at this point in the author's research, the symmetrical behaviorally oriented definitional alternative would appear to have few additional theoretical advantages of significance, except perhaps some easing of the task of empirically identifying the process/postprocess stage boundary. Nonetheless, in that the perceptually oriented definition used by this author is also organizationally based, it too has easily proven to be empirically applicable.

3. More specifically, this illustrates the transborder activity of a representative of an international organization which deviated from the SOPs followed among the international organization and national governments. However, space limitations preclude a discussion of the interesting question of Norstad's empirical, and hence, analytical status.

4. This case study is abstracted from Peyton Lyon, "The Norstad Press Conference," in *Canadian Foreign Policy Since 1945*, ed. J. L. Granatstein (Toronto: The Copp Clark Publishing Company, 1970), pp. 111-14.

5. This case study is abstracted from C. P. Stacey, "The Canadian-American PJBD: 1940-1945," *International Journal*, Vol. IX, No. 2 (Spring 1954), p. 120. It illustrates transgovernmental activity which was encouraged by the joint organizational framework between the two nations in the defense area. In examining transnational and transgovernmental activity in this area, attention should be directed at all seven contemporary U. S.-Canadian defense organizations, which are interesting because they are oriented toward formal political-military negotiation to a lesser extent than may be expected. Of the seven joint organizations, one is directly concerned with active strategic protection (NORAD); two perform planning-recommendatory functions (PJBD and MCC); one is concerned with the economics of defense (Senior Committee on DPSA); one with emergency planning (Civil Emergency Planning Committee); one with

liaison (RPG/NATO); and one with cabinet-level consultation (Ministerial Committee on Joint Defense).

6. This case study is abstracted from James Eayrs, *The Art of the Possible* (Toronto: University of Toronto Press, 1961), pp. 82-85.

7. Ibid., p. 84.

8. Ibid., pp. 84-85.

9. Ibid., p. 85.

10. Even the 1817 Rush-Bagot "Treaty," the rhetorical touchstone of the "undefended border," was not a treaty but an agreement implemented by a U.S.-British exchange of notes, and subsequently confirmed by the U.S. Senate. However, ratifications were not exchanged.

11. Roger Frank Swanson, *Canadian-American Summit Diplomacy 1923-1974* (Toronto: McClelland and Stewart, 1975) pp. 106-110.

12. H. L. Keenleyside, "The Canada-U.S. PJBD," *International Journal*, Vol. XVI, No. 1 (Winter 1960-61), p. 55.

13. C. P. Stacey, op. cit., p. 115.

14. Analyses of the production-sharing agreements have failed to make the case that the agreements are a' discrete unit of analysis. They have not systematically considered the interrelationships between these agreements and the other facets of the larger U.S.-Canadian economic-scientific defense relationship. Because the definitional boundaries are unspecified, it is never clear as to precisely what we are dealing with (e.g., an issue area, the subcomponent of an issue area, a sectoral phenomenon, or a cross-cutting sectoral phenomenon). This lack of definitional precision causes analytical distortions when these discussions consider the agreements as an integrative process. Moreover, these analyses of the production-sharing agreements are unduly restrictive in that, even though they acknowledge the origins of the agreements, they ignore the utility of the historical dimension as a reference point for comparative measurement of integrative and disintegrative processes.

15. To implement the Roosevelt-King 1941 Hyde Park Agreement, a series of joint committees were established during the war: Matériel Coordinating Committee, Joint Economic Committees, Joint War Production Committee, Joint Agriculture Committee, and Joint War Aid Committee. In addition, Canada joined two U.S.-U.K. combined boards: Combined Production and Resources Board and the Combined Food Board.

16. *Canadian House of Commons Debates*, April 28, 1941, pp. 2288-89.

17. Richardson Dougall, "Economic Cooperation with Canada: 1941-47," *Department of State Bulletin*, Vol. XVI, No. 416 (June 22, 1947), p. 1185.

18. Ibid., pp. 1186-1189.

19. H. Gordon Skilling, *Canadian Representation Abroad* (Toronto: Ryerson Press, 1945), p. 315.

20. Ibid.

21. This author has found it useful to distinguish between two hierarchical categories of issues: substantial issues, defined as issues that require resolution at the level of the assistant secretary/assistant deputy minister or above on the part of at least one government; and action issues, defined as issues processed below this level.

22. As background, Canadian curtailment of the CF-105 program suggested its future inability independently to develop major weapons systems, triggering concern about the viability of Canadian defense industry with all the domestic economic ramifications. The U.S. government was concerned about the viability of Canadian defense industry in the overall strategic context of NORAD. However, caution must be exercised in attributing decisional motivation to U.S. and Canadian officials, for it is tempting to oversimplify the dynamics of that period by juxtaposing a purely Canadian economic preoccupation against a purely U.S. strategic one (e.g., U.S. officials also perceived the agreements as having an economic dimension in holding down U.S. procurement costs).

23. To cite one example of a possibly confusing case, Washington State's director of civil defense and British Columbia's civil defense coordinator formally signed a "Letter of Understanding" on October 23, 1968, dealing with civil emergency planning. Their authority for so doing can be found in the *U.S. Office of Civil Defense Federal Civil Defense Guide* (Part G, Chapter 2, Appendix 1), in the *Canadian Emergency Measures Organization Bulletin* (B68-2, International Coordination 5/23/68), and bilaterally in an August 8, 1967, federal exchange of notes (18 UST 1795) which encourages and facilitates "cooperative emergency arrangements between adjacent jurisdictions on matters falling within the competence of such jurisdiction." This therefore illustrates, not a transgovernmental transaction, but a sublevel intergovernmental transaction because it is entirely integrated into the multileveled government processes of the two nations.

24. As developed by this author, these SOPs consist of two dimensions: statutory legitimacy, which refers to written definitions of areas of responsibility and procedural rules of acceptable activity; and operational legitimacy, which refers to unwritten but consensurially defined areas of responsibility and procedures which are organizationally regarded as an acceptable extension of the written dimension. Taken together, they can be subsumed under the phrase organizational mandate. The operational salience of the organizational mandate is a function of the decisional resources (e.g., funding, number of personnel, degree of expertise) available to the actor. Transgovernmental transactions can therefore be defined as all transborder violations of a governmental actor's organizational mandate.

25. See Jon B. McLin, *Canada's Changing Defense Policy 1957-1963* (Baltimore, Maryland: The Johns Hopkins Press, 1967), pp. 38-49.

26. See Keohane and Nye, op. cit., p. 753.

27. "Structural" refers to the organizational environs (i.e., organizational mandates and their execution through organizational roles) and interconnections between these environs, within which the actors function. Indeed, the significance of the transborder activities of individuals, and the transborder movement of tangible items, is also organizationally grounded. The former involves the organizational roles these individuals are performing (e.g., corporate executive, government official, or trade union representative); the latter, the organizational context in which movements of these tangible items take place (e.g., oil, defense, matériel, or money).

VI

INTERGOVERNMENTAL RELATIONS AT THE STATE/PROVINCIAL LEVEL *

An important but relatively neglected aspect of the Canada-U.S. intergovernmental relationship is the relations between U.S. states and Canadian provinces. While state/provincial relations might seem to be a rather abstract phenomenon, they are in fact grounded in "nuts-and-bolts" considerations. Quite simply, in order for a state official to do something in line with his official responsibilities, he considers it necessary to deal with his Canadian provincial counter-

---

* This chapter is excerpted from Roger Frank Swanson, *State/Provincial Interaction: A Study of Relations Between U.S. States and Canadian Provinces Prepared for the U.S. Department of State* (Washington, D.C.: Office of External Research, Bureau of Intelligence and Research, Department of State [Contract 1722-320061]), August 1974. (Neither this monograph, nor this chapter, is intended to represent the conclusions or policies of the Department of State.) The report subsequently appeared as a monograph published by the Natural Resource Institute of the University of Manitoba entitled "The U.S.-Canada Relationship at the State/Provincial Level: A U.S. Perspective," Winnipeg, Manitoba (#R3T2N2), 1976. It was also published in a summary form as an article entitled "The Range of Direct Relations Between States and Provinces," *International Perspectives* (March/April 1976), pp. 18-23.

part in an attempt to establish some mutually useful procedure.

In the simplest sense, this chapter presents an overview of state/provincial relations by answering three basic questions: [1] In sheer numbers, how extensive are these relations? What types of relations are there? (E.g., are they informal procedures or do they take some other form?) What is the functional nature of these relations? (E.g., are they of an economic or cultural nature, or do they involve other functional areas?) The answers to these questions, as will be seen, are noteworthy if not surprising. First, there is a greater number of state/provincial agreements, understandings, and arrangements than might be expected—a total of 766 ongoing interactions. Moreover, these interactions are not confined only to U.S. border states. On the contrary, every one of the fifty states was found to have some form of dealings with the Canadian provinces, with the nonborder states accounting for a full 38% of all state/provincial interactions. Secondly, the state/provincial interactions turn out to be of a more formal nature than might be expected. Though a majority involved informal procedures, 30 percent were formal agreements or semiformal understandings. Finally, state/provincial interactions are more comprehensive and cover a greater range of activities than might be expected. That is, they were found to cover the full scope of governmental activity, including agriculture, energy, and transportation.

It is tempting to regard state/provincial relations as a lower-order replication of relations between nations and thus employ the concepts and theoretical approaches appropriate to the field of international relations. Certainly it is clear that state/provincial relations have implications for international relations as a field of study, but what is less clear is the extent to which they are a component of the field of international relations as opposed to a more discrete unit of analysis, and the extent to which the existing analytical tools of the international relations field are applicable. .

The case can be made that state/provincial relations constitute an analytical supermarket, with something for everyone. The "transnationalists," however defined, can examine nongovernmental or governmentally uncontrolled transborder transactions; the "integrationists" can search out those linkages whereby actors generate increased regularized interactions; specialists in international law can catalogue and sort out the legal status and contractual legitimacy dimensions; specialists in federalism can address themselves to the internal political/constitutional implications; and so on. All these approaches, and mixes of these approaches, obviously contain beneficial and revealing perspectives.

However, one of the findings of this chapter is that the scope, types, and functional range of state/provincial relations are analytically unmanageable with existing approaches. That is, the existing approaches, notwithstanding their utility in illuminating facets of state/provincial relations, are not in the first case able to analytically absorb the full dynamics and implications of state/provincial relations in their totality. Nor is it claimed that this chapter does so, given its preliminary nature. Indeed, the most definitive conclusion that can be forwarded is that the nature of state/provincial relations necessitates more complex analysis beyond the initial conceptualization, mapping, and observations contained in this chapter.

What this chapter does is to develop and apply basic descriptive concepts, typologies, and taxonomies, which, first, impose a sense of order on an elusive and uncharted area of transborder governmental relations; which, second, do so without prejudging the substantive nature and policy implications of these relations; and which, third, do not preclude the application of other analytical approaches once the overall dynamics of state/provincial relations are uncovered and better understood. Hence, this chapter's typology of relations by format (agreements, understandings, and arrangements) permits the unambiguous classification of multifaceted state/provincial relations according to an underlying dimension (degree of formality) while holding in abeyance judgments as to their motivational or legal character.

Equally important, this chapter's development of a taxonomy of the functional range of governmental activity enables consideration of the subject matter of state/provincial relations on a systematic but general basis, while advancing speculative propositions concerning the causes and developments of these relations. Moreover, this taxonomy has the advantages of being applicable to governmental units at other levels, and of having been constructed utilizing an actor-based referent so as to be easily operationalized at all levels. The multilevel applicability, relative specificity, and operationally grounded precision of this taxonomy make it a possible candidate in the exploration of one of the more complex and undeveloped analytical dimensions, that of issue areas.

A third development generated by this chapter, and one whose full analytical implications have yet to be explored, is the conceptualization of the actor contexts of state/provincial relations. State/provincial relations are not, and cannot be, considered solely as a bilateral phenomenon between state and provincial governments. Such a perspective must be supplemented by an examination of the bases upon which states deal with provincial units (multilateral and general), the forms in which they do so, and the involvement of actors of other levels and types in this interaction. Only through subsequent research which further explores these preliminary observations about the actor context of state/provincial relations can analysts begin to offer conclusions on the fundamental analytical question—the extent to which state/provincial relations are a discrete unit of analysis, and the theoretical approaches which its empirical status warrants.[2]

The first section of this chapter discusses the policy implications of state/provincial relations. Because the U.S. states constituted the unit of analysis, this discussion emphasizes a U.S. perspective in examining these policy implications. The second section defines state/provincial interactions and assesses the scope of these interactions among the states. The third section delineates three types of interaction—agreements, understandings, and arrangements—and assesses the extent and significance of them. Section four identifies the functional nature of state/provincial interactions by dividing them into eleven categories, after which the types of interaction are analyzed according to these functional categories. The fifth section of this chapter examines the pairs of states and provinces, as well as the individual provinces, to determine levels of activity. The concluding section presents a summation and raises research questions which go beyond the findings in this chapter. This includes assessments of how states are organized to process these interactions and what transborder techniques have been developed in the dealings between states and provinces.

POLICY IMPLICATIONS

State/provincial relations merit attention at the policy level on three interrelated counts: legal parameters, functional servicing, and bilateral politicization.

Perhaps the most potentially important, but least operationally significant at this point, is the legal dimension of state/provincial interaction. This refers to the fact that state/provincial interaction must, to be legitimate, occur within certain constitutional parameters of the U.S. and Canadian federal systems. Two articles in the U.S. Constitution address themselves to this matter. Article I, Section 10 asserts:

> No state shall enter into any treaty, alliance or confederation. . . . No state shall, without the consent of Congress . . . enter into any agreement or compact with another state or with a foreign power. . . .

Article II, Section 2 asserts that:

> He [the president] shall have power, by and with the advice and consent of the Senate, to make treaties, provided two-thirds of the Senators present concur. . . .

Thus, under the U.S. Constitution, there is in a general sense no doubt as to where the treaty power lies.[3] However, states do partake in transborder interactions having varying degrees of legal formality, and Congress has deemed that not all of them require such consent. In a statement on the Constitution prepared for Congress in its 74th Session and repeated for its 88th Session:

> The terms "compact" and "agreement" . . . do not apply to every compact or agreement . . . but the prohibition is directed to the formation of any combination tending to the increase of political power in the States which may encroach upon or interfere with the just supremacy of the United States. The terms cover all stipulations affecting the conduct or claims of states, whether verbal or written, formal or informal, positive or implied with each other or with foreign powers.[4]

In short, Congress is willing to absorb the functional needs of states in their transborder dealings but is concerned with the "political" power of states and the extent to which this power might erode the centrality of the U.S. federal government. For example, in the case of bridges connecting the United States and Canada, Congress passed an act in 1972 explicitly giving its consent to U.S. states and their subdivisions to "enter into agreements" with the government of Canada or Canadian provinces and subdivisions in matters dealing with these bridges.[5]

The constitutional framework for Canada, as embodied in the British North America Act, (BNA) is quite different from that of the United States. Although written in 1867 when Canada was still a part of the British Empire, the matter of foreign affairs was mentioned in Section 132 of the BNA Act:

> The Parliament and Government of Canada shall have all powers necessary or proper for performing the obligations of Canada or of any Province thereof, as part of the British Empire, towards foreign countries, arising under treaties between the Empire and such foreign countries.

More relevant are those sections of the BNA Act which define in a specific sense the division of powers between the federal government and the provinces. Section 91 gives a comprehensive grant of power to the federal government while also listing certain powers as examples (e.g., regulations of trade and commerce, taxation). Section 92 lists the chief provincial powers (e.g., resources and enforcement of laws); Section 93 gives the provinces the responsibility for education; while Section 95 gives two powers, immigration and agriculture, to both the federal and provincial governments, with the federal position obtaining in the event of a conflict. In short, specific powers are granted to the provinces, and all others are the responsibility of the federal government.

It is ironical that while the intent of the BNA Act was to

create a strongly centralized federation, subsequent judicial decisions reinforced regionalizing political forces, making for a highly decentralized federal structure compared with the United States. The provinces came to have control over the implementation of treaties dealing with powers under their purview. Moreover, as the international system became increasingly interdependent, many of the "domestic" powers of the provinces acquired a high international content (i.e. education and resources). In comparison with U.S. states, the provinces therefore have greater autonomy in conducting transborder relations. The Canadian Department of External Affairs has acknowledged that "there are provincial interests in fields which involve dealings with foreign countries" but that these are or must be either "arrangements subsumed under agreements between Canada and the foreign government concerned" or "administrative arrangements of an informal character . . . not subject to international law." [6]

Notwithstanding the legal implications of the extensive interaction between U.S. states and Canadian provinces, no glaring case or cases were uncovered which would raise major constitutional questions about the U.S. or Canadian federal systems and the concomitant roles of U.S. states and provinces in external affairs.[7] Indeed, from the U.S. standpoint, it is interesting that the state/provincial interaction, given its extensiveness, has not been a major component of the U.S. political/legal debate concerning the role of the states vis-à-vis federal centrality. However, where state/provincial activity could potentially generate questions is not so much in those cases where a state's involvement in this activity is a response to functional needs as it is in those cases in which a state might go beyond these needs in an attempt to register a presence vis-à-vis such extra-U.S. jurisdictions as Canadian provinces. It is in these latter cases involving "international" status that there appeared in the state/

provincial realm some instances of interaction which might at some point raise questions.

Far more important as a matter of continuing policy attention are questions of a servicing rather than of a legal nature. This servicing involves the second area of policy attention, that of functional servicing. This term refers to the capacity of the State Department and, indeed, the other units of the federal government, to respond to and facilitate the constitutionally legitimate and functionally necessary transborder needs of the states.[8]

There is overwhelming evidence to suggest that state governments want to fulfill necessary needs in a manner most appropriate to that functional area in the simplest manner. At the same time, there was the desire to conduct trans-border activity in a manner which fully and categorically meets the constitutional requirements of the U.S. federal system. Here, a sense of frustration was articulated by state governmental officials concerning their inability to easily obtain definitive information from the most appropriate federal agency which would satisfy their latter objective. A lack of responsiveness on the part of the U.S. federal government encourages not so much deliberate directed annoyance as it does a tendency for state governments to proceed on the functionally most appropriate basis in the absence of clear indications that such activity is improper.[9] In short, state/provincial interaction warrants the attention of the U.S. State Department as much in a servicing role, whereby the legitimate functional needs of the states are met by federal authorities, as it does in a monitoring role, whereby the State Department "diplomatically" oversees the transborder activities of the states. Indeed, neglect of the former will procedurally exacerbate the latter.

The third area that merits policy attention, that of bilateral politicization, stems from this need on the part of state governments to meet functional requirements in the absence of the initially desired degree of political and legal clarity. This stems from the fact that state/provincial interactions which proceed within this context can at a later time generate issues that not only require the attention and involvement of the U.S. State Department and federal government but that can also become abrasive as a bilateral issue between the U.S. and Canadian federal governments. It can also refer, in a less negative sense, to the fact that some issues must definitionally become bilateralized because of the constitutional systems of the U.S. and Canada. An example of the latter is the network of civil defense agreements which appear to have provided a generally satifactory statutory and organizational context within which state and provincial units can operate to satisfy their requirements with a minimum of operational, and an absence of political, problems. Still, however responsive the federal governments have been, or may seek to be, the very fact that their involvement occurs at later stages in an interaction process may result in a succession of issues which, by already having been bilateralized, may be less amenable to easy solution.[10] Here it should be noted that in the vast majority of the functional areas federal involvement has taken the simple form of an informational or advisory role, generally to the satisfaction of the parties involved.

In an overall sense, the policy ramifications of state/provincial interactions, and the commensurate U.S. federal governmental attention which it warrants, are grounded not in a patron/client relationship, but rather, in a balanced mutuality grounded in constitutional and functional definitions and requirements. Because state/provincial relations involve fundamental U.S. and Canadian constitutional definitions about the role of states and provinces in "foreign" affairs, every precaution should be taken by U.S. and Canadian officials to operate in a manner consistent with those definitions. This is as important for the two federal governments as it is for the states and provinces. For example, any attempt on the part of the U.S. government to operate outside mutually acceptable channels in dealing directly with the provinces, or for the Canadian federal government to deal directly with the U.S. states, is both undesirable and ultimately counterproductive. In the pursuit of their functional needs, state and provincial officials have their own obligations and should be cautious not to complicate each other's constitutional frameworks. Any debate about the respective role of states and provinces in "foreign" affairs should be a national rather than a bilateral debate, and state/provincial relations should not be a tool whereby states, or provinces, score debating points against their federal governments. This call for adherence to constitutional requirements is not to suggest an undue formality or rigidity in an area of such increasingly complex state/provincial problems as environmental matters. However, unless U.S. and Canadian federal and state/provincial officials pay attention to the constitutional implications of their activities while dealing with these problems, a seriously destabilizing period of bilateral relations could result.

A final policy observation is in order. The fact that state/provincial relations can generate conflict should not obscure the fact that, in the proper context, these relations can be a mutually productive method of meeting state and provincial needs and, as such, can constitute a most useful aspect of the total Canadian-U.S. relationship. Because state/provincial relations are likely to increase rather than decrease in the future, it is as important to the states and provinces as it is to Washington and Ottawa that a balanced perspective is maintained in conducting and assessing these relations. With this as background, it is useful to now examine the scope of state/provincial relations.

THE SCOPE OF STATE/PROVINCIAL RELATIONS

There are a total of 766 interactions between U.S. states and Canadian provinces. A state/provincial interaction is defined as those currently operative processes in which there is direct communication between state and provincial officials on an ongoing basis. A state/provincial interaction must therefore meet three definitional requirements.

First, the interaction must be currently active as of July 1974, when this study was begun, based upon the interactive frequency characteristic of the activity to which a given interaction refers. Second, at some point in the interactive process, state and provincial officials have to be in direct communication. That is, an official of a state has to be in contact—either by letter, by telephone, or face-to-face—with an official of a provincial government concerning a matter acknowledged to be relevant to official responsibilities. Third, the interactive process must involve more than a single exchange: it must be ongoing in the sense that the initial exchange is followed by regularized behavior with reference to more than one case or event.

The 766 state/provincial interactions identified on this basis do not, of course, exhaust the totality of a state government's transborder interactions with an external composite national unit. In the widest perspective, state governments deal directly on a regular, ongoing basis with the full range of actors from Canada, ranging from the national government, through provincial and municipal units, to private corporate and noncorporate organizations and private individuals. For example, a state can interact with the Canadian federal government (e.g, the September 21, 1960, agreement between the Washington State Toll Bridge Authority and Her Majesty the Queen of Canada concerning the use of the ferry terminal at Sidney, British Columbia). A state can also have an interaction with private Canadian financial units (e.g., application and negotiation by the Canadian Imperial Bank of Commerce to Alaska's Division of Banking, Securities, Small Loans and Corporations to establish a banking facility in Alaska). Likewise, a state can interact with Canadian municipalities (e.g., Alaska's Division of Marine Transportation has an agreement with Prince George to supply summer travelers with travel information concerning ferry traffic). And, of course, a state can have a interaction in which mixes of the above three units are operative.

From this extended perspective, 1,057 interactions have been identified and catalogued.[11] These comprise the total direct interaction of U.S. states and Canadian public and private actors. Of this 1,057 total, 766 are currently operative interactions with officials of provincial governments. It is this 766 figure which forms the basis of all the subsequent data presentation and analysis of this chapter.

It is apparent from the accompanying map that the 766 state interactions with Canadian provinces are distributed unevenly across the 50 states.[12] All states have at least some interaction with Canadian provinces, with the maximum being 110 (Maine) and the minimum, one (West Virginia). Eleven states have over 20 interactions, while a full half have 10 or more.

The uneven geographical distribution of state/provincial interaction is rather pronounced. The fourteen border states (Alaska, Washington, Idaho, Montana, North Dakota, Minnesota, Michigan, Wisconsin, Ohio, Pennsylvania, New York, Vermont, New Hampshire, and Maine) [13] account for 61.7 percent of the activity. Indeed, Maine alone accounts for 14.4 percent of 766 interactions. It is, however, noteworthy that a substantial portion of state/provincial interactions (the remaining 38.3 percent) involves states with no contiguous Canadian province. Within the border-state group,

Total State/Provincial Interactions

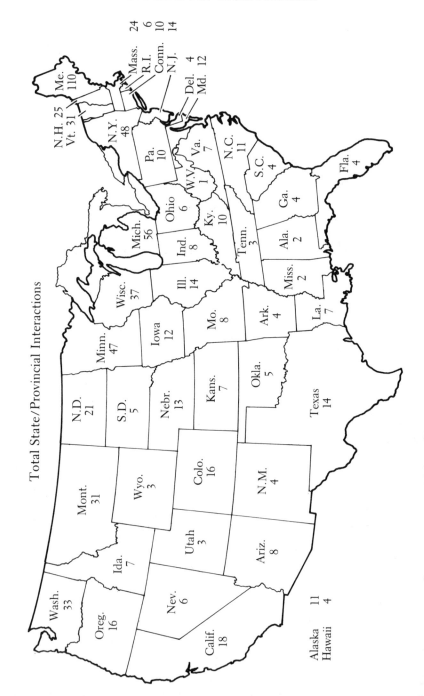

the number of interactions ranges from Maine with 110 to Ohio with six, while the nonborder group extends from Massachusetts with 24 to West Virginia with one. It remains significant, however, that the highest nine states are all border states and together account for 54.6 percent of the total interaction.

The six geographical regions of the United States also display considerable variation in the extent to which they interact with Canadian provinces. The most active region is the northeast with 36.3 percent of the interactions. The Midwest has 30.5 percent, the Pacific has 10.7 percent, the South has 9.8 percent, the Mountain States 8.6 percent and the Southwest 4 percent. The states of the Northeast average 30.9 interactions apiece, those of the Midwest 19.5, those of the Pacific 16.4, those of the Mountain States 11.0, those of the Southwest 7.8, and those of the South 5.4.

TYPES OF STATE/PROVINCIAL RELATIONS

Three types of state/provincial interactions can be identified: agreements, understandings, and arrangements.

An agreement is defined as a jointly signed document setting forth regularized interactive procedures.[14] This is the most formal type of interaction and can be concluded by governors and premiers (e.g., the June 1973 Curtis-Hatfield signed "Joint Agreement" between Maine and New Brunswick "to maintain and foster close cooperation in all relevant areas of concern"). An agreement can also be concluded by other state and provincial officials (e.g., the March 1973 reciprocal agreement concerning licensing of insurance agents between an official of Oklahoma's Insurance Commission and Ontario's Ministry of Consumer and Corporate Affairs).

An understanding is defined as correpsondence, resolutions, communiqués, or memoranda, not jointly signed, setting forth regularized interactive procedures. An example of correspondence is the August-December 1966 exchange of correspondence between an official of Louisiana's Department of Public Safety and Ontario's Department of Transport concerning reciprocity on exemption from registration of motor vehicles and trailers. An example of a resolution is the August 1973 resolution of the New England Governors-Eastern Canadian Premiers for the "development of joint energy policies" through the New England-Eastern Canadian Energy Advisory Committee. An examply of a communiqué is the May 1972 joint communiqué of Maine's governor and Quebec's vice-prime minister setting forth an understanding between Maine and Quebec for cooperation in broadcasting and other areas. Finally, an example of memoranda is the January 1974 Illinois "administrative order" promulgating an understanding between the Illinois Department of Conservation and Ontario for cooperative fishery management in accordance with the Great Lakes Fisheries Commission.

If there is no reported jointly signed document nor any nonjointly signed correspondence, resolutions, communiqués, or memoranda, the interaction is typed as an "arrangement." [15] Hence, an arrangement is any other written or verbal articulation of a regularized interactive procedure. An example would include the arrangement between New York's Department of Environmental Conservation and Ontario's Ministry of the Environment "to discuss mutual air pollution problems" through the holding of "periodic, informal meetings." A second example is the "informal arrangements" between North Dakota's Disaster Emergency Services and Saskatchewan and Manitoba "in disaster emergency preparedness, response, and recovery activities" through the holding of "coordinating meetings periodically" in a "manner of mutual interest without anything in writing."

There remains a fourth category concerning types of interaction—contacts. Although not presented in this report, contacts can be defined as single exchanges in which no regularized procedures are defined, nor any ongoing recipro-cal procedural obligations incurred. These contacts are not reported for two reason. First, they are so numerous and ephemeral that there is no utility in attempting to present, or estimate, them either individually or in the aggregate. Second, since they do not entail regularized procedures, they are of less significance in the dynamics of state/provincial interaction, although they are of course significant when they constitute the basis for possible subsequent ongoing processes.

Table 1 lists the distribution of types of interaction by state. Of the total 766 state/provincial interactions, 5.7 percent are agreements, 23.6 percent are understandings, and 70.6 percent are arrangements. Consideration of the agree-ment-understanding-arrangement distribution for individual states suggest that for most, state/provincial interaction is largely an informal affair.[16] Although only six states (Ala-bama, Mississippi, Ohio, Tennessee, West Virginia, and Wyoming) have all their interactions take the form of arrangements, over half of the states have three-quarters or more of their interactions as arrangements. Thirty-five states have over 50 percent of their interactions as arrangements, five have an even balance, and seven have less than 50 percent. Only one state, Delaware, has less than 20 percent of its interactions as arrangements.

The status of arrangements as the predominant interaction type for most states is reflected in the small percentages accounted for by agreements, which are the most formal of the three interaction types. Twenty-eight states have no agreements, and seven states have 10 percent or less of their interactions as agreements: Maine (2.7%), Massachusetts (4.2%), North Dakota (4.8%), Washington (9.1%), Alaska (9.1%), Kentucky (10%), and Pennsylvania (10%). A further eight states have from 10 to 20 percent of their interactions

TABLE 1 DISTRIBUTION OF TYPES OF INTERACTION

State	Agreement	Understanding	Arrangement	Total	State	Agreement	Understanding	Arrangement	Total
Alabama	0	0	2	2	Montana	4	6	21	31
Alaska	1	1	9	11	Nebraska	0	7	6	13
Arizona	0	1	7	8	Nevada	0	1	5	6
Arkansas	2	1	1	4	New Hampshire	0	4	21	25
California	3	4	11	18	New Jersey	2	3	9	14
Colorado	0	4	12	16	New Mexico	0	2	2	4
Connecticut	0	5	5	10	New York	0	5	43	48
Delaware	2	2	0	4	North Carolina	3	0	8	11
Florida	2	0	2	4	North Dakota	1	3	17	21
Georgia	1	0	3	4	Ohio	0	0	6	6
Hawaii	0	1	3	4	Oklahoma	1	3	1	5
Idaho	0	2	5	7	Oregon	2	1	13	16
Illinois	0	2	12	14	Pennsylvania	1	0	9	10
Indiana	0	2	6	8	Rhode Island	0	4	2	6
Iowa	0	7	5	12	South Carolina	2	0	2	4
Kansas	1	2	4	7	South Dakota	2	1	2	5
Kentucky	1	3	6	10	Tennessee	0	0	3	3
Louisiana	0	1	6	7	Texas	2	3	9	14
Maine	3	46	61	110	Utah	0	1	2	3
Maryland	0	5	7	12	Vermont	0	6	25	31
Massachusetts	1	16	7	24	Virginia	0	1	6	7
Michigan	0	6	50	56	Washington	3	3	27	33
Minnesota	0	8	39	47	West Virginia	0	0	1	1
Mississippi	0	0	2	2	Wisconsin	4	4	29	37
Missouri	0	4	4	8	Wyoming	0	0	3	3

as agreements: Wisconsin (10.8%), Oregon (12.5%), Montana (12.9%), Kansas (14.3%), New Jersey (14.3%), Texas (14.3%), California (16.7%), and Oklahoma (20%). The remaining figures are: Georgia (25%), North Carolina (27.3%), South Dakota (40%), and Arkansas, Delaware, Florida, and South Carolina (50%).

In view of this pronounced weighting of interaction types toward the less formal type activity, both in the aggregate and for most individual states, it is tempting to speculate as to the development of state/provincial interaction. For example, this pattern would appear to be consistent with a developmental sequence in which a state begins with interactions in the form of arrangements and proceeds over time to formalize these arrangements or to conclude other understandings without arrangments on this basis. Although the virtual absence of cases in which there are agreements and understandings without arrangements supports this speculation, caution must be exercised. It is equally possible either that both formal and informal types of interaction are simultaneously a response to a given set of needs which arise at a particular moment or that the distribution of types depends upon the particular characteristics of those specific needs. Equally, the types of interaction could also be dependent upon those operative constitutional parameters which apply to given areas of interaction and upon those other governmental and nongovernmental actors involved. Hence, definitive conclusions as to the dynamic relationship between types of interaction, the temporal evolution of given distributions, and the projective implications this has for future activity are contingent upon a more detailed form of causal anlaysis than is possible within the concept of this chapter.

THE FUNCTIONAL NATURE OF
STATE/PROVINCIAL RELATIONS

The overall activities of governments, including state governments, can be usefully divided into component activities. That is, the organizational subdivions of governments regularly perform diverse but interrelated functions that contribute to the maintenance of the larger whole and serve the needs of the territorial jurisdictions for which they are responsible. These subdivisions can be characterized as functional categories. Eleven such categories have been developed for this report which map the range of governmental activity: [17] (1) Agriculture; (2) Commerce and Industry; (3) Educational and Cultural; (4) Energy; (5) Environmental Protection; (6) Human Services; (7) Military and Civil Defense; (8) Natural Resources; (9) Public Safety; (10) Transportation; (11) Unclassified/General.

Table 2 identifies the transborder activities of states by functional category. Transportation is the category in which by far the most state/provincial activity occurs (27.5%), followed in order by Natural Resources (19.5%), Commerce and Industry (10.4%), Human Services (9.9%), Environmental Protection (8.5%), Educational and Cultural (5.7%), Energy (4.7%), Public Safety (4.7%), Agriculture (3.5%), Unclassified (3.4%), and Military and Civil Defense (2.1%).

Not surprisingly, activity in all functional categories is largely a border phenomenon. Each functional category has at least five border states reporting activity, with five categories (Commerce and Industry, Educational and Cultural, Environmental Protection, Natural Resources, and Transportation) having at least twelve of the fourteen border states reporting activity. Of the states reporting activity in each functional category, border states comprise 100 percent in Military and Civil Defense and 81.3 percent in Environmental Protection. They comprise between 41.2 and 55.6 percent in five categories: Agriculture (55.6%), Energy (52.9%), Educational and Cultural (50%), Natural Resources (46.4%), Public Safety (41.2%), Commerce and Industry (37.8%), Human Services (30.8%), and Transportation (29.5%). The border states account for over half the interactions in nine categories: Military and Civil Defense (100%), Unclassified (84.6%), Environmental Protection (83.1%), Energy (75.0%), Agriculture (74.1%), Natural Resources (72.5%), Educational and Cultural (61.4%), Commerce and Industry (61.3%), and Public Safety (61.1%).

The importance of a border location in generating state/provincial activity is further seen in examining the geographical/regional patterns which characterize the various functional categories. Generally, those regions with no or few border states have the most functionally concentrated activity. The eleven functional categories into which state/provincial transborder interaction can be divided display a noticeable consistency in their patterns. All are unevenly distributed, both in the number of states reporting interactions and in the number of total interactions reported. In virtually all cases the border states account for a disproportionate amount of the activity, and those geographic regions with states located on or near the border are considerably more active than their more remote equivalents.[18]

As Table 3 indicates, the proportion of agreements, understandings, and arrangements varies markedly by functional category. Informal activity is the only type in Agriculture and Public Safety. (These categories have no agreements or understandings.) It constitutes in Human Services (84.2%), Natural Resources (83.9%), and Educational and Cultural (77.3%), all of which have no agreements. Informal activity also characterized Environmental Protection (98.5%), which has a single agreement and no understandings. Of the five categories which have all three types of interactions, informal

TABLE 2   INTERACTIONS BY FUNCTION AND STATE

State	Agriculture	Commerce and Industry	Educational and Cultural	Energy	Environmental Protection	Human Services	Military and Civil Defense	Natural Resources	Public Safety	Transportation	Unclassified/General	Total for Each State
Alabama	0	0	1	0	0	0	0	1	0	0	0	2
Alaska	0	3	1	2	3	0	0	0	0	2	0	11
Arizona	0	1	0	0	0	2	0	2	1	2	0	8
Arkansas	0	0	0	0	0	2	0	0	0	2	0	4
California	2	0	0	0	0	8	0	0	1	7	0	18
Colorado	0	1	2	0	0	1	0	10	1	1	0	16
Connecticut	0	0	0	1	0	1	0	2	0	5	1	10
Delaware	0	0	0	0	0	0	0	0	0	4	0	4
Florida	0	0	0	0	0	0	0	0	0	4	0	4
Georgia	0	2	0	0	0	0	0	0	0	2	0	4
Hawaii	0	1	1	0	0	2	0	0	0	0	0	4
Idaho	0	3	1	0	0	0	0	1	0	2	0	7
Illinois	0	1	0	0	7	0	0	4	1	1	0	14
Indiana	0	0	1	0	3	0	0	1	2	2	0	8
Iowa	0	2	1	0	0	1	0	0	1	7	0	12
Kansas	0	1	1	2	0	0	0	0	0	3	0	7
Kentucky	0	1	0	0	0	5	0	0	1	3	0	10
Louisiana	0	0	5	0	0	0	0	0	0	1	1	7
Maine	9	8	9	6	4	5	7	17	4	30	11	110
Maryland	0	0	0	1	0	1	0	0	3	7	0	12
Massachusetts	0	1	1	1	0	3	0	2	0	15	1	24
Michigan	0	4	1	4	5	2	1	33	0	5	1	56

Minnesota	0	4	1	1	13	4	0	8	4	12	0	47
Mississippi	0	1	0	1	0	0	0	0	0	0	0	2
Missouri	0	1	0	0	0	1	0	2	0	4	0	8
Montana	2	4	1	4	3	0	3	6	2	5	1	31
Nebraska	0	0	0	0	0	1	0	5	0	7	0	13
Nevada	0	1	1	0	0	3	0	0	0	1	0	6
New Hampshire	1	2	6	2	1	0	0	12	0	1	0	25
New Jersey	0	0	1	1	0	2	0	2	0	8	0	14
New Mexico	0	1	0	0	0	1	0	0	0	2	0	4
New York	0	4	1	5	6	9	0	7	9	5	2	48
North Carolina	0	1	0	0	0	1	0	1	0	8	0	11
North Dakota	0	1	0	1	3	5	1	5	1	3	1	21
Ohio	0	2	0	0	3	0	0	1	0	0	0	6
Oklahoma	0	4	1	1	0	0	0	0	0	0	0	5
Oregon	1	1	0	0	1	2	0	4	2	5	0	16
Pennsylvania	0	1	1	1	4	1	0	1	0	2	0	10
Rhode Island	0	1	1	1	0	0	0	2	0	1	0	6
South Carolina	0	1	0	0	0	0	0	0	0	3	0	4
South Dakota	0	1	0	0	0	0	0	1	0	3	0	5
Tennessee	2	0	0	0	0	0	0	0	0	1	0	3
Texas	0	3	0	0	0	0	0	2	1	7	1	14
Utah	0	1	0	0	0	0	0	0	0	2	0	3
Vermont	5	4	3	2	2	0	2	3	1	6	3	31
Virginia	2	1	0	1	0	1	0	0	0	2	0	7
Washington	3	5	1	0	2	7	2	1	1	9	2	33
West Virginia	0	0	0	0	0	0	0	0	0	1	0	1
Wisconsin	0	4	1	0	5	5	0	13	0	8	1	37
Wyoming	0	2	0	0	0	0	0	0	0	0	0	3
Total by Function	27	80	44	36	65	76	16	149	36	211	26	766

arrangements continue to predominate in Commerce and Industry, providing 91.3 percent of the interactions in this category. Arrangements constitute 84.6 percent of unclassified activity, 63.9 percent of the Energy function, and 56.3 percent of that in Military and Civil Defense. Only in Transportation is there more formal than informal activity, with arrangements providing only 30.3 percent of the total.

TABLE 3   TOTAL STATE TABULAR SUMMARY BY
TYPES OF INTERACTION AND BY FUNCTIONAL CATEGORY

Functional Categories	Agreement	Understanding	Arrangement	Total by Functional Categories
Agriculture			27	27
Commerce & Industry	2	5	73	80
Educational & Cultural		10	34	44
Energy	1	12	23	36
Environmental Protection	1		64	65
Human Services		12	64	76
Military & Civil Defense	4	3	9	16
Natural Resources		24	125	149
Public Safety			36	36
Transportation	35	112	64	211
Unclassified	1	3	22	26
Total by types of interaction	44	181	541	766

The marked variation in the distribution of interaction types according to functional category suggests that there is not a general tendency for arrangements to evolve into, or otherwise produce more formal activity, culminating in some "natural" proportion at a terminal point. At the very least it must be acknowledged that any such general developmental sequence occurs at different rates according to the way in which general factors differentially affect each specific functional category. Attention must also be directed at the way in which these same or other factors may operate against formal activity or the formalization of activity, or "freeze" a specific informal-formal distribution at a given point in time. Moreover, it is necessary to consider the way in which formal activity itself may replace, rather than add to, existing informal cooperation, spawn additional informal activity under its umbrella, or be replaced by it.

If lack of knowledge about the causes of state/provincial interaction renders speculation about future activity a hazardous exercise, the lack of specificity on the part of state officials about the interactions themselves restricts the more modest task of describing the temporal evolution of existing interactions. Although the failure of state officials to report the initial date or estimate the duration of many of the arrangements is a revealing commentary on the nature of state/provincial interactions, it makes it difficult to answer questions concerning the increase or decrease in state/provincial interactions over time. Such an exercise is possible only with regard to the agreements category. On the whole, no particular period of intensive activity is apparent. In the field of Transportation, the 35 agreements dealing with motor vehicles were concluded as follows: 3.0 percent before 1955; 6.1 percent, 1955-59; 24.2 percent, 1960-64; 18.2 percent, 1965-69; 42.4 percent, 1970-74; and 6.1 percent undated.[19] The other transportation agreements dealing with a bridge on the Maine-New Brunswick border and ferry service between Alaska and British Columbia were concluded in 1960 and 1971, respectively.

Of the four civil defense agreements, Washington's was concluded in 1968 (with British Columbia), and Montana's three in 1969 (with British Columbia, Alberta, and Saskatchewan). Apart from a 1957 Oklahoma-Ontario Reciprocal Agreement on insurance agent licensing, the four agreements from all categories other than Transportation and Military and Civil Defense have all been concluded within the past two years. These are a July 1972 Washington-

British Columbia "memorandum of cooperation" on oil pollution (Environmental Protection); a June 1973 Maine-New Brunswick Joint Agreement to "maintain and foster close cooperation in all relevant areas of concern" (Unclassified); a December 1973 Massachusetts-New Brunswick Joint Agreement on trade and tourist cooperation (Commerce and Industry); and the June 1974 New England-Eastern Canadian Sugarbush compact on energy supplies (Energy). Thus, the conclusion of agreements has not only increased over time, rising overall from nine in 1960-64 to ten in 1965-69, to 19 in 1970-74, but has recently gone beyond the two traditional functional categories to affirm state/provincial cooperation in "political areas" of both a specific and general nature.

STATE/PROVINCIAL RELATIONS BY PAIRS

Having examined the involvement of states in state/provincial interaction, it is useful for illustrative purposes to consider which pairs of states and provinces are active, as well as which individual provinces. Table 4 lists the states and provinces having interactions.[20] It will be noted on the table that following the listing of the ten individual Canadian provinces, two additional categories are entered, Multilateral and General. Multilateral refers, quite simply, to those interactions in which there was reported the involvement of two or more provinces, while General refers to those interactions reported as having been concluded with such generic designations as Canadian provinces. It is interesting to note that of the total state/provincial interactions, as reported, 45.3 percent are bilateral, 16.1 percent are multilateral, and 38.6 percent are coded as general.

Of the bilateral interactions, Ontario is involved in by far the most, with 29.1 percent, followed by Quebec with 18.7 and British Columbia with 13.3 percent, respectively. To-

(

gether, these three most populous provinces account for 61.1 percent of the total reported bilateral interactions. New Brunswick has 11.5 percent of the bilateral interactions, followed by the three Prairie Provinces—Manitoba (9.8%), Saskatchewan (6.6%), and Alberta (5.5%). Less bilateral activity has been reported with the three remaining Maritime Provinces, which have no land boundary with U.S. states—Nova Scotia (3.7%), Prince Edward Island (1.2%), and Newfoundland (.58%). Regionally, the two central Canadian provinces, Ontario and Quebec, account for 47.8 percent of the reported bilateral activity; the four Western provinces (British Columbia, Alberta, Saskatchewan, and Manitoba) for 35.2 percent, and the four Eastern provinces (New Brunswick, Nova Scotia, Prince Edward Island, and Newfoundland) for 17.0 percent.

The importance of contiguity in engendering the bilateral interactions is dramatically illustrated in examining the most active state/provincial pairs. Maine/New Brunswick leads with thirty two, followed by Michigan/Ontario with eleven, Minnesota/Manitoba with eight, New Hampshire/Quebec and Vermont/Quebec with seven per pair, Alaska/British Columbia and North Dakota/Manitoba with six per pair, and Illinois/Ontario, Louisiana/Quebec, and Montana/Saskatchewan with five per pair. Thus, the 12 most bilaterally active pairs are all contiguous border states, and together account for 48.7 percent of the bilateral interaction. The only noncontiguous pairs reporting five or more bilateral interactions are the culturally linked Louisiana/Quebec pair and the Great Lakes jurisdictions of Illinois/Ontario.[21]

No province is involved in bilateral interactions in all eleven functional categories. Quebec is involved in ten (all but Agriculture), with most of its activity in Educational and Cultural, Transportation, and Commerce and Industry. British Columbia is also active in ten (all but Unclassified), with most of its activity in Transportation, Human Services, and

TABLE 4 TABULAR SUMMARY OF STATE/PROVINCIAL PAIRS

State	B.C.	Alb.	Sask.	Man.	Ont.	P.Q.	N.B.	N.S.	P.E.I.	NFLD.	Multi-Lateral	General	Total
Alabama												2	2
Alaska	6										2	3	11
Arizona			1								1	6	8
Arkansas		1	1									2	4
California	2	1	1	1	2	2	1	1			1	6	18
Colorado		1	1	1	1						6	6	16
Connecticut								1			3	6	10
Delaware					1	1						2	4
Florida		1				1						2	4
Georgia					2	1						1	4
Hawaii					1						2	1	4
Idaho	3										1	3	7
Illinois				1	5						4	4	14
Indiana		1		1	3						1	2	8
Iowa			1	1	1		1	1	1		1	5	12
Kansas					2						2	3	7
Kentucky	1	1		1	1	1						5	10
Louisiana					1	5						1	7
Maine	1	1	1	1	1	20	32	4	1	1	15	32	110
Maryland	1			1	1	1		1	1			6	12
Massachusetts	1	1	1	1	1	1	2	1	1	1	5	8	24
Michigan	1	1			22	1		1			7	23	56
Minnesota			1	8	11	1	1	1			8	16	47
Mississippi						1						1	2
Missouri				1	1						1	5	8

State	1	2	3	4	5	6	7	8	9	10	11	12	Total
Montana	3	4	5		1	1					4	13	31
Nebraska		1	3		2						3	4	13
Nevada	1										1	4	6
New Hampshire				1	7						8	9	25
New Jersey	1			1	1						2	9	14
New Mexico	1										1	2	4
New York	1			1	15	4					9	18	48
North Carolina					2	2		1	1		1	4	11
North Dakota				6		1			1		7	6	21
Ohio					3						1	2	6
Oklahoma	1				2						1	1	5
Oregon	1				1		1				3	10	16
Pennsylvania			2			2					3	3	10
Rhode Island					1	1					4	1	6
South Carolina						2					1	1	4
South Dakota				1			1				1	2	5
Tennessee												3	3
Texas		1		1	1						1	10	14
Utah							1					2	3
Vermont					7	1					6	17	31
Virginia						1						6	7
Washington	22						1				1	9	33
West Virginia					1								1
Wisconson		1	2	1	1		13	1	1		6	11	37
Wyoming											1	2	3
Total	46	19	23	34	101	65	40	13	4	2	123	296	766

Commerce and Industry.[22] Ontario is involved in ten (all but Agriculture), with most of its activity in Natural Resources, Transportation, Environmental Protection, and Commerce and Industry. New Brunswick is also involved in ten (all but Educational and Cultural), mostly in Transportation, and Military, and Civil Defense. The comparable figures are six for Manitoba (mostly Transportation and Human Services); five for Saskatchewan (mostly Transportation and Energy); five for Alberta (mostly Transportation); three for Nova Scotia (mostly Transportation); and one each for Prince Edward Island and Newfoundland (entirely Transportation). The functional pattern of activity is thus roughly the same for all provinces. Quebec's acitivity in Educational and Cultural, Ontario's Natural Resources, and New Brunswick's Military and Civil Defense are the most apparent exceptions.

SUMMATION AND ASSESSMENT

To summarize the findings in this chapter, every one of the fifty U.S. states interacts with Canadian provinces. Although the fourteen border states provide 62 percent of the interactions, four border states alone account for over one-third of the activity: Maine with 14 percent, Michigan with 7 percent, and New York and Minnesota with 6 percent apiece. Regionally, the most active area is the Northeast, with 36 percent of the interaction, followed by the Midwest with 31 percent. The least active region is the Southwest, with 4 percent. The northeastern states average thirty-one interactions apiece, and those of the Midwest twenty apiece.

State/provincial interaction is both a formal and informal affair. Arrangements are by far the most common, accounting for 71 percent of the interaction. Understandings account for 24 percent. Least common are the most formal type of interaction—agreements—which constitute only 6 percent.

Only twenty-two states have formal agreements, with six states providing 45.5 percent of the agreements.

State/provincial interaction is pervasive in scope, extending to all functional areas of governmental activity. The most active area is Transportation, accounting for 28 percent of the total interaction, followed by Natural Resources with 20 percent. The other functional areas, in decreasing order, are: Commerce and Industry (10%), Human Services (10%), Environmental Protection (9%), Educational and Cultural (6%), Energy (5%), Public Safety (5%), Agriculture (4%), Unclassified (3%), and Military and Civil Defense (2%). Significantly, the border states account for over half of the interaction in all functional categories, except Human Services and Transportation. Maine is the most active state in seven categories. New York leads in two categories, and Michigan and Minnesota lead in one each. Generally, the nonborder states have activity in only a few of the eleven functional categories.

The three most populous Canadian provinces are involved in 61 percent of the bilateral state/provincial interaction. From this bilateral standpoint, Ontario is by far the most active partner, accounting for 29 percent of the interactions. Quebec follows with 19 percent, with British Columbia having 13 percent. It is noteworthy that the most active state/provincial pairs are those contiguous to one another. Maine/New Brunswick is the most active pair, followed by Michigan/Ontario and Washington/British Columbia. The most active nonborder pairs are Illinois/Ontario and Louisiana/Quebec.

With respect to further research, four questions might be usefully asked in probing the phenomenon of state/provincial interactions. First, what are the causes of state/provincial interaction? Second, how does state/provincial interaction between the United States and Canada compare with that of the United States and Mexico? Third, how are states (and provinces) organized to process these interactions, and what interactive organizational techniques have been developed? Fourth, what is the extent and nature of governmental and private involvement in state/provincial interaction?

The first two questions continue this chapter's perspective of state/provincial interaction as an aggregate phenomenon between state/provincial subnational actors of two federal nations. The first question involves an exploration of those general factors which cause this interaction.

Here, three components are most in need of explanation: what determines the number of state/provincial interactions; what determines the type of these interactions (agreement, understanding, arrangement); and what determines the functional areas to which the interactions pertain. A variety of factors, considered either across the individual states or over time for all the states, would appear to be directly relevant to these questions. The first factor is those aggregate attributes of the states and provinces themselves, both individually and relative to each other. In this chapter, the importance of contiguity [23] and geographical distance between states and provinces has been stressed as a generator of interaction and a determinant of its functional character. Also of major importance is the size of the states and provinces in terms of population and economic base. Related to this is the size of the state and provincial governments and their attendant capacity and resources for undertaking transborder interaction, and the cultural distribution of the population (particularly the francophone element).

A further related dimension is the various forms of "private" transactions which may require state/provincial interaction, ranging from securities, trade, and tourism to such specific matters as bird and insect movements. Adequate explanations of the level of interaction according to functional category would appear to require the development and use of a wider range and more specific type of aggregate variable than those generally employed in quantitative analyses of international relations. Other sets of factors affecting the level, type, and functional nature of state/ provincial interactions can be dealt with more adequately from other perspectives. These would include the constitutional parameters of both federal systems as they have evolved and been applied over time and the interaction, or lack thereof, of federal governments, which may generate state/provincial interaction of a supportive, complementary, or indeed competitive nature. Particularly relevant concerning this latter dimension are the international, national, and regional profiles and priority levels of various issue areas over time, and the way in which political actors on the state/ provincial level operationally can, and do, respond to them.

A second question which warrants further research involves a comparison of the overall state/provincial interaction of the United States and Canada with that of the United States and Mexico. Such an exercise would permit a determination not only of the extent to which Canadian-U.S. state/ provincial interaction is unusual in volume, type, and functional nature, but also further study of the causes of state/provincial activity, both generically and in the specific Canadian-U.S. case. A systematic comparison with the U.S.- Mexican case would thus more fully suggest the causal role of such factors as the differing constitutional and federal systems, the relationship of the respective national governments in intensity and form, and the "environmental" factors such as relative cultural complementarity. Furthermore, such a study would have an exemplary value in providing insights into the way in which other federal governments respond to state/provincial activity and meet the legitimate needs of the states in a servicing capacity.

The third and fourth questions requiring further research involve an advance from an aggregate perspective to the exploration of the actual organizational processes of state/ provincial activity. This advance from the "what" and "why" to the "how" of state/provincial interaction is of particular significance on two counts. First, an organizational process perspective appears to be best able to describe and analyze the policy and analytically relevant questions of how these interactions operate, and of the multidimensional role of the federal government(s) in them. Second, an examination of the dynamics of state/provincial activity as an organizational process would suggest empirically based answers to the fundamental theoretical questions of whether or not state/ provincial interaction is, and hence can be best viewed as, a self-contained and conceptual whole.

Thus, the third question for further research is the basic question of how states and provinces are organized to process state/provincial interactions. It can be speculated that the vast majority of states do not have specific organizational units, or policies, relating to matters affecting the Canadian provinces. Again, in a general sense, there appears to be no special concern on the part of the governors to encourage, discourage, or centrally coordinate interactions with the provinces as a distinctive policy area. If and when such interactions occur, they generally involve state officials having specific functional responsibilities, whose operational mandate is prescribed either by state statute or via the delegation of authority by the governor to that official to take such actions as necessary to execute his functional responsibilities. In short, state/provincial interaction from an organizational-processing standpoint for most states appears to be organizationally disaggregated into specific state governmental units having particular functional responsibilities.

This organizational posture is primarily a result of the level of interaction with Canadian provinces, and the prominence these interactions assume in the context of a state's policy and functional concerns. Not surprisingly, it is in those states bordering Canada where this level and concern would appear to be greatest, and it is here that an organizational registration of this concern with Canadian provinces as distinct entities can be discerned. It might be noted that the economic size of the state, together with the cultural composition of its population, might be added to proximity as a generator of such organizational forms.

Two forms of organizational recognition which appear to have evolved are functionally specific in scope. The first refers to the development of an organizational capacity within the state government to deal with Canada in specific functional areas such as the field of economic development. The second form refers to the creation of such state-affiliated organizations as specific commissions to promote activity in such functional areas as cultural cooperation with francophone Canadians. An example of the former is Vermont's Agency of Development and Community Affairs, which has an "International Industrial Development Representative" who is the Agency's "liaison" with Quebec on economic matters. As an example of organizationally registered cultural cooperation, fully five of the six New England states (Maine, Vermont, New Hampshire, Rhode Island, and Massachusetts), as well as Louisiana, have some form of an "American and Canadian French Cultural Commission" to promote common cultural activities and exchanges.

The third form of the state's organizational recognition of Canada is more generic in functional scope. This refers to the establishment of a special organizational unit within the governor's office responsible for Canadian relations in general. Maine has pioneered in this area, with the governor first appointing a full-time "Special Assistant for Canadian Relations." In February 1973, the governor established an Office of Canadian Relations as a part of his executive infrastructure, and a twelve-member advisory commission. The office is responsible for "evaluating existing governmental and private contacts in Canada, work to strengthen regional cooperation, and encourage increasing exchanges with the Provinces."

In addition to the three forms in which states organizationally register a recognition within the state itself, five specific techniques have been developed by states for interactively dealing with Canadian provinces. The first is bureaucratic ad hoc meetings in which officials of the states and provinces, ranging from field officials to commissioners and ministers, meet to exchange information on similar problems, discuss common problems, or develop joint projects and programs. A second technique is the development of an organizational presence on the part of the state within Canada through the establishment of state offices, or the appointment of Canadian firms to serve as state representatives. At least eight states have utilized this technique— Georgia, South Carolina, North Carolina, Washington, New York, Vermont, New Hampshire, and Maine. These state presences, which are most often located in Montreal, followed by Toronto, are primarily designed to promote trade and tourism and to encourage economic development.

The third technique developed by states for interactively dealing with Canadian provinces is the creation of state/provincial joint organizations, usually in the form of joint committees, which deal in a systematized manner with the various functional areas. Two examples would include the New England-Eastern Canadian Energy Advisory Committee and the New England-Eastern Canadian Transportation Advisory Committee, which were established in August 1973 by the respective governors and premiers "to develop joint policies" in these two functional areas.

The fourth technique is the development and perfection of a form of "summitry" by state governors and premiers. For example, within the past few years, some dozen U.S. state governors have been involved in some form of summit exchange with their provincial counterparts at least eighteeen times. The most active state in this area is that of Maine, followed by Michigan and Washington State. An interesting variant of this state/provincial summitry is its institutional-ization. For example, the six-governor New England Gover nors Conference held a historic meeting with the five Eastern Canadian premiers in Brudnell, Prince Edward Island, in August 1973, followed by a meeting at Sugarbush, Vermont, in June 1974, with a follow-up meeting in 1975. Finally, the fifth technique developed by states for interactively dealing with Canadian provinces involves legislative exchanges, whereby state and provincial legislators meet with their counterparts for purposes of familiarization and information exchange. For example, both Maine and Washington State have utilized this technique.

The fourth question requiring further research extends beyond the organization and operation of state governmental units to deal with the federal governmental and private organizational involvement in state/provincial interaction. It will be recalled that a state/provincial interaction is one in which there is "direct communication between state and provincial officials." However, this "direct communication" can, and often does, occur in the context of the involvement of other distinct actors, such as organizational units from the U.S. and/or Canadian federal governments. For example, a state may interact with a Canadian province through one of the many subbodies of the joint U.S.-Canada federal organi-zations, such as the International Joint Commission or the Great Lakes Fisheries Commission; through organizational machinery designed to implement federal agreements such as the Great Lakes Water Quality Agreement; or as part of a less institutionalized group which includes officials of one or both federal governments. In order to initially map the extent of the governmental dimension, it is useful to characterize state/provincial interactions as "governmental" when the evidence indicates that officials of the federal governments were actively involved in the state/provincial interaction itself.

Such a preliminary definition of governmental involvement was applied to the data base in this chapter.[24] Of the 766 reported state/provincial interactions, 15 percent were reported and coded as governmental. Twenty-three states account for these governmental interactions. Minnesota has the highest number, followed by New York, Michigan, Wisconsin, and Maine. Together, they account for 53 percent of the governmental interactions. All border states with the exception of Idaho report governmental interactions, providing 78 percent of the activity. Those eight states which border on the Great Lakes provide 61 percent of the interactions. Although this preliminary exercise provides some indication of the extent and pattern of this other-level governmental dimension, it must be pointed out that the definition of "governmental" employed herein by no means exhausts the multifaceted relevance of other-level governments for state/provincial interaction. For example, these figures do not capture a federal role in the form of providing authority, permission, funding, or consequent implementative activity. Nor do they include other-level governmental involvement in the form of other officials dealing with states and provinces prior to or subsequent to the state/provincial interaction, as either a cause or a result of it.[25]

Another dimension of this fourth question is one equally worthy of further attention from an analytical and policy standpoint. This refers to private involvement in state/provincial interaction. Of the private organizations which can be involved as participants in, or serve as the context for, state/provincial interaction, the most active would appear to be professional associations to which state and provincial officials belong, either as private individuals or as representatives of their respective organizational units.[26]

As a preliminary exercise, the data gathered in the research for this chapter were coded "associational" when there was the clear reporting by the state respondents of the presence of associational units in the state/provincial interaction. The results of this preliminary exercise would appear to suggest that the associational dimension of state/provincial interactions is of as great a significance as is the governmental. Associational involvement was reported, and coded in 21 percent of the interactions compared with 15 percent for the governmental dimension.[27] Associational interactions are more widely distributed than are governmental interactions. Nine states provide over half (51%) of the associational interactions: Michigan, Maine, Wisconsin, Vermont, Montana, Colorado, Washington, Nebraska, and New York. A total of forty states report associational interactions, with only the South being significantly underrepresented in this category.

It is the nature, as much as the mere volume, of associational involvement in state/provincial interaction that underlies the significance of this associational dimension. The membership of state and provincial officials in such associations can serve to familiarize them with functional counterparts in transborder jurisdictions, to promote the discussion of common problems, and to promote their reconciliation either within or apart from the associational context. Furthermore, the association itself, through such activities as technical discussion, the sponsorship of cooperative projects, the passage of resolutions, and the establishment of guidelines, can serve as the basis for, or indeed obviate the need for, separate state/provincial interaction.

Thus, even a rudimentary consideration of the information gathered within the context of this chapter strongly suggests the prevalence, if not the nature, of other actor involvement in state/provincial interaction. In addition to its analytical implications, both the volume and nature of this involvement by federal and associational actors is directly significant for the capacity of the federal government(s) to adequately deal with state/provincial activity in both a monitoring and servicing role. However, what remains unclear at this point is the precise form of the existing federal (and associational) involvement in the state/provincial interaction process, its salience in affecting or determining their outcome, and the costs and benefits to all actors of various forms of involvements.

What is required at this point, then, is further study of how federal and private associational actors impact, and are impacted by, the state/provincial interaction process. Such a study would include: first, the development of a typology of these other actors and of the way in which they are involved in, or relevant to, state/provincial interaction; second, a listing of those actors relevant to the interaction; and third, a modeling, based on case studies, of how these other actors characteristically do become involved in state/provincial interaction and thereby affect the outcome of these processes. Apart from its analytical value, such a study would provide the basic informational and analytical tools to enhance the anticipatory and advisory capacity of the relevant federal governmental units and to permit subsequent data-gathering efforts to proceed on a more sophisticated and productive basis.

NOTES

1. The U.S. State Department's Office of Canadian Affairs was not unaware of a number of procedures between U.S. states and Canadian provinces in such areas as motor vehicle registration and environmental matters, but had little knowledge of the nature and extent of these procedures. Thus, while it conceded the value of state/provincial relations within the broader context of Canada-U.S. relations, the Office of Canadian Affairs felt that more detailed information was necessary in order to deal with questions of precedents and guidelines. As a result, the State Department issued a research contract with the mandate of compiling and analyzing a list of the interactions between the states and provinces. The

project report, which is presented in this chapter, gives the first comprehensive picture of the extent and nature of state/provincial relations. To achieve as comprehensive a data base as possible concerning the activity between U.S. states and Canadian provinces, the primary technique was to directly contact relevant officials in every state. After preliminary exploratory letters to each governor from both the U.S. State Department and the author, a questionnaire was posted to 3,434 state officials. These officials, whose names were obtained from the Council on State Governments' publication, *State Administrative Officials* (Lexington, Kentucky, 1973), were administrative heads covering a total of sixty-eight functional areas in every state and U.S. possession and territory. The survey included 100 questionnaires posted to the speakers of state assemblies and the presidents of state senates in order to obtain any information in their records, especially that regarding interlegislative activity. The response to the questionnaire survey was substantial, and constitutes the primary data base of the project. With a response of 55 percent to the original November 1973 mailing, a follow-up letter was posted in February 1974. The overall response to the survey totaled 79.8 percent. On the basis of this return, field research was undertaken in three eastern states (Maine, New Hampshire, and Vermont) and four midwestern states (Michigan, Indiana, Illinois, and Wisconsin).

2. Here it should be noted that state/provincial relations, in which other actors can become involved but in which there continues to be direct state/provincial communication, is but one component of a larger net of transborder interactions not involving direct state/provincial communication, which sublevel governments of nations conduct. The full range of these interactions can be classified under the generic term, "subnationalism." Subnationalism is defined as the transborder interaction of politically and orgainzationally distinct, territorially grounded, hierarchically sublevel governmental units of nations. This political/territorial based definition obviously excludes U.S.-Canada federal/federal and private/private interactions. Perhaps less obviously, it also excludes the bureaucratic interplay of subordinate units of national governments per se, and instead refers to transborder interactions which involve one unit of the spectrum of such hierarchical sublevel governmental units as states (provinces) and municipalities.

3. Specific questions that might arise concerning the role of U.S. states in external affairs would involve, first, the definition of the word "treaty" in the first part of Section 10 of the constitution, and the definition of the words "agreement" and "compact" later in that Section. Second, questions might involve the nature of the "consent" required from Congress, which has been taken to mean the direct active consent of Congress as opposed to the tacit consent of failure to object on being informed of an agreement.

4. Senate Document 39, 88th Cong., 1st Sess., pp. 416-19.

5. As quoted in Richard H. Leach, et al., "Province-State Transborder

Relations: A Preliminary Assessment," *Canadian Public Administration*, Vol. 16, No. 3 (Fall 1973), p. 472.

6. Canada, Department of External Affairs, *Federalism and International Relations* (Ottawa: Queen's Printer, 1968), pp. 26, 28, as quoted in Leach et al., ibid., p. 471.

7. Characteristic of the attention to the legal dimension, and the deference accorded to it, was the attempt of one state in 1961 to enter into a formal "Memorandum of Understanding" with a Canadian province concerning civil defense. However, the formal signing of the memorandum did not take place because the U.S. federal government advised that it could not permit the document to be executed in that it had not been presented to, or concurred in, by the U.S.-Canadian federal authorities. A year later the state and province concluded a mutual understanding with no formal exchange of notes or any written agreements.

8. These needs, as perceived by state officials, are as interactively necessary as they are diverse. To cite just two examples, state officials noted that "fire is no respecter of national boundaries" and that "political boundaries are . . . no obstacle to fish movements."

9. An example of the importance of meeting functional needs lies in the field of disaster emergency preparedness. One state governmental official noted that the activities between his state and bordering Canadian provinces in past disaster emergency situations had been, and could be, suspect at times, because of the federal-level regulations of both countries. The official further noted that his state managed to operate in a manner of mutual interest and expressed the hope that federal authorities would understand that state's particular problems, responsibilities, and needs in disaster emergency work.

10. For example, in the field of transportation, one nonborder state noted that unless some agreement with a province was forthcoming in the very near future, that state would have no alternative except to close its borders to vehicles from the province which maintained nonreciprocal licensing porvisions. In that the state further noted that such a move would be very detrimental to the Canadian trucking industry, it can be assumed that the U.S. and Canadian federal governments would have to become actively involved.

11. This 1,057 figure includes a small number of terminated interactions, and a small number not considered as part of the project research.

12. Excluded from this and subsequent data presentations are those interactions of the U.S. territories and the District of Columbia, and those involving only the Northwest or Yukon territories.

13. Although Illinois and Indiana border the Great Lakes, they do not share a boundary with Canada.

14. Although it would appear probable that all three types would be in accordance with the desires of all parties concerned, acceptable to and understood by all parties, with the intent of being regularly followed by all

parties, such dimensions are not set forth as definitional criteria, and their empirical presence is left as a matter for future research.

15. These three types of interaction (agreements, understandings, and arrangements) were delineated and defined in lieu of usage either by the individual states, or by the U.S. State Department in its diplomatic intercourse. Individual state characterizations of interaction were not found to be useful in a definitional sense given the variance in usage by each state. Nor is diplomatic usage sufficiently rigorous or differentiated to assist in definitions (e.g., "treaties," "conventions," "pacts," "acts," "protocols") on the state/provincial level. See, for example, J. L. Brierly, *The Law of Nations: An Introduction to the International Law of Peace*, 6th ed., ed. by Sir Humphrey Waldock, ed. (Oxford: Oxford University Press, 1963), p. 317. As Brierly points out, "none of these terms has an absolutely fixed meaning. . . .") Definitions were therefore developed specifically for this chapter. Given the differing levels of specificity with which various officials responded, the most useful definitional schema is one based upon format; that is, the observable form which an interaction takes, as reported by state officials. The use of this criterion best permits the unambiguous classification of the very diverse existing data and its subsequent consideration according to other criteria, rather than prejudging and "freezing" the motivational, legal, or other status of all reported interactions as part of the coding exercise.

16. It must be recognized that this individual and overall distribution is to some extent a result of incomplete reported information in conjunction with the coding scheme. (Unless state officials reported that a given interaction takes the form of a jointly signed agreement or meets the definitional requirements of an understanding, that interaction is classified as an arrangement.) This fact poses severe limitations for the degree of quantitative analysis possible with these figures, in the absence of further analytical and empirical work.

17. These functional categories can also be analytically regarded as "issue areas." It should be noted that these functional categories are grounded in actor-based definitions. A total of sixty-eight state governmental subdivisions (according to the Council on State Government's classification scheme) were contacted in the questionnaire survey. To impose a standardized sense of order on these units and their welter of activities, the subdivisions were divided into the above eleven functional categories. An interaction involving a state governmental subdivision is therefore classified accordingly. This has the advantage of providing not only an empirically grounded definition but one in which the categories generally correspond to popular impressions (e.g., the categories are intuitively self-explanatory).

18. This composite pattern, however, is not sufficiently pronounced to prevent the appearance in the different functional categories of different causal combinations of these and other recurrent attributes. Nor does it eliminate the need to look for specific factors which appear to have an

important, if functionally limited, role in a given category. It is this two-dimensional nature of state/provincial interaction which points to the analytical need to view such interaction on a functionally disaggregated basis, and thus address the substantive question of whether such activity is primarily an overall governmental phenomenon or one grounded in the perceived requisites of individual functional areas.

19. This is particularly significant given the natural tendency of state officials to be aware of, and report, the more recent agreements, and given the phraseology of the questionnaire which focused the study on interactions since 1960. These considerations also apply, of course, to agreements in the other functional categories.

20. However, in considering which state/provincial pairs are most active, several qualifications are in order. The use of U.S. states as the unit of analysis, together with the variable specificity with which their officials reported, makes it difficult in some cases to determine which provincial unit(s) are involved in a reported interaction. This difficulty, furthermore, is not simply a coding or statistical problem. Even allowing for information loss in reporting, it is evident that a significant amount of state transborder activity does take place in the context of interaction with several Canadian provinces, For example, states may regularly interact wtih several provinces in such multilateral forums as professional organizations or federally established governmental bodies, or they may simply establish regularized and operative interactive procedures in which various provinces regularly but differentially participate. In short, state/provincial activity is not solely, and may not be primarily, a bilateral phenomenon. Given this substantive nature of state/provincial interaction, multilateral and general interactions have not been disaggregated and counted on a bilateral basis in this data report, even when the reported information provides a basis for so doing. (Thus, generic references were not disaggregated into several interactions, even when the generic characterizations [e.g., "Canadian Provinces," "Eastern Canadian Provinces," "contiguous provinces," or "nearby provinces"] would permit a basis for so doing.) Any attempt to disaggregate and transpose the existing data set for a definitive counterpart province-as-unit-of-analysis approach would result in significant substantive distortion.

21. In the absence of these "special" affinities, nonborder states engaging in state/provincial activity would appear to reply on multilateral forums as much as, if not proportionally more than, their fellow states located on the border.

22. Functional categories are listed in decreasing order according to the number of interactions in that category which the province has.

23. Contiguity refers both to the length of a common state/provincial border and the nature of this border (i.e., land versus water).

24. "Governmental" involvement can include officials of municipalities and international organizations. The active involvement of these actors was rarely reported.

25. Furthermore, if the interactions involving states and other-level governmental actors in Canada but not involving provinces were considered, the 766 interactions identified in this report would be significantly increased.

26. Other private organizations relevant to state/provincial activity would include corporations and unions, service organizations, nonprofit institutions such as universities and foundations, and so on.

27. It must be recalled that the definitional requirements for characterizing an interaction as associational are somewhat less stringent than those for typing it as governmental (i.e., the "presence" of an association in the state/provincial interaction rather than an indication of the involvement of an other-level governmental unit as an actor, coequal in status, in the interaction). Because both are restricted to the requirement that there be involvement in a state/provincial interaction, the relevance of associations is also not fully captured by this coding exercise.

VII

CONCLUSION

This book has concentrated on the mechanics of the Canada-U.S. intergovernmental relationship. In examining Washington and Ottawa, it was shown that the process of translating national policy into operable programs did not involve monolithic bureaucracies, but rather, various constellations of actors drawn from the entire spectrum of each nation's government. In examining U.S. and Canadian diplomatic and consular representation, it was shown that the U.S. Embassy and seven consular posts in Canada constituted a relatively homogeneous operation, while the Canadian Embassy and fifteen consular posts in the United States were more organizationally heterogeneous. In examining the seventeen bilateral organizations active in the Canada-U.S. relationship, it was shown how these organizations supplement, but do not replace, other methods of issue resolution. In extending the Canada-U.S. intergovernmental dimension, it was shown how other actors (transnational and transgovernmental) are active in issues affecting the two nations. Finally, in further extending the intergovernmental perspective to include the role of U.S. states and Canadian provinces, it was found that there is an extensive subnational dimension in the relationship in terms of ongoing state/provincial agreements, understandings, and arrangements.

Given this extremely complex set of actors and interactions, how might the Canada-U.S. intergovernmental relationship be viewed in an overall sense? According to traditional rhetoric, the relationship has been characterized as an example of two nations peacefully settling their disputes—a model of issue resolution which other nations could utilize to their advantage.

"What an object lesson of peace is shown today by our two countries to all the world. ... If only European countries would heed the lesson conveyed by Canada and the United States, they would strike at the root of their own continuing disagreements and, in their own prosperity, forget to inveigh constantly at ours." [1] So declared President Harding in 1923. Canadian Prime Minister King informed Parliament in 1937 that Canada and the United States "in the constitution of the International Joint Commission . . . has set the world the finest example it enjoys in the way of dealing with possible international differences." [2] In 1949 Canadian Minister of National Defence Brooke Claxton allowed that "the relations between our two states show a pattern that other countries could study and follow to their profit, security, and happiness." [3] In 1954 President Eisenhower ruminated that the U.S.-Canadian relationship "stands almost as a model, as I see it, for international relationships everywhere." [4] After becoming prime minister in 1963, Lester Pearson observed that "It is of the utmost importance that the relations between our two countries should be an example to the world. . . ." [5] As recently as 1977, Prime Minister Trudeau declared: "The friendship between our two countries is so basic, so non-negotiable, that it has long since been regarded by others as the standard for enlightened relations." [6]

While one is reluctant to quarrel with decades of such high-level accolades, one is forced to take a less beneficent interpretation of the Canada-U.S. intergovernmental experience. Canada and the United States do, of course, have a meaningful tradition of peaceful coexistence, and the techniques of bilateral issue resolution have been imaginative and successful. However, the model theme is unhelpful on two counts. First, the success of the Canada-U.S. experience is grounded in such indigeneous North American forces as geographical contiguity and isolation, coupled with complementarity of political and cultural traditions, all of which makes its wholesale applicability to other regions of the world at best a dubious proposition. Certainly, Prime Minister King got carried away in the 1940s when he suggested to President Roosevelt that the International Joint Commission would serve as a useful model for the postwar international organization.[7] Second, and more important, the invocation of this model of peaceful coexistence has become, with the passage of time, a rhetorical balloon floating over fundamental and unresolved problems of "peaceful co-existence." In fact, the very success of the U.S. and Canadian governments in amicably resolving their differences has triggered charges from many Canadians that in the process Canada has traded its national sovereignty for bilateral camaraderie.

A more relevant and useful theme of the Canada-U.S. intergovernmenal relationship for the late 1970s is the model of two sovereign nations grappling with the problems, and reaping the benefits, of unprecedented interdependence. This is the essence of the Canada-U.S. intergovernmental relationship—the attempt of the U.S. and Canadian governments to translate national policy goals into operable programs in the context of an interdependent bilateral system that is without parallel in the international community.

In examining this interdependent system, we are not dealing with "good neighbors," but rather with two nations having national decision-making capabilities. This is an important distinction if we are to rid the Canada-U.S. relationship of the rhetorical luggage it has accumulated during the postwar period. Each of the two federal governments attempts to exert control, not only internally within its territorial boundaries, but also outside these boundaries (externally) insofar as it affects its perceived interests. Here we are not assuming that the two governments will necessarily cooperate, or that they have similar interests. Nor are we assuming that the two governments will necessarily compete, or that they will necessarily respect the territorial integrity or interests of the other.[8] The only assumption that is being made deals with sovereignty—that each government will claim the right to control and protect its interest both internally and externally, and this in highly varying degrees and within differentiated political and socioeconomic frameworks.[9]

What we are therefore witnessing in North America is two sovereign nations searching for answers to the problems of managerial interdependence. This book has taken only a first step in examining this intergovernmental phenomenon. Further analytical and empirical work are obviously needed for a fuller understanding of the dynamics of the Canada-U.S. relationship. And of course, further work must include developments in Quebec and the intergovernmental ramifications of these developments. Speculation about the future of the Canada-U.S. relationship, including the future of Quebec, will be useful only to the extent that it is grounded in a firm understanding of this intergovernmental infrastructure. In short, the Canada-U.S. intergovernmental relationship bears watching and further study and should be of concern not only to the U.S. and Canadian publics, but given the importance of Canada and the United States in a global context, to the international community in general.

NOTES

1. Quoted in Roger Frank Swanson, *Canadian-American Summit Diplomacy* 1923-1973 (Toronto: McClelland and Stewart, 1975), pp. 312-13.

2. *Canadian House of Commons Debates*, January 1937.

3. "Canada-U.S.: Good Neighbours But Are We Good Enough," Detroit, May 2, 1949, *Statements and Speeches* 49/18.

4. Quoted in Dale C. Thomson and Roger F. Swanson, *Canadian Foreign Policy: Options and Perspectives* (Toronto: McGraw-Hill Ryerson Ltd., 1971), p. 129.

5. "The North American Partnership," South Bend, Indiana, June 9, 1963, *Statements and Speeches* 63/11.

6. "Canada-U.S. Relations: A Model Admired by Much of the World." Remarks by Prime Minister Pierre E. Trudeau to a Joint Session of the United States Congress. Washington D.C., February 27, 1977. *Statements and Speeches*. No. 77/4.

7. J. W. Pickersgill, *The Mackenzie King Record*, Vol. I (Toronto: University of Toronto Press, 1960), p. 433.

8. See William D. Coplin, *Introduction to International Politics: A Theoretical Overview* (Chicago: Markham Publishing Company, 1971).

9. Although there are hosts of other actors (both nongovernmental, such as corporations and unions, and subgovernmental, such as states and provinces), they are viewed as acting within an intergovernmental framework. In short, the basic framework used in this book consists of the federal governments of the United States and Canada. These may simply be defined as two normatively autonomous, territorially based decision-making components, relatively free to regulate internal actors and who attempt to regulate external actors in the context of perceived interests.

INDEX